Reconstructing Rural Egypt

Other titles in Contemporary Issues in the Middle East

The Communist Movement in Egypt, 1920–1988
Tareq Y. Ismael & Rifa'at El-Sa'id

The Creation of a Medical Profession in Egypt, 1800–1922
Amira el-Azhary Sonbol

Crossing Borders: An American Woman in the Middle East
Judith Caesar

Development and Social Change in Rural Egypt
Richard H. Adams, Jr.

Egypt from Independence to Revolution, 1919–1952
Selma Botman

Egypt's Other Wars: Epidemics and the Politics of Public Health
Nancy Elizabeth Gallagher

Islam: Continuity and Change in the Modern World. Second Edition
John Obert Voll

Khul Khaal: Five Egyptian Women Tell Their Stories
Nayra Atiya

Middle Eastern Lives: The Practice of Biography and Self-Narrative
Martin Kramer, ed.

Naguib Mahfouz: From Regional Fame to Global Recognition
Michael Beard & Adnan Haydar, eds.

Painting the Middle East
Ann Zwicker Kerr

Reveal and Conceal: Dress in Contemporary Egypt
Andrea Rugh

The Rise of Egyptian Communism, 1939–1970
Selma Botman

Women Farmers in Africa: Rural Development in Mali and the Sahel
Lucy E. Creevey, ed.

Women in Egyptian Public Life
Earl L. Sullivan

Reconstructing Rural Egypt

Ahmed Hussein and the History of Egyptian Development

Amy J. Johnson

Syracuse University Press

First Edition 2004
04 05 06 07 08 09 6 5 4 3 2 1

The permission of Aziza Hussein to use materials from the Hussein family archive, including personal papers and diaries, unpublished speeches and other unpublished materials, newspaper clippings, photographs, embassy dispatches, United Nations mission correspondence and technical manuals, family letters and papers, and government documents, is gratefully acknowledged.

Permission to quote from the following sources is gratefully acknowledged:
Full Circle: The Memoirs of Anthony Eden. Copyright © 1960 by Times Publishing Company, Ltd. Reprinted by permission of Houghton Mifflin Company. All rights reserved.
The Middle East Today, by Don Peretz. 5th ed. Copyright © 1988 by Praeger Publishers. Reproduced with the permission of Greenwood Publishing Group, Inc., Westport, Conn.
"The False Hopes of 1950: The Wafd's Last Hurrah and the Demise of Egypt's Old Order," by Joel Gordon. *International Journal of Middle East Studies* 21, no. 2 (May 1988). Copyright © 1988 by Cambridge University Press. Reprinted with the permission of Cambridge University Press.
"Rural Social Centers in Egypt," by Beatrice McCown Mattison. *Middle East Journal* 5, no. 4 (1951). Reprinted with permission.
"Egypt and American Foreign Policy Assistance, 1952–1956," by Jon Alterman. Ph.D. dissertation, Harvard University, 1997. Reprinted by permission of the author.
"Sociopolitical Debates in Late Parliamentary Egypt," by Misako Ikeda. Ph.D. dissertation, Harvard University, 1998. Reprinted by permission of the author.
"Report of the Mission on Rural Community Organization and Development in the Caribbean Area and Mexico." United Nations, 1953. Reprinted with permission.
Egypt's Other Wars: Epidemics and the Politics of Public Health, by Nancy Gallagher. Copyright © by Syracuse University Press, 1990. All rights reserved.

The paper used in this publication meets the minimum requirements of American National Standard for Information Sciences—Permanence of Paper for Printed Library Materials, ANSI Z39.48–1984.∞™

Library of Congress Cataloging-in-Publication Data
Johnson, Amy J.
Reconstructing rural Egypt : Ahmed Hussein and the history of Egyptian development / Amy J. Johnson.— 1st ed.
p. cm.—(Contemporary issues in the Middle East)
Includes bibliographical references and index.
ISBN 0–8156–3014-X
1. Hussein, Ahmed, 1902- 2. Social reformers—Egypt—Biography. 3. Egypt—Politics and government—20th century. 4. Egypt—Social conditions—20th century. 5. Egypt—Economic conditions—1919–1952. I. Title: Ahmed Hussein and the history of Egyptian development. II. Title. III. Series.
DT107.2.H83 J64 2003
307.1'412'092—dc22 2003019658

Manufactured in the United States of America

For my parents, Dennis and Paula Johnson

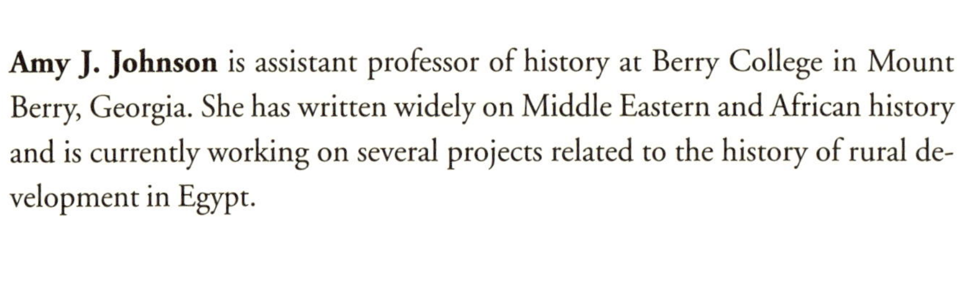

Amy J. Johnson is assistant professor of history at Berry College in Mount Berry, Georgia. She has written widely on Middle Eastern and African history and is currently working on several projects related to the history of rural development in Egypt.

Contents

Illustrations

Tables

Preface

When I first went to Cairo in June 1995, I anticipated writing an institutional history of the Ministry of Social Affairs. While doing preliminary research, two names kept cropping up: Dr. Ahmed Hussein and the Rural Social Centers project. The more research I did on the ministry, the more interested I became in this man and this project. I ultimately switched my attentions to Dr. Hussein and his rural development activities, spending two years on research in Egypt.

The research would not have been completed without the help of my research assistant, Hossam Barakat, who was instrumental in setting up interviews, tracking down sources, and getting into certain libraries when I was denied access. Emad Mahmoud was also a vital help throughout my research in Cairo, helping me with interviews, arranging for copying of documents, and suggesting research strategies. I would also like to thank Scott McIntosh, my tireless and humorous research and editorial assistant at Berry College, for the long hours he spent helping me edit and revise this work. In addition, I would like to express my gratitude to Diane Land, Katie Fowler, Amanda Black, and Scott Greear for their help in preparing the index, and to Christopher Erickson and Jennifer Carman for their assistance with revision and formatting changes in later versions of the manuscript.

Roger Owen and Susan Miller of Harvard University were extremely helpful and generous with their time and advice. Their guidance was essential to this project, and I am deeply in debt to them for their recommendations. I would also like to thank William Granara of Harvard University, Denis Sullivan of Northeastern University, and Mohamed Riad el-Ghonemy of Oxford University for their advice and comments throughout the research and writing stages. Jon Alterman and Misako Ikeda, graduate students at Harvard with me, were invaluable in suggesting sources in Cairo and in providing feedback on my project, as was Iman Ghazalla of the Hubert Humphrey Institute in Minneapolis. The staff at Widener Library of Harvard University were also a great help in my research, particularly in tracking down and obtaining rare materials. The German embassy staff in Washington, D.C., Uwe Jens Nagel of Humboldt University, and Rita Hesse of the Gotha Library were extremely kind in helping me acquire a copy of Dr. Hussein's 1927 dissertation from a now defunct German university. I am also indebted to Catherine Bauer for her assistance in translating Hussein's dissertation and Marjo Vahtola for her translation of Swedish sources.

I would especially like to thank two people without whose intense personal and scholarly interest I would not have been able even to begin this project: Mme. Aziza Shukri Hussein, Dr. Hussein's widow, and the late Hassan Dawood, his lifelong colleague and trusted friend. Both Mme. Aziza and Dr. Hassan were kind enough to accede to a lengthy series of interviews in Cairo, sharing with me their recollections and memories of Dr. Hussein and offering their ideas on further sources. They were both extremely generous with their time and effort, responding promptly to my airmailed and e-mailed requests for further information and reading through various early drafts of this work. Mme. Aziza worked tirelessly to compile a truly staggering collection of materials from the Hussein family library. She encouraged me in every step of my research and work and gathered reports, personal correspondence, pamphlets, books, newspaper and journal articles, photographs, embassy dispatches, and a wide variety of government documents for me. Mme. Aziza and Dr. Ghonemy also introduced me to the Pioneers *(al-Ruwaad),* a group of Dr. Hussein's former students and colleagues, many of whom were kind enough to meet with me several times to answer my questions and provide me with a wealth of personal information about Dr. Hussein, their experiences working with him, and his impact on their personal and professional lives. The information provided by these men was invaluable in completing my picture of Dr. Hussein and his programs.

The staff at the National NGO Council on Population and Development were extremely helpful during my 1998 and 1999 research trips. I would particularly like to thank Salma Salah Ahmed and Laila Shukri, who not only assisted me with everything from research to apartment rentals but also became good friends. Amr Shalakany, Ahmed Hussein's great-nephew, and his mother, Anan Rushdi, were kind enough to provide me with photographs, articles, and family stories about "Uncle Ahmed." I would also like to thank Catherine Maguire Rafferty, Dr. Hussein's secretary at the Egyptian embassy in Washington, for her help and personal recollections of the Husseins. I would also like to express my gratitude to His Excellency Mr. Sabri Beili, former governor of Qalyubiyah, His Excellency Mr. Adly Hussein, governor of Qalyubiyah, Hami al-Islam, general director of research in Qalyubiyah, Gamal Shedid, director general of research in the Ministry of Social Affairs, and Robert Springborg of Development Associates for their valuable assistance with this project.

I would very much like to thank the Center for Middle Eastern Studies and the Weatherhead Center for International Affairs at Harvard University, the PEO Sisterhood, and Berry College for funding my research in Egypt. I would also like to thank Harvard University, the U.S. Department of Education, and the Foreign Language and Area Studies (FLAS) Fellowship for their support. Berry College, the Harvard Center for Middle Eastern Studies, and the Harvard Graduate Student Council were most generous in providing me with funds to attend several conferences and present portions of this dissertation as short papers. Portions of this work were presented as short papers at various conferences and seminars, including ones at the Harvard Weatherhead Center for International Affairs, the University of Chicago, the University of California at Los Angeles, Yale University, the Middle East Studies Association 1997 Annual Conference, the European Association of Middle Eastern Studies 1999 conference, and a 1999 Cairo conference on the history of rural development.

Finally, I would like to thank my family. My parents, Dennis and Paula Johnson, always taught me that I could do anything I set my mind to. Their intellectual, financial, and emotional support and guidance made this project a success and saw me through the difficult stages. I am also greatly indebted to them and to my sisters, Laura Harriss and Amanda Johnson, for reading and offering insightful (and often humorous) criticism on the various rough drafts of this work. Thank you.

A Note on Transliteration

Place Names

Transliterations of place names are taken from the United States Board on Geographic Names, *Gazetteer No. 45: Egypt and the Gaza Strip* (Washington, D.C.: Office of Geography, Department of the Interior, 1959), with a few exceptions: (1) Where applicable, the Egyptian "g" rather than the standard "j" has been used (thus, for example, Sawhag, rather than Sawhaj, and Giza, rather than al-Jizah); (2) the definite article is written as "al-"; and (3) when a place name is found in a quotation from another source, the place name has been left as the original source transliterated it. Place names that frequently appear in English have been left in their familiar forms. Village names that do not appear in the *Gazetteer* appear as found in Egyptian government documents.

Personal Names

Names of individuals are transliterated according to their preference. For the sake of consistency I have uniformly used the definite article "al-" of written Arabic unless the individual uses "el-" in his or her publications. Personal names appearing in quotations from other sources have been left as those sources transliterated them.

In order to distinguish Ahmed Hussein, the subject of this work, from the other prominent figure of the same name, I have used two different spellings. The name of the subject of this work has been transliterated as "Ahmed Hussein," his own preferred spelling. With the exception of transliterations within quotations from other sources, the name of the leader of the Young Egypt Party has been reproduced here as "Ahmad Husayn" in order to distinguish between the two men.

Other Transliterations

Other transliterations of Arabic words are based on the Hans Wehr dictionary. To simplify the text, diacritical markings have been omitted, except for the ayn and hamza. The exceptions to the Wehr transliterations are the use of the more commonly used English spellings of *ardeb, feddan,* and *fellah.*

Abbreviations

ACB	Agricultural Credit Bank
CU	Combined Unit
CWC	Cairo Women's Club
EASS	Egyptian Association for Social Studies
FAO	Food and Agriculture Organization
ILO	International Labor Organization
IPPF	International Planned Parenthood Foundation
LE	Egyptian pound
MEDO	Middle East Defense Organization
MLA	Ministry of Local Administration
NGO	nongovernmental organization
ORDEV	Organization for the Reconstruction and Development of the Egyptian Village
RAS	Royal Agricultural Society
RCC	Revolutionary Command Council
RRS	Rural Reconstruction Society
RSC	Rural Social Center
UAR	United Arab Republic
UNESCO	United Nations Educational, Scientific, and Cultural Organization
UNRWA	United Nations Relief and Works Agency
WHO	World Health Organization

Introduction

Born into one of the most prominent families in Egypt, Ahmed Hussein became a leading reformer and one of the most dedicated and qualified social scientists of his era. After completing his studies in Germany, he began his career in government service as an inspector in the Cooperative Department of the Egyptian Ministry of Agriculture. Though he continued as an official in the Cooperative Department until 1948, his career quickly took on a new dimension. In 1939, Hussein and a group of his colleagues helped formulate plans for a new ministry in Egypt: the Ministry of Social Affairs. As the first head of the Fellah Department of the new ministry, Hussein drew up a plan for the reconstruction of rural Egypt. The linchpin of this plan was a highly successful and internationally acclaimed plan of rural social reform, the Egyptian Rural Social Centers project. Throughout his career in the Ministry of Social Affairs, Hussein worked tirelessly to advance this program.

A pilot project first introduced in 1936 by the Egyptian Association for Social Studies (EASS), the Rural Social Centers program quickly became the focal point of government efforts of social reform in the countryside. It was the first program of its kind in Egypt and served as a vanguard for integrated social reform elsewhere. It dealt with the central social problems confronting the fellah: poverty, ignorance, and disease. A popular catchphrase since the early 1930s, "poverty, ignorance, and disease" had been used to describe the problems of rural life by numerous reformers, including American sociologist Wendell Cleland in his 1936 discussion of Egypt's population problem. "Poverty, ignorance, and disease" gradually became the focus for all discussion of rural reforms. The experiment by the EASS to address these three central problems proved so successful that Hussein, the EASS board member who oversaw the project, adopted the EASS program as part of the Fellah Department's program of rural development.

Stressing its core philosophy of popular participation in reform initiatives and the integration of social services, the Rural Social Centers program achieved immediate and unparalleled success, and the number of centers grew rapidly. The popularity of the centers grew as well, as the centers were able to increase economic prosperity, decrease infant mortality, and improve levels of health and education in the areas in which they were located. Due to the success of this program, Hussein achieved international recognition as a rural social expert, and his project was used as a model for the United Nations' rural social reform projects.

Hussein's long career in the Ministry of Social Affairs culminated with his appointment as minister of social affairs by the Wafdist government of Mustafa Nahas Pasha in 1950. Although Hussein resigned on a matter of principle the following year, his accomplishments as minister were numerous. He introduced a minimum-wage bill for agricultural workers, devised his nation's first social security plan, expanded the Rural Social Centers project, further developed Egypt's agricultural cooperatives, began a program to distribute reclaimed lands to landless peasants, initiated a plan for popular housing, and secured passage of a new law regulating the landowner-tenant relationship.

When revolution erupted in Egypt in 1952, Hussein was on a UN mission examining rural social welfare programs in the nations of the Caribbean. Despite his prerevolutionary affiliation with the Wafdist party, the revolution did not end Hussein's career in government service. He returned to Egypt and was appointed ambassador to the United States in 1953, occupying that post until 1958. During his stint as ambassador, Hussein played an important role in negotiations with the Eisenhower administration on a wide variety of issues. The first priority for the new ambassador was to enlist American support for Egypt's attempt to evacuate the British troops from the Suez Canal Zone. Hussein was instrumental in convincing President Dwight D. Eisenhower and his administration that Egypt had legitimate reasons to insist upon British withdrawal. In addition, Hussein improved Egypt's image in the United States by cultivating good relations with the president, key members of his staff, and the American press. Hussein also forged lasting cultural and educational links between his country and the United States.

Despite these notable successes, the period of Hussein's ambassadorship was a turbulent and challenging one. Egyptian-American relations deteriorated in the mid-1950s as a result of Egypt's growing rapprochement with the Soviet bloc, making Hussein's mission increasingly difficult. He negotiated unsuccessfully for the acquisition of American armaments and for American support and funding for the Aswan High Dam project. As ambassador, Hussein explained the nationalization of the Suez Canal Company to the American people and played a key role in urging Eisenhower to oppose the tripartite aggression of Britain, France, and Israel in the Suez Canal War of 1956.

Never one to withhold his opinion, Hussein was not a typical diplomat. As a result, his relations with Egyptian president Gamal 'Abd al-Nasir were often difficult, and the two rarely saw eye-to-eye on policy issues. Differences between the two reached a crucial point two years after the Suez war when 'Abd al-Nasir announced the formation of the United Arab Republic of Egypt and Syria. Telling the president that he was unable to represent what he saw as two very different countries with very different interests, Hussein asked to be recalled. After completing his ambassadorial assignment, Hussein returned to Egypt. He resisted substantial pressure to continue serving his country in the diplomatic corps, resigning from public service in 1958 to devote himself to his family, friends, and private studies until his death in 1984 at the age of 83.

In addition to providing valuable information on the man himself and his revolutionary approach to social welfare, a study of Hussein's life is useful in four broader contexts. First, it is one of the only political biographies of a senior Egyptian official. While biographies of 'Abd al-Nasir, Sadat, and even the decadent King Faruq abound, very few other Egyptian officials have received the attention their lives and works deserve (one notable exception is the biography of Sayed Marei by Robert Springborg). Rather than concentrating on the actions of presidents and kings, biographies of officials like Hussein allow projects and policies to be seen from the perspective of those who implemented and evaluated them. In this way, a more thorough and complete understanding of Egyptian history and politics can be achieved.

Second, Hussein was one of the few foreign-trained social specialists of his era at the start of his career in the Ministry of Social Affairs. Therefore, he served as a crucial transmitter of social science thinking, introducing social reform ideas from the West into Egypt and adapting them to local conditions. His pioneering work on the Rural Social Centers project was the culmination of this transfer of knowledge. A study of his social reform work provides a glimpse of how Western ideas of social science entered into and became part of Egyptian reform projects.

Third, this biography examines Hussein's role as ambassador during the 1950s, in the context of the cold war and 'Abd al-Nasir's increasingly anti-American policies. The book presents Hussein's ambassadorship as primarily an exercise in public relations. Although Hussein was involved in negotiations on many important issues during his tenure, 'Abd al-Nasir wanted Hussein in Washington mainly for the image he could present to the American public. Hussein made every effort to advise the Egyptian president on policy and to influence American policy toward Egypt, but, with few exceptions, neither 'Abd al-Nasir nor American officials listened. Hussein's biggest success was in improving cultural and social ties between Egypt and the United States.

Finally, this biography is important for students of development in contemporary Egypt. The study does not conclude with Hussein's death in 1984 but instead continues into the 1990s and beyond and chronicles the attempts currently being made by several organizations to revive Hussein's reform agenda and methods. Thus, the book provides an important link between past and present efforts at socioeconomic development in Egypt, a link that is largely absent from discussions of Egyptian development.

This work is not intended as a full biography of Hussein. Very little personal information is known about his childhood and his years in Germany. Those close to Hussein in his youth have passed away, and few records exist of Hussein's childhood and formative years. Rather than trying to present a complete view of Hussein himself, this biography is a type of memoir that chronicles Hussein's career and locates him within the larger context of Egyptian history and the politics of his era. It is a biography of Hussein in his public persona—a history of his actions, policies, successes, and failures. It does not seek to nor can it provide a full account of Hussein's thoughts, feelings, or his private persona. Hussein left few records of his private life and thoughts; most information must be reconstructed based upon interviews with family members, friends, and colleagues. Hussein himself carefully guarded his privacy and categorically refused all interviews after retirement.

Although this study seeks to provide an objective view of Hussein, it must nonetheless be noted that a significant portion of the sources used are from the Hussein family library and Hussein's widow, and many of his former colleagues have assisted the author with this project. As a result of circumstances beyond the author's control (and in fact for reasons never disclosed to the author), the Egyptian government declined to make any of its records available. All Egyptian government documents used in this study are either publicly available or were made available to the author by Hussein's widow, Aziza Hussein.

This work is divided into six chapters. Chapter 1, "Origins of Hussein's Reform Ideas," looks at Hussein's upbringing and family life and his education in Egypt and in Germany, and how his experiences and education affected his ideas of social reform. Chapter 2, "The Professor and the Inspector," deals with Hussein's career in the 1920s and 1930s when he was both a university professor and an inspector in the Ministry of Agriculture. The chapter analyzes his early reform efforts and the formation of a cadre of students who became his disciples. Chapter 3, "The Ministry of Social Affairs and the Rural Social Centers Project," examines Hussein's involvement in founding the Ministry of Social Affairs in 1939 and his career in that ministry until 1950. It focuses on Hussein's signature reform effort, the Rural Social Centers project, and locates it within the context of prerevolutionary reform debates. Chapter 4, "Gaining International Recognition," begins with Hussein's appointment as minister of social affairs in 1950 and the expansion of development programs until his resignation in 1951. It also looks at his involvement in international and nongovernmental reform programs from 1951 to 1952. Chapter 5, "After 1952: Hussein and Gamal 'Abd al-Nasir," looks at Hussein's career after the 1952 revolution. It includes both an account of his tenure as Egyptian ambassador to the United States (1953–58) and what 'Abd al-Nasir's government did to Hussein's social reform projects. Chapter 6, "Hussein's Legacy," begins with a brief account of Hussein's retirement years from 1958 until his death in 1984, then focuses on attempts currently being made in Egypt to resurrect Hussein's approach to development and concludes by providing an analysis of Hussein's importance to Egypt and the world.

Reconstructing Rural Egypt

1

Origins of Hussein's Reform Ideas

Ahmed Hussein was born in November 1902 in Helwan, a southern suburb of Cairo, to 'Ali Hussein Pasha and Khadija al-Nagdaliya. 'Ali Hussein Pasha and his family were originally from Upper Egypt, while Ahmed's mother's family was of mixed Tunisian and Turkish descent. Growing up in Helwan with three brothers (Hussein, Muhammad, and 'Abd al-Aziz) and two sisters (Namizar and 'Aisha), Ahmed was part of a wealthy family that owned a considerable amount of land in the countryside and was of the social and political elite. Ahmed's mother was a cousin of the poet Ahmed Shawki, who helped raise young Ahmed. One of Ahmed's uncles was Osman Muharram Pasha, a minister of public works who developed Shari' al-Haram (Pyramids Road) in Giza. Ahmed's father was a prominent Wafdist politician, a founding member of the party. He was also minister of religious endowments and minister of justice in different Wafdist cabinets.

While not much is known about Hussein's early life, his family appears to have provided the initial impetus toward public service. From an early age, Hussein was encouraged to become involved in national affairs, to be educated, and to find a suitable career. While the boys in the family were encouraged to pursue their educations and make their fortunes in the world, the girls in the family were raised in a more traditional, conservative manner. Although they were educated, Hussein's sisters were not encouraged to leave the house, and the boys of the family were treated preferentially. In Aziza Hussein's words, "They were very kind people, very wonderful people, but the women were treated differently from the men and they had to take a secondary role. [Ahmed] was supposed to be the star of the family."[1]

Ahmed Hussein and his parents, ʿAli Hussein Pasha and Khadiga al-Nagdaliyah. Courtesy of Aziza Hussein.

The boys attended the Tawfiqiyah School in Cairo, a well-known and highly regarded secondary school at the beginning of the century, and they went on to prominent careers in both the public and private sectors. Hussein ʿAli Hussein studied to become a medical doctor. ʿAbd al-Aziz pursued a career as a professor in the field of food processing and was later minister of agriculture in the government of President Anwar Sadat. Hussein's brother Muhammad pursued a career in business, while his sisters Namizar and ʿAisha married and raised families, Namizar remaining in Egypt and ʿAisha traveling abroad as the wife of an ambassador.[2]

Hussein's Early Education

Hussein's early education must be seen against the backdrop of the British occupation of Egypt. Throughout the nineteenth century, the descendants of Muhammad ʿAli, "founder of modern Egypt," continued the program of

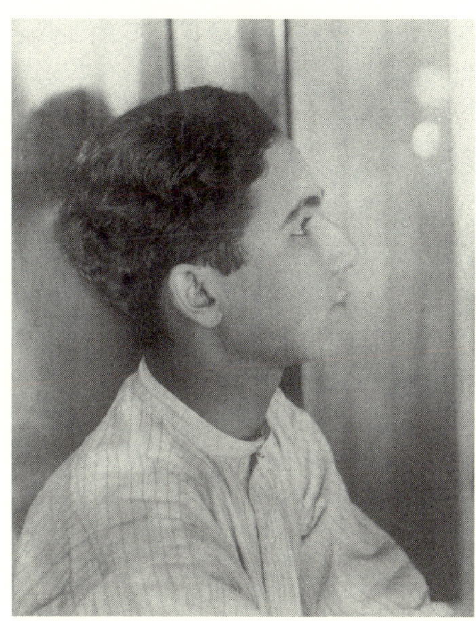

Hussein as a young boy. Courtesy of Aziza Hussein.

modernization begun when Muhammad 'Ali served as Ottoman governor of Egypt (1804–1849). Spending freely on development initiatives, these leaders, Ibrahim, 'Abbas I, Sa'id, and Isma'il, began projects to improve roads, railways, and bridges and to create a postal system, telegraph system, and an enhanced educational system. Unfortunately, Egypt did not have the capital to pay for their projects, and the spending habits of its rulers pushed Egypt deep into debt with the European powers. Sa'id was responsible for the agreement with the French engineer Ferdinand deLessups to build the Suez Canal, which was finished in the reign of Isma'il. To finish the canal, Isma'il pushed Egypt so far into debt to Europe that he sold Egypt's shares in the canal to the British government. By 1876, Egypt was officially bankrupt, and the Ottoman sultan formally deposed the khedive three years later. Six years later, Britain felt that its financial interests dictated direct intervention in Egypt. In 1882, Britain sent military forces to Egypt in response to a nationalist uprising led by Ahmed 'Urabi, and Britain defeated 'Urabi at the battle of Tell al-Kabir. The British motives were not only military but also political (protecting the legitimate ruler, Isma'il's son Tawfiq) and economic (protecting the Suez Canal and hence the route to India and securing a British hand in restoring financial stability in Egypt).

During this period of British occupation, which would last until formal independence in 1922, very little public money was spent on education, since the primary goal of British policy in Egypt was to "secure [Britain's] route to India. . . , keep the country quiet, minimize European objections to [Britain's] policies by repaying European creditors, and make Egypt pay for its own occupation. . . . Whatever funds [British consul general Sir Evelyn Baring, also Lord] Cromer could spare went for irrigation works to increase agricultural prosperity."[3] In keeping with this philosophy, Cromer (who held his post from 1883 to 1907) "permitted Egypt only three state secondary schools, which until 1902 were together graduating fewer than 100 students a year."[4] In the decade before World War I, state spending on education increased, but at its peak it only reached 3.4 percent of the national budget.[5]

The Tawfiqiyah School was one of Egypt's few government-run schools. Education had been free of charge until the 1882 occupation; during Hussein's childhood, education came at a price. State-run primary schools were neither compulsory nor free again until 1922, and secondary schools continued to charge tuition until 1950.[6] The policy of requiring students at all levels to pay tuition for their education was in keeping with Cromer's notion, shared by his educational adviser Douglas Dunlop, that "Egyptian students and their parents took education seriously only if they paid tuition."[7] Tuition for secondary schooling was set at LE 15 per student per year, an amount that meant only the well-to-do were able to educate their children. Cromer's educational policy was driven also by his belief that "the poor should stay in their place" and that, based on his experience in India, "Westernized schools manufactured nationalist malcontents, particularly among those who failed to obtain the government posts to which they aspired."[8] Therefore, according to his view, schooling should be kept to a minimum.

Hussein, then, was one of the minority of young Egyptians who came from a family both willing and able to pay for the education of its children. Although little is known about his early life, Hussein's experience in the Tawfiqiyah School must have been typical of the era. The primary aim of the state-run schools at the beginning of the twentieth century was to train public officials, officials who would be "unintelligent and docile," and the ethos of the schools ensured this.[9] The dominant values of the education system under British occupation were "submission to authority, passiveness, and lack of

Hussein and his brother Muhammad.
Courtesy of Aziza Hussein.

courage and independent thought."[10] Freethinking was not encouraged, memorization was the most common method of learning, and "politics was strictly forbidden under heavy penalties."[11]

In order to buttress the goal of producing passive bureaucrats, the curriculum of the schools was restricted to essential subjects. While instruction in Egyptian schools during this period was primarily in English, Arabic and French were taught as well. Hussein somehow learned German, although it is unclear whether this was at school or in private lessons.[12] Geography, mathematics, and basic science rounded out the curriculum of the schools, but those courses took a back seat to language instruction, in keeping with the mission of training government employees.[13] Muhammad 'Abduh, writing in 1905, described the curriculum as follows: "Of all the other sciences of which human knowledge is composed, the Egyptian may sometimes obtain a superficial notion at the preparatory schools, but it is almost impossible for him to study them thoroughly, and often he is compelled to ignore them. For example, Social Economy, with its branches, historical, moral, and economical; Philosophy, ancient and modern; Literature, Arabic and European, and the Fine Arts are not taught in Egypt in any school."[14]

'Abduh summed up the net effect of this system of education, saying, "The result is that we possess judges and lawyers, physicians and engineers more or less capable of exercising their professions; but amongst the educated classes one looks in vain for the investigator, the thinker, the philosopher, the scholar, the man in fact of open mind, fine spirit, generous sentiments, whose whole life is found devoted to the ideal."[15] In light of the prevailing spirit of public education in Egypt during Hussein's childhood, it is all the more remarkable that he was able to become not a submissive bureaucrat but essentially the sort of man for whom 'Abduh was vainly searching.

Hussein's Studies in Germany

Until the establishment of Fu'ad I (later Cairo) University in 1908, secular higher education choices in Egypt were limited to teacher training and the study of engineering, law, and medicine.[16] The new university provided increased opportunities for higher education within Egypt. Hussein, however, did not opt to remain in Egypt. After finishing his baccalaureate he decided to continue his studies abroad. By the time Hussein was ready to begin his higher education, Fu'ad I was still a small young university. In the academic year 1919–20, the university had a staff of fourteen professors and an equal number of courses. The university's orientation was geared toward the liberal arts, with only seven courses being taught on a regular basis: geography, philosophy, Islamic history, ancient history, and Arabic, English, and French literature.[17] Courses in other subjects were offered on an irregular basis depending on funding and staff availability. For a young man like Hussein who wanted a specialized higher education and had no inclinations toward the fields offered, attending university abroad was the only logical choice.

Owing to international economic conditions following World War I, education in Germany was particularly affordable, and many sons of prominent Egyptian families chose to pursue higher education there, including young Ahmed. He enrolled at the Landwirtschaftliche Hochschule in Berlin, where he studied agricultural economics. After completing his undergraduate education, he stayed at the Hochschule to pursue his doctorate in the same discipline. He was awarded his Ph.D. in agricultural economics in 1927.

When Hussein arrived in Germany, World War I had recently ended, the Treaty of Versailles and its attendant reparations payments had been imposed on Germany, Bismarck's state had collapsed, and the Weimar Republic was

As a student in Berlin, 1920. Courtesy of Aziza Hussein.

newly born. Inflation was rampant, the socialist movement was gaining ground, and the socialists struggled with the parliamentary parties and the communists for the loyalty of the German populace. A growing sense of aggressive nationalism was evident in many aspects of German society, including new Prussian school texts that "not only denied that Germany had any share in causing the war but insisted that its armies had not been defeated" and "placed all the responsibility for all of Germany's present misfortunes at the door of foreign Powers and the republican government."[18] By 1923, the NSDAP *(Nazionalsozialistische Deutsche Arbeiterpartei,* National Socialist German Workers Party, or Nazi Party) had been outlawed, and Adolf Hitler was writing *Mein Kampf* while serving a prison term following the Beer Hall Putsch in Munich.

German society was in flux when Hussein traveled to Germany, and its universities were in crisis. At the beginning of the twentieth century, the German educational system at all levels was "in many respects the envy of Europe."[19] Both traditional, liberal arts universities and the more technical educational institutes flourished because "it was recognised that Germany's powerful industrial growth depended on soundly based educational provision."[20] Education was largely specialized, technical, and narrow; the German university was the prototypical ivory tower, where, "engrossed in his narrow studies, a student often became estranged from his fellow men and indifferent to questions of society and state, and of the world at large."[21]

After World War I, the situation changed somewhat. More and more students flocked to the universities and the *Hochschulen* (technical universities), seeking higher education for lack of other alternatives. The increasing numbers of students "were driven not by any passion of the intellect but by the attempt to save themselves from economic destruction in the lower levels of the social structure from which, for the most part, they came. The illusion of climbing to safety on academic 'privileges' lodged itself in their minds."[22] As enrollments in the universities and the *Hochschulen* increased, a debate began about the role of the university in German society. Both the traditional, narrow focus of study and the burgeoning enrollments were widely criticized. With the influx of students came the creation of more student groups. As a result, university students came to have more outlets for their energies and more interest in the world outside the university.[23] Indeed, "a number of minor reforms and innovations were actually introduced in the universities and a considerable literature in the 1920s testifies to the concern which the future of the institution aroused not only in academic but in government circles as well."[24] Despite these minor changes, however, no wholesale reform program was instituted.

The steadily increasing numbers of students into the university system had far-reaching social and political consequences in Weimar Germany. The overcrowding of the universities and the *Hochschulen* reached its peak between 1925 and 1930.[25] By the early 1930s, its effects had become evident. As the students graduated, they found that their higher education was of little practical use in Germany's depressed economy. They "had completed their training only to find themselves among the growing ranks of an 'academic proletariat', embittered and disillusioned."[26] As one scholar remarks,

> The result of increased enrollments meant an overproduction of intellectuals and an intensification of competition in professional fields, which led to re-

> sentment first against the traditional scapegoats, the Jews. Disillusioned and despairing for the future the students . . . entered politics. After 1918, as after 1806, the majority of students became the protagonists of nationalism and nationalist emancipation, but unlike their predecessors the students of the Republic took up not the cause of liberalism but of reaction.[27]

This was the educational system of which Hussein became a part when he arrived in Germany. As a foreign student without plans to remain in Germany after his education, it is unlikely that Hussein was greatly influenced by the debates surrounding the university system in Germany during this time period. As a student in a specialized *Hochschule,* studying agricultural economics rather than one of the more overcrowded professional fields (dentistry, medicine, engineering, etc.), Hussein was on the fringe of the turmoil of the German universities in the 1920s. Nonetheless, he must have been aware of the mounting problems associated with the overcrowding of Germany's system of higher education. Although Hussein himself was never a political activist per se, coming from Egypt after the 1919 revolution he must have viewed the minimal involvement of German students outside the ivory towers as rather strange. Indeed, he most likely saw the growth of student clubs and associations in the 1920s as more in keeping with his own experience in Egypt.

Hussein's most important intellectual influence in Berlin was his professor, adviser, and mentor, Friedrich Aereboe, of whom he often spoke with great respect throughout his life. Educated in Bonn, Aereboe held teaching positions at several institutions before coming to Berlin and teaching at the *Hochschule.*[28] Aereboe was a prolific writer and well-known scholar in the field of agricultural economics, and Hussein held both the man and his scholarship in high esteem. Some of Aereboe's works include *Agrarpolitik, ein Lehrbuch* (Agricultural policy, a textbook), 1928; *Allgemeine landwirtschaftliche betrieb-slehre* (General agricultural management theory), 1923; *Der Einfluss des Krieges auf die landwirtschaftliche Produktion in Deutschland* (The influence of the war on the agricultural production of Germany), 1927; *Handbuch der landwirtschaft* (Handbook of agriculture), 1929; and *Die Taxation von Landgutern und Grundstucken: Ein Lehrbuch für Landwirte, Volkswirte, Kataster-und Steuerbeamte* (The taxation of landed estates and real estate: A textbook for farmers, economists, and land registry and tax officials), 1912.

Ali Hussein Pasha. Courtesy of Aziza Hussein.

Aside from Aereboe's influence on Hussein, very little else is known about Hussein's experiences in Germany. Correspondence between Hussein and his father during this period speaks only in general terms of Hussein's life. Hussein told his father of his initial difficulties understanding lectures and readings in German and requested increases in his allowance; 'Ali Hussein Pasha responded with typical fatherly advice and encouragement, offering to have Hussein's study materials translated into Arabic, urging Hussein to write home more often, instructing him to be more frugal in his expenditures, and warning him to stay away from the ladies and focus on his studies.[29]

Although he found plenty of time for a social life in Berlin (including entering and winning several ballroom dance competitions and avidly following the early stage successes of budding German star Marlene Dietrich), Hussein appears to have heeded his father's advice. In 1927, he earned his doctorate from the *Hochschule* with a dissertation entitled *Der Genossenschaftliche Bezug Landwirtschaftlicher Bedarfsartikel. Sein Aufbau, Seine Durchführung, sowie Seine Bedeutung f.d. Einzelbetrieb u.f.d. Volkswirtschaft* (The cooperative purchasing of agricultural consumer goods: Its structure, its execution, and its significance for individual businesses and for the national economy). Although the thesis examines the development and functioning of the cooperative systems in Germany, many of the ideas expressed by Hussein were later applied in his own work with Egyptian cooperatives.

In his thesis, Hussein divides farmers' cooperatives *(Genossenschaften)* into two categories, both of which handle cooperative purchasing and marketing of agricultural goods. The first type are specialized purchasing cooperatives, *(besondere Bezugsgenossenschaften),* which undertake the cooperative purchasing of agricultural inputs (seed, fertilizer, etc.) for their members. Farmers purchase goods directly from the cooperative, paying cash for the merchandise within a certain amount of time after delivery. Some of these cooperatives handle the purchasing of household goods on the same basis. Most purchasing cooperatives also handle the sale of agricultural produce, although cooperative sale is unpopular with and rarely required of members. Hussein distinguishes purchasing cooperatives from agricultural credit cooperatives *(landwirtschaftliche Kreditgenossenschaften),* which are associated with savings and loan institutes *(Spar- und Darlehnskassen).* These cooperatives buy and sell goods

On a sailboat with German friends. Courtesy of Aziza Hussein.

Hussein and friend in front of German castle. Courtesy of Aziza Hussein.

through the savings and loan institutes, with the risks carried by those institutes, not by the members of the cooperatives. Rather than paying cash for goods purchased directly from the cooperative, members buy goods from the cooperatives on credit given by the savings and loan institutes. Given the increased inputs necessary in modern agriculture, these types of cooperatives were becoming increasingly common in Germany.

In the first part of his thesis, Hussein looks in detail at the structure and execution of cooperative purchasing, examining issues such as the reasons for the increase in cooperatives in Germany, the differences between local and specialized purchasing cooperatives, and the form of communal purchasing of agricultural consumer goods. He evaluates the advantages and disadvantages of limited and unlimited liability, observing that in Germany, the proportion of cooperative associations with unlimited liability had been steadily declining as more and more farmers became reluctant to risk joining such groups. He concludes that cooperative associations work best in small areas where all farmers own roughly the same amount of land and there is a strong sense of community. The importance of a sense of community in the success of rural programs that Hussein highlights in his study of German cooperatives is something he would later apply to his own reform programs in Egypt.

He also reviews the circumstances in which specialized purchasing cooperatives are advantageous, the legal forms cooperative associations can take, and the various other organizations through which purchasing can be done, before discussing the formation of central cooperatives, or cooperatives whose members are primarily other cooperatives rather than individual farmers. After stating his own preference that cooperatives enact measures to make it more financially difficult for farmers to cancel their membership, Hussein briefly comments on the cooperative purchase of agricultural machinery, noting that cooperative purchasing of machinery has been slower to develop than cooperative purchasing of consumer goods because machinery is infrequently bought and there are often disagreements on the utility of various machines. Hussein identifies clear advantages in such purchasing, though, and recommends that it be expanded. In his view, the main advantage is that in a cooperative, the purchase of machinery would be done by experts who would be better able to get a good deal and less likely to be taken advantage of than an individual farmer would be.

Hussein then presents an overview of the administrative structure of these purchasing cooperatives before dealing at length with the actual execution of the cooperative purchasing of agricultural consumer goods. He summarizes the two different ways in which a cooperative purchases goods: either by filling preplaced orders for its members or by establishing and running its own warehouses. Concluding that the former is easier and cheaper, while the latter is more advanced and allows the cooperative to get better bargains for its members by buying off-peak, Hussein recommends that German cooperatives return to the system of filling prepaid orders for their members. His recommendation is primarily based on the state of the postwar German economy; Hussein notes that cooperatives tended to use the warehouse system in times of high inflation (e.g., after World War I). He argues that when inflation began to decline somewhat and interest rates remained high, the cooperatives abandoned the warehouse system in order to free up all monies for current transactions.

The remainder of the first section of the thesis is devoted to three topics: the setting of prices for purchasing cooperatives, payment for cooperatively purchased raw materials, and the buying of household necessities through the purchasing cooperatives. Hussein appears to be in favor of cooperatives tying the prices of their goods to their current market values rather than charging members exact purchase prices, ensuring that members all pay the same price for the same goods. He also pays particular attention to payment policies in the cooperatives, arguing that in agriculture lenient credit options are essential since farmers do not get returns on their investments until up to one year after making their initial investments. Hussein argues that providing credit should not be considered a problem, and he particularly urges further credits for the purchase of fertilizers and concentrated feeds because the use of these materials would allow the farmers to get higher returns on their investments. Hussein states that it is convenient for agricultural purchasing cooperatives to become involved in the purchasing of household items as well; consumers would get better deals through cooperatives because the retail system is not well developed in the countryside and because no additional personnel or expenditures would be required. Thus, in the first part of this thesis, Hussein expresses three ideas that would become central to his later programs in Egypt: a focus on community identity and cooperation, reliance on local experts, and the importance of access to credit and advanced agricultural technologies.

In the second part of his thesis, Hussein examines cooperative purchasing of agricultural consumer goods for both individual businesses and for the national economy. He attributes the development of cooperative purchasing in part to the introduction of new scientific and technological discoveries (such as mineral fertilizers, concentrated feeds, higher quality seed, modern machinery, and tools) into agriculture. He argues that another impetus driving the spread of cooperative associations was the desire of owners of small- and medium-sized farms to avoid the monopoly of traders of agricultural goods.

Hussein then spends considerable time demonstrating how cooperative purchasing helps create an economic upturn in agriculture through higher quality goods, better delivery conditions and lower prices, sale of agricultural products through the purchasing cooperatives, and the advice given to farmers through the cooperatives. He argues in favor of purchasing cooperatives also engaging in the sale of agricultural produce, particularly in remote areas where farmers often have little choice in where to sell their produce. He also emphasizes the need for cooperatives to provide sound purchasing advice to farmers. Though Hussein notes that the staff of local cooperatives are economic experts, he stresses that, even more important, they are people who are knowledgeable about the daily conditions of farming in the areas where they work. Emphasis on local experts and the importance of a thorough knowledge of local conditions are themes that Hussein would later develop and apply in all his rural reform projects, particularly in his Rural Social Centers program. He also stresses the advantages of speeches, exhibitions of goods, mailings, and prizes for good work in furthering the spread of agricultural cooperatives. These methods also were adopted by Hussein in later projects.

With respect to the national economy, Hussein stresses that since agriculture is such an important part of the German economy, the development of agricultural cooperatives, which has significant positive economic effects on agriculture, should be given more attention. Arguing that agricultural purchasing cooperatives have regulated the market for agricultural consumer goods, rationalized agricultural business, promoted modern science and technology, and improved agriculture as a whole, Hussein concludes:

> According to all we have seen so far, the cooperative purchasing of goods is basically significant for agriculture and national economy in three aspects. First of all, the individual farmers have joined together at the start in local purchasing cooperatives out of pure defense against the poor state of affairs in the newly developing market for raw materials. Here, we are talking only about a promotion of the individual. The purchasing cooperatives then developed further into institutions that would aid the farmers in preserving their interests before producers of agricultural raw materials, which were united in rigidly structured syndicates, especially in the areas of fertilizers and fuel. Here, we see a promotion of farmers as a whole. Finally, the cooperative purchasing organizations have not only benefited agriculture alone, but also have had direct effects on the different sectors and occupations within the whole of the national economy.[30]

Thus, as his thesis demonstrates, Hussein was a staunch advocate of the expansion of the cooperative system in Germany. He saw agricultural cooperatives as beneficial to the individual farmer, to farmers as a group, and to the

Practicing target shooting. Courtesy of Aziza Hussein.

national economy. His study of German agricultural cooperatives served as a basis for his subsequent work in the Cooperative Department upon his return to Egypt.

Why Rural Reform?

As the son of a privileged family, Hussein, like others of his generation and class, was expected by his family to make a useful career for himself. But the key question is why this young man from such a prominent and wealthy family chose to study and work in the arena of rural reform. Although Hussein's mother's family had land in the Egyptian countryside, young Ahmed did not enjoy visiting rural areas. Even in adulthood, his wife recalls that he would spend the night in rural areas only rarely, as he found them uncomfortable and did not rest well there.[31] While it may appear ironic that a man who would devote the majority of his professional career to work in the countryside did not enjoy spending time there, it was perhaps his own recognition of the poor standard of living in rural areas and his own discomfort there that were precisely the factors that motivated him to spend most of his life trying to alleviate rural poverty. Religious motivation seems to have been absent from the equation. Though raised in a conservative, Muslim family, Hussein himself was not a practicing Muslim, only rarely praying, fasting, or celebrating the *eids*. He was not ignorant of religion, however, and believed Islam (and many other belief systems) contained much of value.

Admittedly it is difficult to determine a person's intellectual influences, particularly after that person has passed away. However, both Aziza Hussein and Hassan Dawood, Hussein's lifelong colleague and friend, attributed Hussein's pioneering approach to social reform in Egypt to his Western education. Aziza Hussein states categorically that "it was the influence abroad, in Germany" that inspired her husband to get involved in rural social reform in Egypt.[32] Similarly, Dawood ascribes Hussein's interest in social reform, particularly his strong belief in popular participation and the minimal role of government, to the influence of his studies in Germany. As one of the leading Western-educated public servants of his generation, Hussein served as a crucial transmitter of social science thinking, introducing social reforms ideas from the West into Egypt and adapting them to local conditions. Yet both

Sitting on a wall at a friend's *'izba.* Courtesy of Aziza Hussein.

Aziza Hussein and Dawood were quick to point out that Hussein was no blind imitator of Western ideas of social reform or methods of social science. Dawood recalls that although Hussein's ideas were influenced by experiences of social reform in the West (particularly by his own studies in Germany), he would frequently caution his colleagues and pupils that "the very excellent and advanced technology of the West is not enough for us, or is not ready to help us. We have to have our own technology that is maybe taken from Western technology but adapted to the conditions of our country."[33]

Evidence of Hussein's insistence on adapting foreign ideas to local conditions can be found in his development of the program of Rural Social Centers while director of the Fellah Department. Hussein's own training in Germany convinced him of the necessity of thorough research. Accordingly, his first step when appointed director of the Fellah Department was to conduct a thorough study of different methods of social action in rural areas. Projects from the Balkans and India were among those evaluated, as were programs in the American South. Aziza Hussein, remarking on her husband's development of the project, noted that the involvement of the government in this program was a

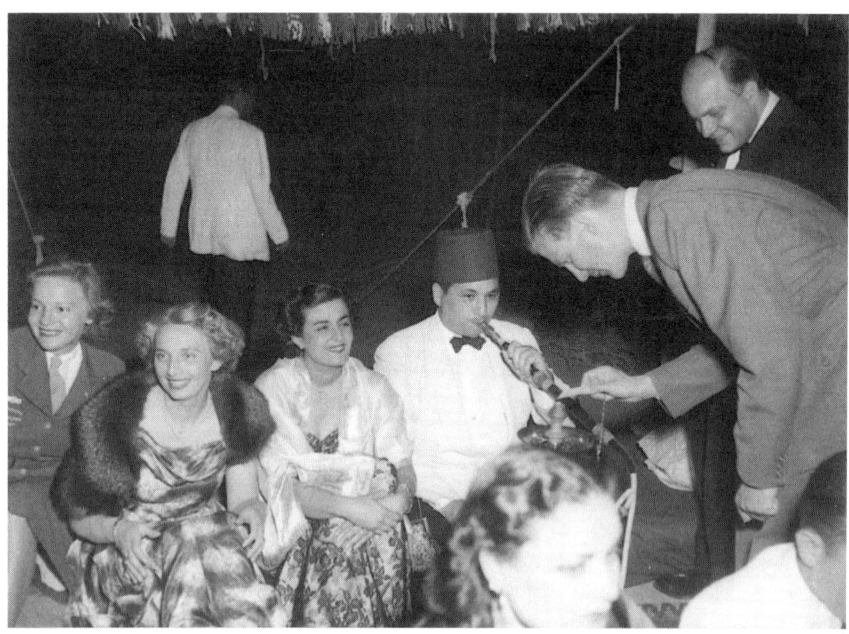

With friends, smoking *shisha.* Courtesy of Aziza Hussein.

completely Egyptian innovation.[34] The other self-help programs studied had been aided by nongovernmental organizations. In switching to government-aided self-help, Hussein was adapting these useful programs to Egyptian realities. As will be seen in more detail in later chapters, other aspects of the project, such as the existence of a separate female health visitor to address the needs of the village women, informal talks on religion, and incorporation of influential village leaders such as the *'umda* into the conciliation committees of the centers all are further examples of the program being adapted to meet the needs of the Egyptian villages. Hussein's ability to combine the best elements of his foreign training with his knowledge of local conditions was a significant factor in the success of his programs of rural reform.

2

The Professor and the Inspector

Upon completing his education in Berlin, Hussein returned to Egypt, where he began working as an inspector in the Cooperative Department of the Ministry of Agriculture. He was quickly promoted to the position of head inspector before becoming undersecretary of the department. He was appointed as head of the Fellah Department in the Ministry of Social Affairs in 1939 and retained a concurrent post in the Cooperative Department (which had been transferred to the Ministry of Social Affairs in 1939),[1] serving as that department's assistant director until 1948.[2] As undersecretary and later as assistant director in the Cooperative Department, Hussein helped guide the cooperative movement in Egypt. At the same time, he was also pursuing an academic career at Fu'ad I University, where he encouraged his students to become involved in rural reform projects of their own design. From 1927 to 1939, Hussein's most valuable contribution to rural development came under the auspices of the Egyptian Association for Social Studies. As one of the organization's most active members, Hussein oversaw a pilot project of rural reform that he would later adopt as the centerpiece of his development efforts in the Ministry of Social Affairs.

To set the stage for Hussein's return, this chapter begins with a brief look at events in Egypt while Hussein was finishing his studies in Germany. It then presents Hussein's work as inspector and his involvement in the cooperative movement in the 1920s and 1930s and examines how those experiences helped Hussein formulate his reformist agenda. The chapter then discusses Hussein as professor, his role in early rural development projects, and how such projects fit into the political and social climate of interwar Egypt.

Egypt in the 1920s

Hussein left Egypt on the heels of a revolution. Following World War I, an Egyptian nationalist politician, Sa'ad Zaghlul, asked the British for permission to attend the Paris peace talks, where the victorious allies were deciding the fate of the areas previously under Ottoman control. When the British refused, Zaghlul responded in 1919 by calling for complete independence for Egypt, and the British promptly deported him to Malta. Large-scale demonstrations against the British broke out, culminating in an unsuccessful revolution in 1919. When Hussein left Egypt, he left a country recovering from world war and a thwarted revolution, and a country on the verge of becoming a monarchy. Fu'ad I (who ruled from 1917 to 1936) was Egypt's first king, although real power continued to rest with the British high commissioner.[3]

While Hussein was away from Egypt, the political situation in his native land changed again. The British protectorate ended in 1922 when Egypt officially became an independent nation. Independence was not total, however; Britain reserved the right to security of communications, the defense of Egypt from foreign powers, the protection of foreign nationals in Egypt, and control over the Sudan. Sa'ad Zaghlul was permitted to return from exile in 1923, the same year a new constitution was completed. The constitution, modeled on the constitution of Belgium, vested the monarch with extensive powers:

> Only a two-thirds vote of the members of parliament could override the king's veto on all legislation. In case of a disagreement with parliament, the king could dissolve it and rule by decree. Although ministers were responsible to parliament, they were appointed and could be dismissed by the monarch. The elected Chamber of Deputies was balanced by a Senate in which two-fifths of the members and the president were appointed by the king. The rest of the senators were elected indirectly. All had to be men of considerable property or of high position.[4]

The first elections were held under this constitution in January 1924. To no one's surprise, the elections resulted in a significant victory for Zaghlul's new Wafd (Delegation) Party, a primarily middle-class, anti-British party. The Wafd won 188 of 215 seats in the lower house of parliament. Other parties participated in the elections as well, most notably the Liberal Constitutionalist Party (primarily composed of old Ottoman elites; their primary goal was to limit monarchical power in the government) and the Union *(Ittihad)* Party (a party with no popular base, formed by the king to counterbalance the power of the Wafd, and popularly known as the King's Party).[5]

The victory of the Wafd in this first round of elections and the enormous mass support enjoyed by the party signaled the emergence of a new force in Egyptian politics. The British and the Palace were established centers of influence; now the Wafd was a third factor in the struggle for power. Throughout the prerevolutionary period, these three groups competed for control of the government, two of them sometimes allying against the third and at other times all openly competing against each other. This three-way power struggle would be played out in a variety of settings, including social service provision.

The British governor-general of the Sudan, Sir Lee Stack, was assassinated in November 1924, setting off political clashes that ultimately resulted in Zaghlul's resignation as prime minister. Parliamentary elections were held later that year and brought about a defeat of the Wafd by a coalition of Liberal Constitutionalists, Union Party members, and independent candidates. The confusion of Egypt's political situation and the effect of the three-way power struggle can be illustrated by a description of the events surrounding the 1924 elections:

> The first overt clash between the Egyptian nationalists and the British after independence followed the assassination of Sir Lee Stack, governor general of the Sudan. [Egyptian prime minister] Zaghlul rejected [British high commissioner] Lord Allenby's ultimatum to punish the killers, pay an indemnity, and remove Egyptian troops from the Sudan. Reprisals, which had the effect of again converting Egypt into a British protectorate, caused Zaghlul to resign. His initial showdown with King Fuad occurred after the Wafd defeat in the 1924 elections. . . . Despite the defeat, the Chamber of Deputies elected Zaghlul its president, whereupon the king dissolved parliament. Zaghlul retaliated by forming a rump parliament in a nearby hotel. This time British High Commissioner Lord [George] Lloyd backed the nationalists because he feared a popular uprising. In the 1926 elections the Wafd won a sweeping

> victory, but Lord Lloyd now convinced Zaghlul to compromise by turning the prime ministry over to the middle of the road Liberal Constitutionalists.[6]

In 1927, the year Hussein received his doctorate, Sa'ad Zaghlul died, and the leadership of the Wafd Party was assumed by Mustafa Nahas, who, in 1950, would persuade Hussein to accept a post in the last Wafdist cabinet before the 1952 revolution.

Inspector Hussein

To this tumultuous political environment Hussein returned in 1927, not as a political activist but as a civil servant determined to help improve the living conditions of rural Egyptians by involving himself in the cooperative movement. The cooperative movement in Egypt had begun approximately two decades earlier, in 1909, when 'Umar Lutfi Bey, inspired by his studies of cooperatives in Italy, began canvassing the countryside, urging the formation of agricultural cooperatives.[7] Lutfi argued that agricultural cooperatives, which

Aboard ship. Courtesy of Aziza Hussein.

he called agricultural unions, had the potential to raise both the economic and the social standards of living in the countryside.[8] Lutfi and the committee he formed were responsible for the drafting of the first law of cooperation in Egypt in 1909. This bill proposed forming a permanent government body to supervise and to promote agricultural cooperatives.

Several types of cooperatives subsequently developed in Egypt. In the German context (Hussein's area of expertise), the primary defining characteristic of the cooperatives was whether they were associated with credit-granting institutions. In Egypt, on the other hand, there were several types of cooperatives: agricultural credit cooperatives, which handled cooperative purchasing of agricultural inputs (the primary form of cooperatives and, except where noted, the type discussed in this chapter); consumer cooperatives, which handled cooperative purchase of consumer goods; and marketing cooperatives, which collectively marketed agricultural produce (primarily potatoes, onions, and other fruits and vegetables).[9]

Lutfi's enthusiasm and hard work bore fruit, and many societies were organized within two years. By 1911, Lutfi had succeeded in organizing the Cooperative Financing Company in Cairo and seventeen cooperative agricultural societies, and his work had earned the support of Prince (later sultan) Hussein Kamel.[10] However, the program started by Lutfi did not last. Hussein, summarizing the beginnings of the movement in a 1955 speech, remarked that "the whole program, however, rested on this man's zeal and hard work. When he died in 1911, there was unfortunately no one to carry the movement forward. The lack of trained leaders and credit facilities caused even the cooperatives he had organized to collapse."[11] Hussein may have seen this early failure of the cooperative movement as significant; in his own programs, he relied not on his own efforts but instead made certain to build up a corps of specially trained and educated personnel who could carry out his reformist agenda.

When 'Umar Lutfi Bey passed away, his brother, Ahmed Lutfi Bey, took up the cause of the cooperative movement. Ahmed Lutfi succeeded in creating the General Central Union, a body that was to serve as a general federation for all cooperatives, to oversee all commercial transactions of the cooperatives, and to act on the cooperatives' behalf in all financial dealings with the Central Bank of Cooperative Institutions. The laws drafted by the Lutfi brothers and their supporters were eventually passed by the parliament after much study and reworking.[12] However, the advent of World War I interfered with their application. The war and the events of 1919 (and the resulting lack of government interest in passing supporting cooperative legislation) coupled with the lack of funding for the cooperatives and the fact that they were still a new institution all combined to undo the work of the Lutfi brothers.

The movement remained dormant for twelve years, until the Egyptian government passed the first cooperative law in 1923 (while Hussein was beginning his studies in Berlin), one year after Egypt became nominally independent from Britain.[13] This law gave legal recognition to the existing cooperative societies in Egypt. It also allowed them to borrow money. Finally, it incorporated Lutfi's call for the creation of a governmental body to regulate, supervise, and coordinate the cooperatives, creating a Cooperative Department within the Ministry of Agriculture that same year.

The new cooperative law resulted in the speedy creation of numerous cooperative societies in rural areas. By 1925, there were 139 agricultural cooperative societies registered in Egypt, with 10,673 members and total capital of LE 35,404.[14] Yet, these societies were largely unsuccessful. Although farmers joined them and paid their dues to the societies, "they had no real grasp of the meaning of a cooperative. They were not convinced it would serve their interests. They did not know how to run it once they had it. The general low level of education increased the difficulties of keeping the cooperatives' books in order. No wonder then, that the scheme evaporated as fast as it sprang up."[15]

Four years later, in 1927, the government tried again, and the Cooperative Department was enlarged. Hussein himself was part of this expansion, joining the Cooperative Department as a new employee the following year. In addition, a High Cooperative Advisory Council was formed with representatives from both the government and the various cooperatives.[16] New legislation governing cooperatives was also passed that allowed for the creation of cooperative societies in nonagricultural sectors and changed the system of financing the societies: "Whereas they previously borrowed money from the Government credit account for industrial advances in Bank Misr, [after the passage of the new law] the Government opened a special credit account to the sum of LE 350,000 for loans to cooperative societies."[17] As a result of his studies in Germany, Hussein was asked to participate in devising a plan for the forma-

Hussein near the beginning of his career. Courtesy of Aziza Hussein.

tion of the new Agricultural Credit Bank. The foundation of this bank in 1931 furthered the expansion of the cooperative movement, as it took over from the government the lending to cooperative societies and eliminated the "maximum limit on total loans granted."[18]

The new provisions resulted in a rapid expansion in the number of these societies. By 1930, the number of cooperatives in both agricultural and nonagricultural sectors had increased from 135 to 514, and by 1931, there were 539 societies with more than 53,000 members and total capital of more than LE 150,000.[19] However, like the increase after 1923, this rapid increase was deceptive, as Hussein himself admitted:

> The movement expanded and the number of societies increased ten-fold. But, in the process, our enthusiasm had gotten ahead of sober planning. We cared more for the increase in numbers and volume of business than for intensive basic cooperative education of the members. The individual peasant did not understand his responsibilities and democratic privileges as a member. The land distribution system raised several problems. The big landowners were not ready to accept the principle of equal vote. The smaller peasants

> were too weak to insist on their rights. The former soon monopolized the management, services, and advantages of [the cooperative] societies. The relatively easy terms of credit tempted members to borrow in excess of their real needs and their ability to repay.[20]

Indeed, one of the reasons for the rapid expansion of cooperative societies during the 1930s was the desire of the large landowners to take advantage of the easy credit offered by government banks. This was an especially attractive option during the crisis years of the Great Depression.

These difficulties were only overcome through the passage of time, overall economic improvement, and the concerted efforts of the Cooperative Department to educate the population about the nature and benefits of cooperatives. As Hussein recalled, "Specific cooperative education through dissemination of literature; through lectures by qualified officials; through our cooperative schools for society officers; through actual participation by the farmers in discussions, prepared the way for progress."[21] The lessons Hussein learned from this experience were later applied to the expansion of his Rural Social Centers (RSC) program. Rather than focusing on rapid expansion of the program, Hussein, drawing upon his experience with agricultural cooperatives, focused on the participation and education of the peasants, involving them directly in the program and allowing the program to evolve and expand naturally.

Politics in the Interwar Years

In 1928, the year after Hussein returned to Egypt and began working in the Cooperative Department of the Ministry of Agriculture, the Wafd, which had been sporadically negotiating with the British with an eye toward achieving complete independence for Egypt, lost power. Accusations of influence peddling were lodged against Mustafa Nahas and other Wafdists, and King Fu'ad took advantage of the situation to dismiss the Wafdist government. Muhammad Mahmoud, a Liberal Constitutionalist, was named prime minister. After one month in power and without garnering a parliamentary majority in support of the government, the government simply dissolved the Chamber of Deputies. A state of emergency was declared, and the 1923 constitution was suspended, including Article 4, which had stipulated that the king would govern through his ministers. The suspension of the constitution meant that the king was now able to function as an absolute monarch and to govern directly, rather than through ministers or parliament. The events of 1928 were referred to by many observers as a royal coup d'état.[22]

The Wafd response to events was to denounce the suspension of parliamentary life in speeches in both domestic and foreign venues. Popular opinion still overwhelmingly supported the Wafd Party. Public demonstrations against the suspension of the constitution and in favor of the Wafd, however, were repressed by Mahmoud with the cooperation of the British. In an attempt to smother opposition, several newspapers were shut down by the government, and, as Jacques Berque explains, "The Government tried to discredit its adversaries by suing them for embezzlement, with a signal lack of success. Disappointed in this direction, it sought to strengthen its hold on its own officials, by passing an order of 'protection of public functions' which penalized any attack against an official in the exercise of his duties, while forbidding officials or students to take part in political demonstrations."[23] Shortly thereafter, in March 1929, a law was passed making it illegal to protest against the suspension of the constitution.

Mahmoud's own struggle for power with the king led to his resignation later that year.[24] A caretaker government under Adli Yakan Pasha took over until new elections were held in December 1929. These elections, predictably enough, brought the Wafd to power yet again, this time for only six months. Negotiations with the British were resumed, and the party committed itself to protecting the constitution. The negotiations appeared to be succeeding until the issue of the Sudan was addressed, and here the talks broke down. The Wafd had again failed to resolve the key issue of British control.

At the same time that successive governments were being appointed and dismissed with alarming rapidity, the world economic crisis, later to become known as the Great Depression, was beginning. By this time, Egypt was actively involved in the world economy, and the depression had similar effects in Egypt as it did elsewhere in the world. The Egyptian economy was dependent on agricultural exports (primarily cotton), and the depression had serious socioeconomic consequences. Agricultural exports declined, and prices of agricultural products followed suit; this agricultural crisis played a major role in bringing Egyptian rural poverty to light and in generating support for various types of rural reform plans. With the decline in agricultural exports that resulted from the depression came an increased interest in industrial projects, both to offset losses in agriculture and because industry was seen as essential to the economy of a modern nation.[25]

Yet despite the growing awareness of the need for progressive social and economic reform in Egypt, political affairs were taking a decidedly antiliberal turn. By June 1930, Isma'il Sidqi and his People's *(Sha'ab)* Party had replaced the Wafd, and the parliament was again adjourned. Sidqi had "already become a symbol, in all eyes, of anti-constitutionalism," and his government quickly became authoritarian.[26] A new constitution was written in 1930 that made a number of important changes to the structure of government. Drafted in secret and in haste, the new constitution limited the number of seats in the parliament to 150 and restricted voting rights to those paying tax.

> An indirect election by notables was therefore rigged. [The constitution] contained a number of odd clauses: for instance, members of the liberal professions were not eligible [to vote] if they practised outside Cairo. It was hoped in this way to restrict their political activity to the chief towns of the *mudiriyas.* The rural electorate naturally received favoured treatment. The Senate was considered too large; it consisted of three-fifths of elected members and two-fifths appointed by the Government. This proportion was to be reversed, this securing a majority of docile members in the Upper Chamber. Results that could not have been obtained by direct manipulation would thus be achieved by discretionary means. Moreover, the text of this Constitution, imposed without national consultation, precluded any amendment for a period of ten years. If the Government thus acquired an almost total freedom to manoeuvre, the King took his share of the spoil. His veto could henceforth eliminate the discussion of any project under consideration; postponement to the next sitting would make it possible to negotiate an eventual majority. The monarch had secured something else, which he valued greatly, and which Zaghlul had striven so hard to wrest from him: the right to nominate the shaikh of al-Azhar and the leaders of religious orders. He thus gained control over these important connecting-links between the established order and popular religious observance.[27]

The government now had the legal means, embodied in this new constitution, to effectively repress all dissent. Sidqi took over the portfolios of interior and finance in addition to his post as prime minister.

Although the means existed, repression was not wholly successful. By 1932, Berque wrote, opposition had grown so violent that "every journey made by the [Prime] Minister proved an occasion for fresh clashes, when people were injured and sometimes killed." Government response was directed against the Wafd, which it viewed, with some justification, as the source of the unrest. Government repression reached such proportions that the entire apparatus of government seemed to function solely to discredit the opposition. Berque continued, "People realized that in many trials, whether political or civil, the prosecution made use of a sinister police department which specialized in the faking of evidence. If you were a member of the opposition, or merely a journalist or intellectual, you had to take care lest a police spy should slip into your car or into your pocket a packet of cocaine, so as to involve you in an unpleasant scandal."[28]

By September 1933, Sidqi's government had proved to be another disappointing failure, and it too was dismissed by the king. The unusual constitution he had drafted was abrogated the next year, and "Egypt became a constitutional country without a constitution," where "all power was vested in the Cabinet."[29] After Sidqi fell from power, Adli Yakan Pasha took the helm and was prime minister during King Fu'ad's illness (which resulted in his death in 1936) and the resumption of constitutional life. In January 1936 the royalist 'Ali Maher took power but was ousted by May of that same year. However, during his hundred days in office, Maher managed to establish the Higher Council for Social Reform, the precursor of the Ministry of Social Affairs (established when Maher came to power again in 1939). In addition, the Constitution of 1923 was reinstated, and Maher put together a delegation to resume negotiations with Britain. "The [delegation] was cleverly representative: it consisted of seven Wafdists, three Independents, and one delegate from each of the other three parties."[30]

The elections of 1936 ousted Maher and replaced him with another Wafdist government, under Nahas's leadership, which concluded negotiations with the British on a new Anglo-Egyptian treaty. The agreement signed in 1936 was a considerable improvement over the 1922 pact. The new treaty abolished the office of high commissioner, set a date for abolishing the capitulations and consular courts, and gave the Egyptian government jurisdiction over non-Egyptians. It ignored the thorny issue of control over the Sudan, but it still reserved for the British the defense of the Suez Canal and the right to station troops in the canal zone and in other Egyptian cities in the event of war. The other major event in Egyptian politics in 1936 was the death of King Fu'ad and the assumption of the throne by his son, the sixteen-year-old Faruq. The young and handsome Faruq was initially hailed as a nationalist and was immensely popular with the people. Circumstances soon changed, however, and the popular Wafd Party was dismissed from power a year and a half later, in December 1937. Faruq, like his father, preferred more tractable ministers. 'Ali Maher returned to power on the eve of World War II.

During the interwar period, Hussein stayed aloof from political affairs. Despite familial Wafdist affiliations and despite his hopes that 'Ali Maher's Higher Council for Social Reform might prove effective, Hussein joined no political party. Although Hussein's primary career from 1928 until 1939 was as an official in the Cooperative Department of the Ministry of Agriculture, he was also, at the same time, organizing independent reform associations, giving weekly lectures in the Faculty of Agriculture at Fu'ad I University, gathering together groups of his students for discussions about rural social reform and encouraging them to use their summer vacations to carry out reform projects of their own design in the villages. He was also one of the founding members of the Egyptian Association for Social Studies (EASS), a private, voluntary social studies organization in Cairo.[31]

Professor Hussein

While a professor at Fu'ad I University in the 1930s and 1940s, Hussein started a student association called al-Ruwaad (the Pioneers) within the Faculty of Agriculture. Founded in 1931, the Pioneers dedicated themselves to studying methods of social reform, particularly social reform in rural areas, and the group held periodic discussions about issues of rural life. The main purpose of the group was to study, discuss, report on, and design projects to address problems facing the Egyptian countryside. With the motto "The strength of the nation is in the strength of the individual, so with ourselves we

Ahmed Hussein. Courtesy of Aziza Hussein.

must start,"[32] the organization founded branches in both Cairo and Alexandria. In addition to carrying out studies of rural areas, the group also "experimented with some [reform] projects by working with the people rather than for the people."[33]

Under Hussein's tutelage, the students designed summer projects to be carried out in rural areas. Each project was to research and address various aspects of the farmers' problems, such as illiteracy, wages, or the shortage of land. At the beginning of each term, the students would meet and discuss the results of their projects. Hussein's own ideas of the importance of studying the farmers themselves, of technology as merely a means to raising the standard of living for the people, and of the importance of popular participation guided the work of the group. In addition to designing and carrying out summer projects in rural areas, the group also began literacy classes for university employees. The students had been struck by the incongruity of people with doctorates and workers who were illiterate working in the same institution, and they sought to address the problem with these classes.[34]

Muhammad Fu'ad Galal, speaking at the Second Social Welfare Seminar for Arab States of the Middle East in 1950, praised the Pioneers for their help in forming a college to train teachers in rural schools, saying, "This work was connected with the activities of the Rowad (Pioneers of Social Reconstruction), which is a voluntary body that prepared a rural camp near one of the villages of Fayoum for the study of the problems of rural life. From among those volunteers the teachers [for the new college] were selected."[35] Writing in 1950, Karl de Schweinitz praised the group, saying that the Pioneers "banded together to find ways in which they could serve Egypt and . . . have since then contributed much to their country."[36]

By the late 1930s, Hussein saw an opportunity to expand the activities of the Pioneers outside the university setting. In conjunction with a group of prominent, reform-minded figures in Egypt, Hussein helped establish the Egyptian Association for Social Studies (EASS). Founded in 1937, the goals of the EASS, as determined by Hussein and his colleagues, were "1) To study the social problems of Egypt and to arouse the active interest of the general public in the aims and methods of Social Works. 2) To carry out social projects as practical experiments to show the results of the scientific methods in Social Work. 3) To train professional social workers with special reference to local conditions."[37] Since one of its primary goals was the establishment of exemplary projects to find the best methods of social reform, the association developed a plan for integrated village reform, known as the Rural Social Centers project. The original plan was a product of the collaboration of all the association's members and was placed under Hussein's supervision. Hussein directed the experiment and periodically visited the villages where the project was to be carried out in order to ensure things were working properly.

The EASS chose two vastly different villages as sites for the first two social centers: the village of al-Manayil, located fifteen miles northeast of Cairo in Markaz Shibin al-Qanatir in the province of Qalyubiyah, and the village of Shatanuf, located about thirty miles from Cairo in Markaz Ashmun in the province of Minufiyah, both in Lower Egypt. Al-Manayil was a small, traditional village, isolated from almost all "modern progress," while Shatanuf was a larger village and had more connections to economic and social activities in the region. These two villages were chosen because EASS considered them to be representative of the two kinds of villages to be found in the Egyptian countryside.[38]

The 1937 census statistics for al-Manayil and Shatanuf illustrate the differences between the two villages. Shatanuf, with a population of 4,731, was approximately three times the size of al-Manayil, and its population density was higher as well. Its literacy rates were somewhat better than al-Manayil's, with Shatanuf boasting a male literacy rate of 29.6 percent and a female literacy rate of 8.2 percent compared to al-Manayil's male literacy rate of 22.6 percent and female literacy rate of 2.6 percent. Shatanuf's economy was more diversified than al-Manayil's, and the percentage of its population working in agriculture was approximately 20 percent lower, although in both villages the majority of the working population was engaged in agriculture, fishing, or hunting. Both villages were overwhelmingly Muslim. Shatanuf did have an almost 10 percent non-Muslim (primarily Coptic Christian) minority, while al-Manayil's religious minority (entirely Coptic) comprised a mere 0.9 percent of its population.

Edwin Muller, an American researcher who visited al-Manayil prior to the beginning of the pilot project, described the village in the following terms:

> Manayil was perhaps a little worse than the average village, but not much. The streets were rutted and piled with filth. Three stagnant ponds were literally open cesspools. No school. Not even a mosque; the tumble-down old mosque had been condemned. Nearly 90 percent of the villagers were afflicted with Egypt's peculiar curse, bilharzia, worms which live as parasites in the human body, weakening the victim and stupefying him. More than 50 percent of the villagers had hookworm and malaria. Illiteracy was 83 percent. General misery, 100 percent.[39]

More detailed is the description of the village of al-Manayil written by social worker Mohamed Shalaby. Shalaby recorded his observations in his 1950 publication *Rural Reconstruction in Egypt,* which includes both his own memories of the project and his recommendations for future reform:

> El-Manayel is a small village fifteen miles northeast of Cairo on the east side of the Nile Delta, about a mile west of the Ismailia Canal in the Province of Kalubia. Living conditions in this brilliantly green, beautiful village compared most unfavorably with many other villages in Egypt. Houses are

> damp, dark, ill ventilated and badly constructed of sundried bricks or stones, with roofs covered or made of cotton stalks, floors are of packed clay; doors are roughly made and windows are too small and rarely have glass. . . . The streets were filthy, narrow and irregular passage ways and usually dusty and full of mud. In the surrounding area there were three dirty ponds, an active focus of disease and source of malaria. Piped water was almost unknown and there were no supplies or even stand-pipes in the streets. Drinking water was often taken from the small irrigation ditch running from the Nile through the various villages. It was also used for washing and even for bathing of men and children. Internal sanitation and arrangements for sewage disposal were equally rare, baths were non-existent. . . . Some families have beds and chairs, others use mats and rugs for both sitting and sleeping. . . . No decent clothes were used by most of the *fellaheen* except one suit, usually used when going any place outside the village, when expecting a guest or in a feast. . . . The village had no school although children, by law, were obliged to go to school. The nearest school was more than a mile away from the village. . . . The old mosques were used for prayers. Their washing rooms were unhealthy and were closed for several months of the year by order of the public health inspector. Few children received medical care since there were no local services and it was not easy to reach the free crowded hospital (about ten miles from the village) or afford the services of a private physician. Diets are monotonous, high in starch, low in protein and fats and lacking in milk, meat, fruits, or even vegetables. Diarrhea and other illnesses were frequent among the children owing to the lack of sanitation. All these factors mean a low standard of living which undermines resistance and makes the *fellaheen* an easy mark for disease. In brief, the whole village was completely neglected.[40]

Clearly, the village of al-Manayil was ripe for some sort of reform project, and given such overwhelmingly bad conditions, the EASS had its work cut out for it.

As formulated by the board of the EASS, the original plan was created with four basic assumptions in mind:

> 1. That certain changes in village life are desirable to improve health, increase physical comfort, add to knowledge, develop personality, and build

> up helpful social relations. 2. That any change, in order to be effective, must spring from within and be in the direction of people's own desires. If these desires do not exist, they should be created. 3. Changes must not destroy existing values, which must be considered by the reforms to be adopted. It is not to be assumed that whatever [exists] is bad although plenty of it may be. 4. That while introducing such changes under controlled conditions, their effectiveness in raising the standard may be measured and evaluated.[41]

In addition to these basic assumptions, there were two central ideas guiding the project. One was to get the people to participate actively in every aspect of reform. The other was to ensure that the reform was integrated—that it would address medical, economic, social, agricultural, health, and cultural issues in the village at the same time. As Hussein later explained:

> Above all, the strategy is based on the doctrine that people must learn to help themselves if they are to be helped at all. And the central notion behind the great forward push [for reform] is that it must be made on all fronts at once. For it is useless to attack the health problems of families who must remain hungry, or to preach sanitation and cleanliness to those who lack the means of purchasing such simple things as soap and adequate clothing.[42]

The work began in both villages in October 1938, and other sites for experimental reform projects were added later.[43] The EASS began pilot projects similar to the ones in al-Manayil and Shatanuf in the villages of al-Agayza, Bahtim, and Umm Khunan Minufiyah.[44] However, these projects were not full-fledged social centers. In al-Agayza, the Egyptian Land Mortgage Bank donated funds for a reform project, and the villagers pledged participation, money, and the necessary buildings. By November 1941, the EASS had sent an agricultural-social specialist and a health visitor to the village, and the Ministry of Health had promised to provide a temporary field hospital. The Royal Agricultural Society (RAS) sponsored the project in Bahtim and sought financial cooperation from the factories and firms in the area. The RAS requested that the EASS and the Ministry of Social Affairs advise it on what the village needed and how to implement the project. The National Bank of Egypt also contributed by beginning a reform program in the village of Umm Khunan

Minufiyah.[45] These three projects were started several years after the al-Manayil and Shatanuf projects began. It is important to note that each village reform project had a primary sponsor from the nongovernmental sector. Only after the Fellah Department, under Hussein's leadership, took over the project was the project changed from one of nongovernmentally aided self-help to one of governmentally aided self-help. This section will focus on the pilot program in al-Manayil for two reasons: first, the al-Manayil project was the larger and more significant of the two initial projects, and second, documentation on the al-Manayil project is more extensive.[46]

Support for the projects in al-Manayil and Shatanuf came from many sources. The Ministry of Health donated medicine and medical supplies, the Ministry of National Defense contributed a number of old military blankets, and the Royal Agricultural Society, private citizens, and businesses gave financial and material support to the project.[47] Most important, of course, were the contributions made by the EASS and by the villagers themselves.

The first stage of the pilot program in al-Manayil was the selection of a male agricultural-social specialist and a female health visitor to serve the village. After renting two houses to serve as the buildings of the social center, the EASS sent Mohammed Shalaby, a graduate of the Faculty of Commerce at Fu'ad I University[48] and graduate student at the new School of Social Work in Cairo,[49] and 'Aida Kabil, a nurse, to establish residency in the village. Initially, their mandate was rather vague. Their first step was to compile a thorough social, health, and economic survey of the village.[50] After that the project would, it was hoped, grow naturally from the comments and ideas of the villagers. To complete the survey, however, Shalaby and Kabil had to win the trust and confidence of the people, and this proved to be a slow and difficult task. Shalaby recalled that gaining the trust of the villagers was an uphill battle. "It was not an a easy job because social work in its modern form was not known even to many well educated persons in the area, and because of the suspicion of the *fellaheen*. . . . They used to see government officials coming to carry out the laws, to gather taxes, to follow criminals, or to fine them for their actions, which are usually the result of their ignorance and misunderstanding of the state laws."[51] Though Shalaby and Kabil were not government officials themselves, they believed they would be perceived along the same lines—as outsiders sent from Cairo to interfere with village life.

After several abortive attempts to draw the village men into conversation, Shalaby obtained a radio from Cairo and began listening to it in the evenings. He began tuning in to the broadcasts of the Qur'an from Cairo, and eventually a few men began to wander near the house.[52] The first man Shalaby was able to establish a friendly relationship with was Hassan Abou al-Nasr, a seventy-year-old villager who began listening to the radio with Shalaby and who in time brought with him his seven sons and six sons-in-law.[53] After this, more and more of the village men began to listen with them, and a sort of "men's club" was born. Kabil's friendships with the village women were also slow to develop. She began teaching the children new games and from there began to have regular contact with their mothers and sisters. The basis of the project thus became mutual trust and friendship between the specialists and the villagers.

The project was not without its difficulties, even after friendships with the villagers were established. One of the wealthier villagers began to request favors from Shalaby, and when Shalaby did not grant them, the villager became hostile and obstructive. Muller recounts the tale as follows:

> The rich man of the village—he owned nearly five acres—had rented the benches and chairs [in the center's buildings] to Shalaby. He was the kind of man who is always on the make. He began demanding favors of Shalaby, to get his son a job in Cairo, and so forth. When Shalaby didn't respond, he got mad. One day he came around with a camel and carted the furniture away. For a time the Men's Club had to sit on the floor, until the growing pressure of public opinion brought the rich man around.[54]

This kind of incident occurred in other locations later on, when some village elites began to resent the growing respect of the villagers for the staff members of the centers. But as in the al-Manayil project, such situations were generally defused by the patience of the staff members, by the results achieved by the centers, and by public opinion in the village.

Since the cornerstone of the project was the active participation of the villagers, the two specialists in al-Manayil did not directly suggest reform projects to the villagers. Instead, they waited until the people themselves began to talk about the conditions of life in their village. Shalaby phrased it as "waiting all the time for the right opening, some spark of discontent which [I] could fan into a flame."[55] A good example of this is the process by which the village of al-Manayil came to have its own primary school.

One night while listening to Shalaby's radio, the village men began commenting on the government's compulsory schooling program. Since al-Manayil did not have a school of its own, the children were required by law to attend school in another village, more than a mile away. The predictable result was that many of the children of al-Manayil did not attend school. That particular day a truant officer had arrived in al-Manayil and fined the parents of truant children the equivalent of three days' wages. Shalaby asked the men why al-Manayil did not have its own school and asked whether the village men did not think the government might build one there.[56] The discussion then continued into broader issues such as the justice of compulsory education laws and the real value of education for the children and their families.[57]

The result of the discussion sparked by Shalaby's query was remarkable. The men of the village, without Shalaby's knowledge or direction, drew up a half-page petition to the government complete with three pages of thumbprints as signatures requesting that the government build a school in the village of al-Manayil.[58] Shalaby sent the petition to Hussein and his colleagues on the EASS committee in Cairo; the committee then brought up the issue with the governor of the province, a man who had been interested in the reform project from the beginning.[59] The petition was successful. The government agreed to build and maintain the school, provided the villagers would locate and clear an appropriate site.[60]

Initially, the problem of finding a site was a challenge. All the productive land owned by the village was used for agriculture, and the rest was taken up by houses and roads. At Shalaby's suggestion, the villagers chose a stagnant pond and filled it in with refuse and earth obtained by leveling the village streets, thereby creating a site for the new school. The result of the conversation following the truant officer's visit, therefore, was not only the building of a village school but also the removal of a significant source of disease (the stagnant pond) and an improvement in village infrastructure and hygiene (leveling the streets and removing the refuse from them).[61]

While the villagers were in the process of filling in the pond, the project suffered another setback, this time at the hands of the provincial government. The men began filling in the pond in their spare time, but the requirements of farming and the weakness brought on by the diseases endemic to the community combined to make progress extremely slow. The governor of the province, impatient with what he perceived as the laziness of the villagers and anxious to have this new project succeed, sent ten policemen to al-Manayil, who dealt with the situation by assembling the men and forcing them to fill up the pond that day using "anything that came to hand, including the cotton and corn stalks that were stored on the flat roofs for fuel."[62] While this action did succeed in filling in the pond, it also nearly destroyed the villagers' confidence and trust in Shalaby, who then had to spend weeks trying to gain back their goodwill.

In the end, however, the school was built, and Shalaby was able to reestablish good relations with the villagers. The presence of a school in al-Manayil increased school attendance dramatically, but the benefits did not end there. Plans for a new sort of rural school had been in the works since 1926, but they had not been realized. The EASS in conjunction with the Modern Education League of Cairo established a school board for al-Manayil consisting of representatives of their two groups and representatives of the Qalyubiyah Provincial Council. The aims of the board were to continue to teach the standard elementary school curriculum (described by Shalaby as "the 4 R's—reading, 'riting, 'rithmetic, and religion")[63] as well as to broaden the scope of education to include practical subjects.

According to these new ideas, more subjects, such as sewing, poultry raising, modern agriculture, weaving, and furniture making were added to the standard school curriculum. Students spent half their day inside the schoolhouse learning "the 4 R's" and the other half in the workshop learning practical lessons for rural life. While the village girls used the classroom, the boys "worked in the fields and workshops, planting crops, vegetables, etc., starting a garden or dairy farming, breeding animals, bees, making furniture (from grasses and split palm branches) and weaving cotton and rugs." While the boys received academic instruction, the girls "took silk culture (there being silk worm food in the village's mulberry trees), fruits and vegetable preserving, sewing and poultry."[64] The school also became a center for adult education, and Shalaby successfully persuaded the villagers of the benefits of literacy.[65] As the EASS board member responsible for overseeing the al-Manayil pilot project, Hussein was aware of the progress being made in the village, and he served as liaison between Shalaby, the EASS itself, and the government in Cairo. Hussein was particularly interested in the new village school, and when he adopted the RSC project for the Fellah Department, he incorporated the new model into the government's rural social centers.

In the meantime, Kabil's friendship with the village women had progressed to the point where pregnant women not only came to her for health advice but almost all delivered their babies in her house, which was converted from a home into a maternity and child welfare clinic. Infant mortality, which had been almost 30 percent, decreased, and Muller reported that most of the new baby girls born to al-Manayil mothers were named 'Aida in gratitude to the hard-working nurse.[66]

The women of the village also came to the clinic to learn embroidery, tricot, and needlework, and one day each week the social center building was turned over to the women so that they might gather there and listen to the radio.[67] Unfortunately, all the anecdotal accounts of the al-Manayil project were written by men, who naturally had very little access to and knowledge of the projects being carried out to benefit the village women. Consequently, there is a dearth of information on the women's projects in al-Manayil and Shatanuf compared with the amount of information available on the primarily male activities. However, Shalaby did include in his memoirs an account of how the women of the village pushed for—and gained—membership in the village cooperative society.

The idea of founding a cooperative society in al-Manayil, which would, according to tradition, be an enterprise restricted to the male population, was introduced about two months after the project in al-Manayil began. While it is unclear from existing literature on the pilot project why this idea was introduced, it is likely that Hussein played an important role in pushing for the establishment of such a society. It took fifteen months before Shalaby was able to convince the villagers that a cooperative society would serve their needs. After that time, sixty-four villagers contributed LE 57.50 for shares in the new cooperative society.[68] By the time the cooperative society caught on, the Ministry of Social Affairs had been founded and the Cooperative Department transferred to the new ministry from the Ministry of Agriculture. Hussein was at that time both head of the Fellah Department and assistant director of the Cooperative Department; at his urging, the ministry waived the legally required minimum group subscription of LE 100 and allowed the al-Manayil cooperative society to be registered with the ministry.[69] With Shalaby serving as the elected secretary-general of the society and the *'umda* elected as the chairman, the cooperative society began its own projects:

> [The cooperative society] started its activities by distributing to the members a quantity of kerosene oil on the government ration basis and price. (This article was subject to the black market and its price reached four times the fixed price). The society moved on to supplying the members with their needs of soap, matches, cotton clothes, and household utensils, etc., at a great saving. In the agricultural field of activities, the society started to supply seeds, fertilizers, chickens for poultry raising, etc., moving to collective means of selling their crops.[70]

Despite the progress of the society, the village women were unhappy. They resented not being included in the group, and they felt that it did not represent their interests. The women asked Kabil to help them form their own cooperative society because their husbands, fathers, and brothers would not allow them to join the cooperative society founded by the village men. However, these women did not simply ask for help in forming a cooperative; they had already raised a significant amount of money for their cooperative before coming to Kabil with the proposition. Shalaby reported:

> One day the health visitor [Kabil] came to [me] with a serious problem. Twenty-two women from the village visited her with the request that she start a women's cooperative society. They gave her their subscriptions and promised to assemble the other women of the village. Thirty pounds was the first part of the capital, more than half of that gathered in 18 months from the men, and more subscriptions were to follow.[71]

Shalaby himself preferred that the women be allowed to join the established cooperative, rather than forcing the formation of a second society. After numerous discussions between Shalaby, Hussein, and the EASS in Cairo and between Shalaby and the men of al-Manayil, it was agreed that the village cooperative would be open for membership to all villagers regardless of gender.[72]

The membership in the village cooperative society grew rapidly as women were admitted to the group and as its successes continued. In less than three years, the capital invested in the society grew approximately sevenfold, and the membership increased to almost eight times its original number. The society was so successful that the people of the neighboring village of Sindiwah, two miles away, asked Shalaby's help in establishing a cooperative society for their village. The Sindiwah cooperative was created as a "sister society" to the al-Manayil organization, and the al-Manayil society was subsequently recognized as a model project by the Cooperative Department of the Ministry of Social Affairs.[73]

Due to the success of the village school, the maternity clinic, and the cooperative society, the people of al-Manayil developed more projects. Citizens who had initiated the original projects formed a village council and began to suggest additional programs to help the community, including a contest for the cleanest house in the village and creation of a village charity organization. The cleanest-house contest (which was instituted in later centers as well) was begun by the children of al-Manayil, who were encouraged and excited by the prospect of winning a badge if their house was chosen as the cleanest home in the village. Later, this project was taken over by the village adults, and the winning house was given a free whitewash (or pink-or blue-wash).[74] Shalaby recalls "how proud the wife was when visitors came to see her white walls and the well swept floors" and adds that "prizes of other types [also] were given to the owners of the cleanest houses in the village, such as building a new healthy latrine, giving a certain number of chickens, or a head of sheep or cattle." In time, cleanliness became a habit for the villagers, and it was no longer necessary to give prizes as encouragement.[75] In addition, the charity organization raised enough money from voluntary contributions throughout the village to buy a loom and threads, which the poorer members of the community began using to generate their own income.[76]

Despite such progress, health concerns remained paramount in the minds of the two staff members in al-Manayil, and one of the most important tasks was the establishment of a clean water supply for the village. Persuading the villagers of the necessity of using clean water proved to be a daunting challenge. Shalaby hit upon the idea of using a microscope to show the villagers all the organisms living in the irrigation ditches and river water.

> Presently, he was sending [the village men] for specimens of the ditch water, putting a drop on the slide, showing them the bilharzia larva swimming merrily around. He described in colorful detail how it bores through the skin and enters the blood stream, grows into a worm, then makes its way into the urinary tract, living on its host and draining away his strength. But it was hard, hard work to persuade anyone. They had always drunk the water of the Nile brought to them by the ditches. As one of the headmen stated it: Allah had put the water there and the worms in it. "Oh Sheikh," said Shalaby, "you speak words of wisdom. Now tell us this: if you were walking on the railroad track and heard a train approaching, would you continue to walk or would you leave the track?" [The man responded,] "Only a fool would continue to walk on the track." [Shalaby agreed, saying,] "You speak wisdom, Oh Sheikh. And these worms are like the train. A wise man will avoid them."[77]

Despite Shalaby's use of the microscope and his debating skills, changing the villagers' attitudes toward the use of irrigation ditch water was a slow process. Eventually, however, the villagers became convinced that they needed a new source of clean water, and they asked Shalaby to contact the EASS in Cairo, saying that if that group would provide the pumps and the pipes to construct a new water system, they would build and use it. All families in the village helped to dig a well and to install the three water pumps provided by the EASS. For the first time, residents of al-Manayil had a source of clean water. Later, the villagers took the initiative to raise money and contact the provincial council to improve and to expand their clean water system.[78]

Health projects were not limited to the provision of clean water and attempts to persuade the villagers to use it. The health clinics in both al-Manayil and Shatanuf began smallpox and diphtheria vaccination campaigns. Thanks to the presence of the center, all villagers received free medical examinations, and sick patients in each village were examined and transferred to local hospitals.[79] Combined with the provision of clean water, the improved health care in al-Manayil reduced the rate of bilharzia from 90 percent to 30 percent.[80] Shalaby summarized the changes made in health care in al-Manayil, saying:

> Now each family has complete medical service. There is no difficulty about getting necessary medical service. If hospitalization is indicated, arrangements can be made for it at the nearest hospital. Pregnant women can secure prenatal care with no difficulty because they can walk to the doctor's office or go to the nurse. . . . A school health clinic was also developed. A medical examination was given to every child and daily health inspection was made . . . The health unit (the doctor and nurse) provided a weekly clinic for the control and treatment of venereal diseases. In the beginning many families were reluctant to use the medical services but now they are delighted. The change in the water supply, filling the ponds and the great improvement in the sanitation conditions are also of considerable value [to public health].[81]

The villagers also began several economic projects, including the establishment of a dairy in Shatanuf, where the agricultural-social specialist helped the farmers increase milk and cheese production, the establishment of the cooperative association in al-Manayil, and the acquisition of better cotton, wheat, maize, and vegetable seeds and fertilizers at reduced prices through the good offices of the EASS. Al-Manayil also established its own local market to sell the vegetables now grown in the village, while Shatanuf established small factories for weaving and batiste (a variety of sheer fabric) projects as well as a beekeeping industry complete with both modern and traditional apiaries. Shalaby reported that the value of the land in and around al-Manayil had increased, production had improved, and new crops were being raised.[82]

The centers also began recreational activities, including lectures on health, religion, and agriculture, and organized athletic events and contests. A library was established within the social center building, and although Shalaby reported that very few adults used it, the children of the village visited the library regularly.[83] In addition, the agricultural-social specialist in Shatanuf was able to convince the owner of the weaving factory to raise the wages of his workers and to end evening and weekend work. The specialist also acted as a mediator between the villagers and the government during negotiations for placing an access bridge near Shatanuf.[84]

The benefits of the pilot projects in al-Manayil and Shatanuf were clear just six years after they began. Muller, who had observed the conditions in al-Manayil before the project began, returned to the village in 1946 and gave an entirely different picture of village life there:

> I saw the community center, the child-welfare center, maternity ward, community shower baths, etc. I walked through streets swept of debris. I went into houses which, although still mud huts, were nearly as clean as a Connecticut farmhouse. It wasn't what would be called a model village in America. There were no sidewalks, there was no running water in the houses. . . . They were still poor people—they couldn't be otherwise with the limited land at their disposal. But compared to the average Egyptian village, it was a paradise. And, much more impressive than the physical appearance of the village was the aspect of the people. In Egypt you get so used to the typical bilharzia look that you take it for granted. The shambling gait, the dull, lackluster eye with no interest in anything. The half-alive, apathetic inertia. But these people look alive, alert. They look as if they are going places. They are.[85]

The changes wrought in the village of al-Manayil were incredible. The overwhelming success of the project, despite the difficulties posed by the local elite and an impatient provincial administration, prompted increased interest in the project. Hussein's personal experience with the al-Manayil project and his personal knowledge of its success led him to champion the project as a model for future reform efforts. After the founding of the Ministry of Social Affairs in 1939, the government, in the person of Ahmed Hussein, first director of the Fellah Department, committed itself to promoting rural social welfare, using the al-Manayil pilot project as the basis of its plans. Hussein's early reform projects thus established him as Egypt's leading rural social reformer, and these projects were a basis for his future reform projects within the framework of the Ministry of Social Affairs.

3

The Ministry of Social Affairs and the Rural Social Centers

Some commentators in Egypt during the prerevolutionary period tended to dismiss all social reform efforts before 1952 as poorly disguised attempts to deceive the people. This point of view, shared by many postrevolutionary scholars as well, is a common misconception of Egyptian history—that prior to the 1952 revolution Egyptian society was essentially stagnant, that little or no social or economic progress was being made, and that there was no real interest among the elite in reforming the country. Such a perspective posits a sharp division between pre-and postrevolutionary Egypt. It argues that the 1952 revolution ushered in a new era of progress and reform, sweeping aside all elements of the prerevolutionary regime, and bringing light to a country stumbling in the darkness of corruption and despotism.

Although it is true that little tangible progress was made in the area of social reform, efforts were made to improve the living conditions of the poor, to increase levels of health and education, and to bring about a program of land reform. The 1930s and 1940s in Egypt were not a time of darkness and despotism—rather, they were a time of great intellectual ferment and a time when many members of the social and political elite were advancing programs designed to reform the country. When the Free Officers seized the reins of government in 1952, they benefited from these prerevolutionary reform ideas. Their programs of land reform, minimum wages, and social, health, and economic services were neither original nor revolutionary—they were natural outgrowths of decades of social reform thinking and programs. The Free Officers inherited from Egyptian intellectuals and social reformers a rich legacy of ideas on how the government ought to address the country's ills. The programs begun by Ahmed Hussein in the Fellah Department of the Ministry of Social Affairs were an important part of this rich legacy. In order to locate Hussein's programs within the larger context of reformist debates prior to 1952, this chapter begins with an overview of some of the major groups, individuals, and parties offering reforms in late parliamentary Egypt. It then presents the 1939 establishment of the Ministry of Social Affairs as, at least in part, a result of the emerging reformist debates and discusses how World War II influenced these debates. The remainder of the chapter analyzes Hussein's Rural Social Centers project and argues that amidst the lively discussions of reformist ideas, this program was a uniquely successful program of integrated rural development.

The Emergence of Reformist Ideas

Around the time Hussein returned from Germany, a new force entered Egyptian politics. In 1928, in the canal city of Isma'iliyah, a religious scholar named Hassan al-Banna founded al-Ikhwan al-Muslimun, the Muslim Brotherhood. Socioeconomic conditions in the interwar period helped attract many to the group: "Al-Bana's [*sic*] disarmingly simple program to revive Islam by combating secularization through social justice had wide appeal for the urban proletariat, impoverished students, and the *fellahin*. . . . the organization and its leaders were imbued with a social idealism that could attract those most disaffected by the increasingly complex economic pressures of modern society."[1]

Originally a socioreligious movement concentrating its efforts on religious revival and provision of social services, the Brotherhood eventually grew to become a potent political force in Egyptian society. During the depression years of the 1930s, however, the group's activities were primarily charitable and religious in nature. Prominent elements of the Brotherhood's program of reform included using the Qur'an and *shari'a* as the bases of government as well as more general goals such as decent wages, more and better education, and the availability of social services to all Egyptians. The Brotherhood was one of many groups actively involved in formulating plans for the reform of society (in this case, along Islamic lines) during the prerevolutionary period.

During World War II, difficult political and economic conditions resulted in massive gains for the Brotherhood, and as membership ranks swelled with new adherents, the Brotherhood became an increasingly political organization. Rather than concentrating its efforts on the social and religious reform fronts, the Brotherhood began using violent methods in an attempt to achieve its political goals: "During the postwar turmoil, the group reached the zenith of its power through the organization of violent strikes and demonstrations. Its political murders, student riots, and bombings of public places so terrorized Egyptian politicians that they listened seriously to Brotherhood demands."[2]

Alongside the Brotherhood's plans for reform of society on religious lines, many intellectuals—one of them being Ahmed Hussein—were devising various plans and programs for secular reform. The appalling conditions of life in rural Egypt were becoming widely recognized. A brief summary of rural living conditions indicates why reformers often targeted rural areas for their programs:

> Egypt's peasants were among the world's most poverty-stricken, with an annual per capita income of $55 to $65. They lived in disease, filth, and on the verge of starvation. . . . Possessions were limited to some reed floor mats, a few simple cooking utensils, and a garment or two per person. Food was cooked over dung fires whose smoke irritated the eyes, usually already infected with trachoma. Most of the rural population was infected by the liver fluke, bilharzia, whose parasites weakened its victims, making them easy prey to dysentery, malaria, and tuberculosis. Most peasants were old at forty, and nearly 80 percent of those of military draft age had to be rejected for service. Disease was spread by the use of filthy Nile water for drinking and washing. Unskilled workers earned the equivalent of about five cents for a twelve-hour day; and real income had actually declined since World War I. This was indicated by the decline in total consumption of tobacco, coffee, meat, textiles, and cereals, despite a 25 percent increase in population.[3]

It is no surprise, then, that rural areas became the primary focus of reformist debate.

The issue of rural poverty and rural reform became a popular topic of concern and debate during the agricultural crisis in the 1930s. When international economic conditions caused agricultural prices to fall, both poor peasants and wealthy landowners felt the loss of revenue. The crisis helped direct attention to the countryside, as did the conclusion of the 1936 Anglo-Egyptian treaty. Although not a nationalist's dream, the treaty was welcomed in all quarters as a distinct improvement over the 1922 treaty, and as a result of its conclusion, attention began to be focused inward rather than on the foreign enemy. Books dealing with the conditions of rural life and containing recommendations for reform began to appear in Cairo, and more interest developed in the sciences that would permit a thorough study of rural problems.[4]

Agricultural economics became an increasingly popular field of study, and statistics on rural areas began to be kept. Population studies were made and data on landholdings, land rents, and crops were collected with increasing frequency.[5] Many of the people scientifically studying the conditions of rural life were colleagues and students of Hussein. Mohamed Riad el-Ghonemy, for example, published a statistical analysis of landownership in 1948 in *al-Mujtama' al-Jadid*,[6] in which he argued against the inequalities in landownership, which he blamed for the decline in agricultural prosperity. Another protégé of Hussein, 'Abbas Ammar, was also at the forefront of those doing statistical analysis on rural conditions in the 1940s. In his two-volume work on conditions of life in one Egyptian province, he criticized lack of government action in the countryside, the fragmented approach to social service provision, the unequal distribution of land, and the growing debt among the fellahin.[7]

The centrality of agriculture to the Egyptian economy, the recognition of rural problems, and the fact that the majority of the country's population still lived in rural areas combined to make rural reform a key issue. However, although rural reform was a political issue, inhabitants of these areas were rarely participants. The people who debated how to address rural problems were almost exclusively urbanites, although many had rural family backgrounds or ties to rural areas.[8] As one scholar commented, "For all parties, and above all for the Wafd, the peasantry formed a basis and provided a stake that could not be ignored. It was discussed and studied, its fate was said to be bound up with that of the whole country." Beginning in the late 1930s, political speeches referred to the king as an "honorary *fellah*," and politicians were quick to identify themselves and their parties with the rural population and to praise the fellahin as the true backbone of Egypt.[9]

Founding the Ministry of Social Affairs

By the late 1930s, these developments led to a growing awareness in Egypt that the government needed to take a hand in addressing the social problems of its people. In 1936, Prime Minister 'Ali Maher Pasha founded a formal governmental body, the Higher Council for Social Reform, as a first step in governmental reform efforts. Maher, who was also the first president of the EASS, was a conservative and a royalist, but he was also concerned with the growing social problems in Egypt.[10] Hussein and his colleagues in the EASS envisioned the government taking an active role in social service provision, thus moving away from the trend of social services being provided as charitable services by nongovernmental organizations. They believed that the government should not only become involved in the social sphere but should also be the leader in the development of the country. Accordingly, this group drew up a plan to establish a larger governmental body whose purpose would be to address all social and labor issues in both urban and rural Egypt. This governmental body was the Ministry of Social Affairs.

The Ministry of Social Affairs was officially established in 1939, and many prominent officials, including 'Abd al-Moneim Riad, 'Abd al-Wahid al-Wakil, and Ahmed Hussein, quickly joined its service.[11] The ministry was established in the historical context of the Great Depression, mounting social discontent worldwide, and growing government concern with the welfare of its citizens. With the adoption of the Constitution of 1923, Egypt regained control of its internal affairs from Britain. Yet government efforts to address social and health issues remained minimal. As Nancy Gallagher reported in her comprehensive history of public health policy in Egypt, "The Great Depression, however, severely aggravated existing social and economic disparities in Egypt, and in response, the Wafd party added an internal social reform program to its nationalistic objectives during its 1935 party congress."[12] Hussein, writing in 1950, explained that the establishment of the ministry was largely due to the growing realization that private agencies were inadequate to address the social problems of the country and that the government had a duty to provide social services to its people. As he said:

> The creation of the Ministry of Social Affairs in the latter part of 1939 was a necessity dictated by the social evolution in the country. It was felt at the time that it was no longer wise to leave the various social problems to be dealt with by haphazard efforts curtailed by opposing currents and conflicting opinions. It was a supreme duty of the State to observe and record social conditions and their development, to diagnose social diseases and defects and to study the methods of treatment; to plan, in the light of these observations and studies, a comprehensive and permanent policy of social rehabilitation with a view to uplifting the poor classes, raising the standard of living of the individual as well as the family, and finally assuring the biggest share of social justice to the people. It is on these grounds that the Ministry of Social Affairs was created and its tasks planned out.[13]

Thus, the welfare state emerged in Egypt for much the same reason it emerged elsewhere in the early part of the twentieth century: a growing governmental and public desire to help the poor, particularly in the interwar period.

But what were the underlying reasons for the emergence of such a desire? Did all the people involved in founding the new ministry have altruistic motives, or were other factors at work? Jeremy Bentham, writing in the eighteenth century, argues that legislation has two primary ends: the provision of subsistence and the protection of security. Discounting as mere justification the argument that governments serve their citizenry out of commitment to religious, moral, ethical, or philosophical beliefs, he argues that failing to provide subsistence for the few risks the security of the many; legislation providing social services is thus not merely a matter of providing charity but rather a utilitarian approach to preventing the uprisings of the dispossessed.[14] Adam Smith, writing about motivations for providing charity and social welfare, agrees with this view. In *The Theory of Moral Sentiments,* Smith allows that humanitarian concerns and sympathy for the less fortunate do indeed play a role in the provision of social welfare. However, he stresses that another important, though less idealistic, motive is the desire to prevent the poor and disenfranchised classes' "impulses from leading to the use of violent means to enrich themselves."[15]

Eric Midwinter has applied this view to the development of the welfare state. Noting an expansion of government services in the late 1800s and early

1900s in countries as diverse as Prussia, France, Finland, Japan, Holland, Denmark, and tsarist Russia, he argues that the common rationale for providing services in all nations was to prevent uprisings resulting from the growth in industrialization and urbanization of the era. Amid the economic crises of the 1920s and 1930s, governments worldwide continued this trend, providing an ever-increasing array of social welfare policies.[16] The involvement of prominent conservatives like Maher in the EASS and the movement to found a Ministry of Social Affairs may be seen as partial support for this view. Social reform had been needed for many years. The Great Depression brought with it increased social and economic dislocation, and fear of its effects may have been the impetus for much of Egypt's wealthy elite to support governmental reforms in the social sphere.

Examining the relationship between private and governmental provision of social services and pursuit of economic development, Joseph Jabbra contends that in the Arab states, bureaucracy expanded primarily to carry out social and economic development programs. In his view, the Arab states differed from those of Western Europe and the United States because the task of economic and social development was left entirely in the hands of the government. Whereas the private sector made substantial contributions to social and economic growth and development in the West, political instability in the Arab states made the private sector unwilling to invest in social and economic development projects at home. The desire for secure profits drove Arab monies into Western investments, leaving the governments of the Arab states to assume sole responsibility for social and economic development schemes.[17] In the case of Egypt, while it is true that many charitable organizations (e.g., Mubarrat Muhammad 'Ali and the Red Crescent Society) had been active for decades in Egypt, development projects per se had not been initiated by these societies.

There are similarities between each of these models and events in Egypt; however, the Egyptian case fits none of the models precisely. While it is true that Egypt, like the nations analyzed by Midwinter, began a program of social services in response to the difficult economic conditions in the interwar period and attendant concerns about potential uprisings, there were other factors at work. There was, for example, a sincere belief on the part of officials like Hussein that the government had a moral obligation to alleviate poverty and to take steps to improve the standard of living of its population. In Hussein's case, this belief was divorced from any utilitarian concerns.

Jabbra's conclusion that in the Arab states governments were the only entities interested in and capable of providing social and economic services does not apply completely to Egypt. The development of social policy in Egypt was not an enterprise restricted to the government. Throughout the monarchical period, many nongovernmental agencies competed for popular support by establishing social and economic aid programs. Assuming that the people would tend to support whatever person or entity that provided them with the most tangible benefits, various groups began their own systems of social and economic service provision. These programs often competed with one another, and even different branches of the government strove to develop programs of social service provision. However, integrated development programs, as distinct from charitable services and small-scale service provision, did not begin until after the Ministry of Social Affairs was founded in 1939.[18]

Robert Bianchi has argued that in Egypt, neither simple concerns about popular uprisings nor a genuine desire for social reform led to the creation of the Ministry of Social Affairs. In his view, the ministry was created as a way to control different sectors of society. He contends that "during the 1920s and 1930s the state chartered no new corporatist organizations and provided no legal guarantees for the freedom of association. Each government tolerated a shifting assortment of private, voluntary groups that could be manipulated in an arbitrary and discriminatory manner."[19] According to this view,

> Only in the late 1930s, when mass movements reached new levels of organized violence, did the aristocratic dictatorships begin to advance corporatist strategies for restructuring associational life. As powerful clandestine organizations superseded the discredited party system, pluralism developed revolutionary potentials that demanded innovative countermeasures. Gradually, the regime began to abandon palace pluralism in favor of new state-sponsored groups that were intended to serve as supporting elements of a more popular authoritarian order.[20]

This argument is similar to Smith's and Midwinter's in that it posits the fear of uprisings as a motivating factor for government policymakers. However, Bianchi takes the argument a step further, contending that the government not only sought to provide enough services to dull the threat of uprisings, it also sought to establish the ministry as a means of controlling associational life in Egypt. Bianchi writes, "The 'reform' governments of 'Ali Maher (1936 and 1939–40) signaled the first attempt to bolster authoritarianism by sponsoring a legitimist set of interest groups and creating the illusion of a modern welfare state. . . . 'Ali Maher established the Ministry of Social Affairs to control private voluntary groups, including labor unions, which were on the verge of recognition."[21]

Smith's theory and Bianchi's arguments might well explain why the government embraced the idea of creating a new ministry. It is likely that both utilitarian concerns about potential unrest and the desire for further control of society played a central role in the decision to found the Ministry of Social Affairs in 1939. These reasons, however, are not sufficient to explain the involvement of Hussein and his colleagues in the formulation of a plan for this new ministry. While conservatives like Maher may have sought to establish the ministry as a means to control society, liberals like Hussein envisioned the new ministry as a means to a very different end.

For a variety of reasons, then, the ministry was officially established in 1939. Before this time, the government of Egypt was primarily concerned with the commercial, technical, and financial aspects of agriculture. The working conditions and standards of living of farmers and farm laborers received little attention, despite the fact that approximately two-thirds of the population were engaged in agricultural work. Pronouncements by various prime ministers and other government officials showed some concern for social welfare, both in rural areas and in the cities. The majority of the ministry's development activities before the revolution took place after 1942 and were focused on the countryside, where most of the population lived. Creation of the Ministry of Social Affairs in 1939, however, did not silence the reformist debates in Egypt, nor did the beginning of World War II the same year. A variety of groups, parties, individuals, and movements began calling ever more loudly for full independence from Britain and wholesale reform for the people.

Egypt and World War II

With the outbreak of World War II in 1939, the British, within their rights according to the 1936 Anglo-Egyptian treaty, used Egypt as their main base in the Middle East. The British also forced the king to sever relations with Hitler's Germany, and censorship was imposed. The use of Egypt as a major base had some short-term economic benefits:

> Industry was vastly expanded to supply Allied troops. At one time, Allied expenditure represented a quarter of the national income. About 200,000 Egyptians were employed in British workshops and camps. Small local industries were encouraged to develop to produce such products as textiles, preserved foods, chemicals, glass, leather, cement, building materials, petroleum, and machinery. War profits increased bank deposits from 45 million pounds in 1940 to 120 million by 1943, and the country's 50 millionaires became 400. Prosperity made Egypt a creditor nation to the extent of 300 million pounds.[22]

Yet neither these economic benefits nor the fact that Britain was within its treaty rights to station troops in Egypt resulted in much Egyptian support for the Allied cause. The massive influx of foreign troops was disruptive to Egyptian society, and it reminded the people that their country was not truly free. Admiration for the achievements of German field marshal Erwin Rommel's Afrika Korps was widespread, and many Egyptians sympathized with the Axis. The strength of British influence and the weakness of the king were brought to light in a way no Egyptian could forget in February 1942.

Prior to 1942, a series of prime ministers had been appointed and dismissed by the king. Prime ministers were either mildly pro-Axis or carefully neutral, but none were pro-British. When Husayn Sirri showed signs of Allied sympathies by severing relations with Vichy France in 1941, the king dismissed him. At this point, the British decided to put an abrupt end to pro-Axis governments. Former prime minister 'Ali Maher, known for his Axis sympathies, was arrested and charged with espionage, and the king was given a choice by British ambassador Sir Miles Lampson (by then Lord Killearn): either appoint a pro-British prime minister (meaning a Wafdist) who would uphold the 1936 treaty or give up the throne. To demonstrate the seriousness of the British position, Lampson ordered British tanks to take up positions near Abdin Palace, where the king was deliberating his next move, and went armed into the palace to hear Faruq's decision. Faruq, a practical man in this instance, decided to save his throne, and the Wafd was thus brought back to power.

The incident at Abdin aroused widespread contempt for the king, resentment against the Wafd, and further hatred of the British. Whereas the Wafd had previously been seen as the party of the nation, the incident discredited it in the eyes of many nationalists, and it increasingly was seen as the party of the British. The economic benefits brought by the onset of war began to dissipate, and this situation resulted in further widespread discontent:

> The apparent prosperity was deceiving. Only a relatively few Egyptians grew richer while the masses became more impoverished than ever. Wartime inflation caused prices to spiral upwards until by 1944 they were nearly three times those of 1939. Nearly 1,200,000 farmers had to seek tax exemption in 1942 because of poverty. Most hard hit were the unskilled urban and rural workers and the salaried middle class, who suffered severe privation. Expansion of the industrial proletariat by 35 to 40 percent created major urban problems. In Cairo when starved mobs attacked wheat shipments in 1942, a Wafdist leader commented that, "On the eve of the French Revolution the people of Paris shouted, 'We want bread.' The people of Cairo have done just the same thing. . . . The situation in this country can be described as revolutionary." Despite the 300 million sterling credits, the country was left with nearly a quarter million urban unemployed when the Allies withdrew after the war.[23]

The poor economic conditions and unpleasant political situation fostered the growth of two alternative political movements that gained ground during World War II: the communists and the Young Egypt Party (Misr al-Fatat). Until 1942, the communist movement in Egypt had been fairly weak, its popularity confined largely to non-Muslim intellectuals. The Soviet entry into World War II combined with Egypt's economic deterioration gave the communists greater prominence. Immediately following the war, communist leaders began organizing a series of strikes "to demonstrate their new power.

Textile and transport workers, police and hospital employees rebelled against the deterioration in postwar economic conditions." The growing influence of the communists was limited, however. Membership in the party was never higher than 7,000, and although "Communist leaders in various labor groups controlled about 60,000 workers," the party never had enough support to pose any serious threat to the government.[24]

Young Egypt was founded by Ahmad Husayn (although the two bear the same name, this Husayn is not to be confused with and was no relation to Ahmed Hussein). Prior to World War II, Husayn organized a group of young men into the Young Egypt Party. Initially modeled on Italian and German fascist groups and called by the nickname the "greenshirts," Husayn's organization changed ideologies after the defeat of Nazi Germany. It first became the Islamic Nationalist Party and then, in the post-World War II era, adopted socialism as its philosophy. In all its manifestations the group, like the communists, never succeeded in gaining enough support to threaten the government, although its terrorist tactics and threats of assassinations did arouse a degree of fear.[25]

Against this backdrop of world war, economic depression, and continued low standards of living, by the mid-1940s it was rare to find any politician who was (or could afford to be) thoroughly antireform. Social reform had become "politically correct," and it was an idea few challenged. Makram Ubayd tried to draw attention to rural poverty and the inequitable distribution of land during a three-day speech in parliament in 1945.[26] Ahmad Abd al-Salam al-Kirdani called attention to the problem in a series of articles in *al-Thaqafa* in 1945, where he blamed the poor living conditions of the fellahin on the oppression of feudal landowners. Marxist writings similarly blamed the privileged elite, and they often advocated widespread government intervention in economic and social life to improve conditions. Hafiz Afifi, the general director of Bank Misr, also contributed to the debate on rural issues but from a more conservative standpoint. Viewing land reform as a sure way to spread poverty to all Egyptians, Afifi instead advocated increased agricultural production, increased education, and programs to improve health conditions as the proper means to address the problems of rural life.[27]

Epidemic diseases sweeping through rural Egypt during the early 1940s also helped thrust rural areas into the limelight, and many attributed the epidemics to the poor living conditions of the fellahin.[28] Virtually all alternative political groupings formed action committees to fight the cholera and malaria epidemics, both as a means to combat the diseases themselves and as a means to gain adherents to their causes. While political parties used the epidemic as yet another excuse for argument rather than action, the Muslim Brotherhood and Young Egypt both volunteered their services. The Brotherhood "offered to distribute leaflets issued by the Ministry of Health, to help people understand them, to care for patients, and to help in cordoning off the infected areas. . . . The Students' Section of the General Headquarters of the Muslim Brotherhood sent a letter to the Ministry of Health declaring the readiness of thousands of its members to curb cholera by whatever means it suggested."[29] In addition,

> Members of Young Egypt formed a committee to fight cholera in the Sharqiyya province, where they placed themselves at the disposal of the Ministry of Health. The committee organized teams to go to the mosques to explain how to fight cholera. . . . Ahmad Husayn, president of Young Egypt, called on every member to make himself a soldier against cholera, to spread correct health procedures among people, to teach methods of resistance, to organize assistance, and to lead the campaign through local committees on every street, izba, and town.[30]

In contrast, the opposition parties limited themselves to words rather than engaging in productive action: "Makram Ebeid, the leader of the opposition Kutla party, announced that the party's newspaper would participate in the epidemic by publishing any and all complaints against the Ministry of Health." For their part, the Wafdists "formed a committee to study the cholera crisis and published a report on the government's shortcomings in dealing with the epidemic. The report focused on weaknesses in containing the disease and claimed that the Wafd government had contained malaria in Aswan and Qina and had kept the death rate at 8 percent."[31] Rhetoric of the parties during the epidemics shows that party leaders recognized the importance of rural issues, while their inaction brought to public attention their overall inaction on issues of social reform.

In various ways, then, diverse groups began to realize the centrality of the countryside in both health and politics.[32] Although the epidemics did spur short-term relief, longer term and more thorough plans of reform were also advanced. Ahmed Hussein proposed reforms dealing with the distribution of state lands to landless peasants, the establishment of a minimum agricultural wage, the regulation of the landowner-tenant relationship, progressive taxation on arable land, the expropriation of a limited amount of land from large landowners, and the various programs carried out through his Rural Social Centers project. The Ministry of Health also began a program of rural health units during this period.

Many other people, including members of parliament, were also concerned with social reform issues. The issue of land rents preoccupied several members of parliament, and they urged their colleagues to take action to limit rent charges. 'Ali al-Shishini harangued his fellow deputies during one of his speeches in December 1945, calling for reform of agricultural rents.[33] Other deputies, including Muhammad Fikri Abaza, leader of the Nationalist Party, and 'Abd al-Fattah Azzam also spoke in the Chamber on the same day in favor of restricting land rents.

King Faruq got into the act as well. From the day he took the throne, he took care to present himself as the friend of the fellah. The growing prominence of rural issues on the national political scene meant that regardless of his inclination, political expediency demanded that he pay some attention to the issue of rural reform. The king made his own estate at Inchass a model of what an agricultural estate could be and a model of the humane treatment of agricultural workers. He also attended government meetings on the issue of rural poverty.

Although no prerevolutionary government passed a land reform bill, the controversial issue was addressed in parliament and in the press. Senator Muhammad Khattab's proposal, first submitted to parliament in 1943, is the earliest example of a prerevolutionary attempt at land reform. Khattab, a Sa'adist Party member, proposed that agricultural landholdings be limited and that anyone owning 50 *feddans* of land or more be legally prohibited from acquiring additional land, except through inheritance. Khattab's proposal was rumored to have been influenced by Marxist thinkers, and it predictably met with a solid wall of opposition in parliament. The bill went through several revisions and in its last manifestation was finally defeated in 1947.[34]

In 1945, Mirrit Ghali published his influential book *Al-Islah al-zira'i* (Agrarian reform) in which he presented a concrete program of agrarian reform. In the book, Ghali addressed four essential elements of reform: the extension of small landownership, its preservation, the limitation of large landownership, and the reform of land rent and labor. He argued that each fellah needed a minimum of 3 *feddans* to support himself and his family, and he urged the government to distribute land parcels to the fellahin. In order to accomplish this, the government, according to Ghali, had to increase irrigation and land reclamation projects. It also had to redistribute land currently held by large landowners. Alongside these agricultural reforms, Ghali advocated the expansion of industry to meet the anticipated increase in peasant purchasing power.[35] The program of land reform instituted after the 1952 revolution owed much to Ghali's proposals.

The same year, another book advocating land reform, *The Problem of the Peasant,* was published by a communist writer, Ahmad Sadiq Sa'd. Sa'd criticized Ghali's program of reform for being too limited. He argued that the problem lay not only in the concentration of land in the hands of a few landowners but instead was part of a broader problem of a monopoly of political and social influence. Sa'd proposed to set 50 *feddans* as the maximum allowable agricultural holding and advocated the immediate imposition of the ownership ceiling. He also urged the foundation of more agricultural cooperatives and the passage of protective legislation for the peasantry.[36]

Rashid al-Barrawi, professor of economics at Fu'ad I University, presented a program for land reform similar to Ghali's in a 1948 speech. Al-Barrawi recommended setting the maximum allowable individual landholding at 50 *feddans* (also Sa'd's ideal maximum, and while a much lower ceiling than the revolutionary regime's initial cap of 200 *feddans*, 50 *feddans* was the maximum holding eventually settled on by the 'Abd al-Nasir government). He also argued for the regulation of land rents, the improvement of agricultural output, and the aggregation of small farms into some sort of cooperative farming arrangement.[37] The same year, Sayed Marei, who would later become director of the Higher Committee for Agrarian Reform and minister of agriculture under the 'Abd al-Nasir government, spoke in parliament about the need for land tenure reform.[38]

The religious establishment also entered the debate on land tenure. The same year that al-Barrawi made his proposal for limits on agricultural holdings, the Grand Mufti of Egypt issued a fatwa (religious opinion) on the subject of land ownership. In response to a document presumably issued by the Muslim Brotherhood condemning the inequitable distribution of land, the mufti, a state appointee, predictably came down firmly on the side of the landowners and presented alternative methods of alleviating rural poverty. The fatwa reiterated the role of almsgiving in Islam as a means of addressing poverty, stressed the rights of individuals to property ownership, and argued that Islam gives the individual the right to defend his or her property against aggressors.[39] The position of establishment Islam on the issue was refuted by Brotherhood member Muhammad al-Ghazali in a series of articles in the group's newspaper, *al-Ikhwan al-Muslimun*.[40]

In 1950, during the Wafdist government in which Hussein was minister of social affairs, two bills were presented to parliament on the land reform question. One was drafted by Mirrit Ghali, the other by the parliament's lone socialist member, Ibrahim Shukri. Ghali's proposal, which was very similar to the program outlined in his 1945 book, would have established the legal limit of ownership at 100 *feddans* by means of a limitation on new land purchases similar to that of Khattab's bill. Shukri's draft law was, predictably, more radical in its provisions. It stipulated the immediate confiscation of holdings in excess of 50 *feddans* and their redistribution to peasants holding fewer than 5 *feddans*.[41] The owners whose land was confiscated would be repaid in long-term government bonds, a feature that reappeared in the revolutionary land reform law after 1952. Both bills were defeated.

Although land reform met with no official encouragement during the prerevolutionary period, the fact that so many proposals for it were advanced during this period is testimony to the centrality of rural issues in the minds of intellectuals, reformers, and politicians. The stress put on other aspects of rural reform, such as rents, wages, cooperatives, and the treatment of the peasantry, is also evidence of intellectual effort put forth to address the myriad problems of rural life. It is within this context of a vibrant debate on how to remedy rural ills that Ahmed Hussein's activities should be examined. Hussein did not advance a wholesale program of land reform, nor were his other reform programs designed to be radical or rapid. In an era characterized by political unrest, intellectual fervor, and plans for sweeping reform, Hussein's programs stand out as moderate and gradual. They are also distinguished by their success.

Hussein's Marriage

In the midst of the social, economic, and political turmoil of the 1940s, Hussein somehow found the time to begin looking for a bride. He found Aziza Shukri, who was to become not only his wife but also his partner in reformist initiatives in Egypt before the revolution and an invaluable asset in his diplomatic career after 1952. Ahmed Hussein and Aziza Shukri met in Aswan through mutual friends in 1942 when Shukri was a student at the American University in Cairo and Hussein was director of the Fellah Department in the new Ministry of Social Affairs. Hussein wanted to marry a woman who was modern and intelligent, yet morally conservative. Having heard favorable reports about Shukri's intelligence and character from mutual American and Egyptian friends, Hussein formally proposed to Shukri in 1944.[42]

For her part, Shukri was flattered that a man as prominent as Hussein would be interested in marrying her. Considerably younger than Hussein, Shukri had not been thinking of marriage at the time Hussein proposed, and she had to make a fairly quick decision whether to accept or reject this suitor. Shukri admired Hussein's accomplishments and sense of purpose. She also believed that since Hussein chose her because of her education, energy, and modern outlook, he would appreciate her and love her for herself, and she therefore agreed to the marriage.[43] The couple were formally engaged, with the wedding date set for a year later so that they could get to know each other better. On June 17, 1945, Dr. Ahmed Hussein and Miss Aziza Shukri married, and the newlyweds moved into a top-floor apartment in the same building as Hussein's parents in the affluent Cairo neighborhood of Zamalek.[44]

Although both Hussein and Shukri came from wealthy and respected families, their upbringings had been radically different. Hussein came from a very conservative family, while Shukri's parents, particularly her father, were extremely liberal and progressive. In Hussein's traditional family, boys were preferred to girls, and the females in the family essentially took second place to the males. In sharp contrast to this was Shukri's own upbringing. Aziza Shukri Hussein described her father as a feminist who constantly stressed to his

Ahmed and Aziza Hussein on the beach in Alexandria. Courtesy of Aziza Hussein.

family the importance of education, self-reliance, self-esteem, and the dignity of women.[45]

Shukri's father, Sa'id Shukri, grew up in the village of Mit Ya'ish in Markaz Mit Ghamr, in the Nile Delta region. His father died when Sa'id was a young boy, and his mother lived in the village *'umda*'s compound. Sa'id Shukri was interested in medicine and went to Cairo to study, where he lived with one of his brothers who was an engineer. While a student in Cairo, Sa'id Shukri became involved in anti-British protests and was something of a revolutionary. As an opponent of the British, he was not chosen to study abroad on educational missions as were many students of that era. Determined to continue his studies, Sa'id Shukri financed his own higher education. He went to Dublin to study, received diplomas in gynecology and surgery, and then continued his education in France. Upon returning to Egypt, he participated in the Libyan war before settling in his village. Although many students returning from studies abroad went to Cairo to seek their fortune, Sa'id Shukri believed he should return to his village and serve his community. He set up modern medical clinics in Mit Ghamr and the nearby town of Zifta, and to this day the regional hospital is called the Shukri Hospital in honor of his contributions to the community.[46]

Ahmed and Aziza Hussein sipping coffee in a café in Alexandria. Courtesy of Aziza Hussein.

Sa'id Shukri met his wife, Aziza's mother, Hekmat Aref, through his relatives in Cairo. Although Sa'id Shukri preferred to marry a woman of his own choosing, he eventually decided to let his relatives find a suitable bride for him. Aref was the daughter of divorced parents of Turkish origin, each of whom subsequently remarried. As a result of this, Aref always felt somewhat alienated and out of place in both her mother's and her father's houses.[47] She was a very sensitive, musical, and artistic woman, and Sa'id Shukri was devoted to her. In spite of this, she found village life to be very difficult, and her health declined after the birth of the couple's five children, three girls (Aziza, Esmat, and Leila) and two boys (Hussein and Mohamed).[48]

As a result of his wife's ill health, Sa'id Shukri played the major role in bringing up the couple's five children. Aziza Shukri Hussein recalls that her father was often prejudiced in favor of herself and her two sisters and that her brothers felt oppressed by this favoritism. Tangible evidence of Sa'id Shukri's beliefs is seen in his efforts to provide a good education for his three daughters. Although the family was Muslim, the girls were sent to the local convent school in Mit Ghamr because Sa'id Shukri believed it would provide the best available education for his daughters. For high school, Sa'id Shukri sent the girls to the Mère de Dieu School, a French secondary school in Cairo, where they lived as boarders. Before the last year of Aziza's secondary education, Sa'id Shukri decided that the girls should change schools. He believed that the Mère de Dieu School's teachings were too antiquated, and he felt his daughters should have a better, more modern education. His close friend Aziz al-Masri (who later became a prominent figure in Egyptian politics) and his American wife recommended the American College for Girls, and as a result, Aziza spent her last year of secondary school at a new institution.[49]

By this time Aref's health had declined even further, and Sa'id Shukri decided to move to Cairo so that his wife could be closer to her family. He was offered a job as director of the medical department of the Railways Administration, and the family made the move to the capital. Aziza Shukri continued her education at the American University in Cairo, and it was during her student days that she first met Hussein. Sa'id Shukri always taught his daughters not to rush into marriage. He believed that women should be independent and educated and not be in a position where they were forced to rely on their husbands. According to Aziza Shukri Hussein, "He would tell us that unless you are totally pleased with the [proposed] marriage, then don't get married. He saw all the women who were being pushed into marriage, and he hated that."[50]

Aziza Shukri was totally pleased with the proposed marriage to Ahmed Hussein. Hussein was influenced by his family's conservative view of the role of women,[51] but despite the differences in their family backgrounds and the occasional difficulties posed by them, the two found that their beliefs basically coincided. Both believed strongly in the need for social reform, in the importance of popular action, and in the benefits of altruism. From the start of the marriage, and in part because the couple did not have any children, Aziza Shukri Hussein was very active in community affairs. She became involved in the Cairo Women's Club, which encouraged its members to propose projects to help the community. At the same time, her husband was director of the Fellah Department in the Ministry of Social Affairs and was busily expanding the department's program of rural social centers. Inspired by this project and with her husband's support and encouragement, Aziza Hussein proposed that the Cairo Women's Club work in conjunction with one of the rural social centers to help village women. The collaboration between Ahmed and Aziza Hussein

Ahmed and Aziza Hussein atop mountain in Switzerland, 1950.
Courtesy of Aziza Hussein.

on the Sindiyun project (detailed later in this chapter) illustrates their common commitment to social reform and popular action. Throughout their thirty-nine-year marriage, each encouraged the other to pursue their own interests, and both remained active and committed to social service. Even after Hussein's retirement, he continued to encourage Aziza Hussein in all facets of her career.

Aziza Hussein remembers her husband as a very wise, very private man. She also remembers that he was uncompromising on matters of principle, steadfast in his integrity, and very obstinate—a quality that proved useful in his career but somewhat frustrating in personal life.[52] Aziza Hussein recalls one incident during her marriage that illustrates better than any other Hussein's unwillingness to compromise on matters of principle. One time when the couple was in Geneva, they encountered a friend, the prominent feminist and writer Amina al-Said. Al-Said invited them to dinner that night with her relatives. In the Egyptian context, this implies that the person doing the inviting is the person who will pay. Aziza Hussein recalls, "[Ahmed] said, 'Are you joking? You want to invite me? What do you mean? There is no such thing as you inviting me. I don't get invited by women.' " Al-Said responded by saying that was fine, she just wanted Aziza and Ahmed to come to dinner, and it was not important who paid. Aziza remembers the events that occurred:

> So we went and as soon as we sat down, [Ahmed] realized that [al-Said and her relatives] had all prepared this in advance and they had sort of organized it so that they would be the hosts and they would have paid. And [Ahmed] left the place! He left us! And he wasn't ashamed! He felt more ashamed [at the idea of a woman paying for him] . . . I felt very frustrated with him, but that is an example of how he gets something in his mind about something important and never changes.[53]

Hussein's obstinance and devotion to principle might give one the idea that he was a rather dull, overly serious man. However, friends and family alike remember him as a jokester. The suit-and tarbush-clad Hussein was talkative, animated, and often funny. Fond of expensive cognacs and good cigars, Hussein was no drab, somber academic. With his sense of humor and winning smile, Hussein made friends easily, though he rarely spoke to them of personal matters. Instead, Hussein enjoyed discussing literature, playing golf, going to the opera and the cinema (particularly to see Greta Garbo's films), listening to the latest hits of Umm Kulthum, and simply partaking of a hearty *baladi* meal with his pals.[54]

Still, Hussein's stubbornness and dedication to principle despite consequences, while fodder for amusing stories, were important aspects of Hussein's personality and influenced how he dealt with turmoil in his professional life. Despite being occasionally difficult, Hussein was a role model in his family and was respected and loved by family members, students, and colleagues.[55] His dedication to professional ethics and his own philosophy of reform can be seen most clearly in his signature social reform project, the rural social centers.

The Rural Social Centers Project

Social reforms in the prerevolutionary era are popularly considered, at best, half-hearted attempts at window dressing and, at worst, outright frauds designed to deceive the Egyptian people and the world into thinking the Egyptian government actually concerned itself with the welfare of its citizens.[56] While it is true that reform projects in the prerevolutionary period were, on the whole, extremely limited in scope and did not succeed in remedying all the ills brought on by the inequitable distribution of land and attendant rural

Hussein, explaining methods to colleagues.
Courtesy of Aziza Hussein.

problems, not all social reform efforts in this period can be so easily and cavalierly dismissed. Hussein's Rural Social Centers project was a prime example of a well-intentioned and effective program. Although limited in scope and slowly implemented, the project was from the start a well-planned and well-organized attempt at improving the lot of the fellahin, who made up approximately two-thirds of the country's population.[57]

The Rural Social Centers (RSC) program was envisioned by Hussein as the centerpiece of his plan to reconstruct rural Egypt. The centers were to accustom the peasants to participating in governance, setting priorities and making decisions, and implementing their own projects, but they were not to operate in a vacuum. In addition to the RSCs, Hussein planned a widespread network of agricultural cooperatives, limited land reform, the establishment of a minimum agricultural wage, and the regulation of the landowner-tenant relationship, and he saw all of these elements as essential parts of the reform of the Egyptian countryside. One of the first departments of the Ministry of Social Affairs was the Fellah Department, created to regulate farmers' affairs and, more broadly, to address issues of social reform in the rural areas of Egypt. The mission statement of the department, issued by the cabinet in 1939, defined its work as follows: "This Department shall be concerned with the study of problems connected with the life of the *Fellah,* in an effort to improve his lot, and to raise the standard of living of the Egyptian village either through direct action or the support of local bodies interested in village welfare work in order to make their work more effective and far-reaching."[58] The problems confronting the Egyptian peasant that the Fellah Department was created to address were many. Beatrice Mattison described them in 1951, basing her analysis on studies from the 1940s:

> [The Egyptian peasant] is, on the average, one of five children, representing the survivors of 8 to 10 births, and has a life expectancy of 38 years. He lives in a one-to two-room mud brick house which accommodates all members of his family, including probably several relatives and such livestock and poultry as he may possess. He may own some land since over 50 percent of those actively engaged in agriculture are also landowners. However, the area will be small because 72.1 percent of those owning agricultural land in Egypt . . . owned less than one acre, and 94.2 percent owned under five acres. Therefore he must supplement his income by working as a day laborer on a large estate or by becoming a tenant or a sharecropper or cash-rent basis. Due to rapid increase of population in proportion to available land, rents are very high, frequently exceeding net farm income. In such a case, the Egyptian tenant farmer receives, in effect, no compensation for his labor or that of his family or livestock. With a current average rent of about LE 30 per acre of agricultural land and average revenues of about LE 55 per acre, it is obvious that the *fellah* is going to have a hard time keeping out of debt, particularly in view of the fact that for approximately 95 percent of the agricultural families, annual per capita income is less than LE 10.[59]

To deal with these problems Hussein, already recognized as Egypt's premier expert on rural social reform, was chosen as the department's first director. In the first annual report on the RSC project, in 1942, Hussein denounced the conditions of life forced upon the majority of his nation's population by decades of governmental neglect of rural areas and an unjustified focus on urban centers. In the report he stated:

> Rural life having been neglected for generations, the standard of living has been lowered to a deplorable extent, although by far the majority of the pop-

> ulation of Egypt (twelve millions out of sixteen millions) is engaged in farming. This majority is actually the most productive class of the Egyptians, yet, the village has been reduced to a collection of miserable mud-hovels surrounded by narrow dirty crooked lanes, while urban districts and cities have been developed and raised to match those of other countries.

In Hussein's view, it was the government's responsibility, particularly in the absence of action by the landowning pasha class, to alleviate the misery of the rural population. He believed that "poverty, illiteracy and disease have become so widespread as to endanger the very life of the *fellah;* a matter that demands quick, drastic and reconstructive measures. Thus it has been considered that the most essential and urgent duty of the Ministry of Social Affairs is to deal with these social defects on sound bases."[60]

In accordance with Hussein's desire to establish reform projects on a firm, scientific foundation, the Fellah Department began a study of social welfare legislation in India and several Balkan states, reviewed social welfare schemes already in place and proposed in Egypt (including the al-Manayil project), and

Ahmed Hussein. Courtesy of Aziza Hussein.

compared the projects in order to determine a course of action for the future. Preliminary studies for the project began on May 5, 1941.[61] Hussein's own experience in the EASS pilot programs at al-Manayil and Shatanuf, combined with the department's examination of other reform schemes, convinced him that "the best remedy was to attack the problem from all angles simultaneously, viz., economic, sociological and medical, since remedying one phase and neglecting the other would be abortive."[62]

After conducting this study, the first project of the new department was to begin a program of rural social centers based on the al-Manayil model to serve as the centerpiece of the new rural reform efforts. As Hussein put it, "Experience has shown that this scheme is the best comprehensive reform scheme devised; it is not liable to failure from guesswork and haphazard judgment, it is inexpensive to operate and will not burden the Government budget so much as to prevent its general extension."[63] The department decided to launch forty such centers, distributed throughout the country. However, with Egypt's entry into World War II, all new projects were canceled. Not only was the project to create forty rural social centers canceled, but the Fellah Department itself was almost eliminated. Hussein, well aware of the potential benefits of the social centers scheme, refused to accept this decision, despite the advent of world war. By pressuring the prime minister, cabinet members, and various officials, Hussein was able to convince the government to retain the Fellah Department. Even more impressive was his ability to get it to retain the Rural Social Centers project. In 1942, as a result of Hussein's lobbying efforts, the government approved funds for six rural social centers to be built and staffed on an experimental basis.[64]

The experiment proved to be a success. With the initial allocation for the project in 1942, there were six rural social centers serving 25 villages; by 1946, the number had grown to eleven. Then, when Isma'il Sidqi Pasha was asked by King Faruq to form a new government in 1946,[65] he made a speech emphasizing the three main threats to social progress in the countryside: poverty, ignorance, and disease. As a result of this speech, a formal governmental body was created and named, appropriately enough, the Committee to Combat Poverty, Ignorance, and Disease. Hussein was named secretary of the committee,[66] which included members from the Ministries of Health, Social Affairs,

Agriculture, and Education and which was seen from the outset as a real and positive step toward social reform.[67]

King Faruq officially supported the Rural Social Centers project as well. Although popularly lampooned as a profligate, gossip-mongering wastrel interested only in fast cars and loose women, without an intellectual thought in his head and with a total lack of either training in or concern for the affairs of government and the welfare of the nation he ruled, Faruq did manifest a degree of concern for the fellahin. In fact, the king personally attended one of the first meetings of the committee, a rare event for the slothful monarch.[68] As noted earlier, the king also made his own royal estate at Inchass a model for the humane treatment of the agricultural laboring class. Gallagher detailed the reforms made on the royal estates:

> The *fellahin* had been given fired (rather than mud) bricks to build their houses and had sanitary facilities and potable water. The land was irrigated by machine. The *fellahin* shared the crops with the landlord at the unusually favorable rate of 60 percent for the *fellah,* 40 percent for the owner. The royal estates had hospitals, social services, physicians, and nurses. Workers on the royal estates in Qina and Aswan were paid more than the minimum wage.[69]

With the support of the Palace, one of the first steps of the committee was to solicit proposals from each ministry concerning the steps to be taken to improve the standard of living in both urban and rural areas. The Ministry of Health proposed various methods of improving the standard of living in urban areas. These proposals included obligatory social insurance against illness, old age, invalidity, and death (a precursor to Hussein's later program of social security), the creation of urban social centers complete with sports facility, lecture hall, library, medical clinic, and restaurant, the foundation of orphanages, the establishment of hospitals for "occupational diseases," and support for public restaurants and baths to encourage proper nutrition and hygiene among the urban poor.[70]

Despite the attention paid to proposals for urban reform, the focal point of the proposals introduced to the committee by the Ministry of Social Affairs was the establishment of an expanded program of rural social centers. One of

At an exhibit of crafts produced at RSCs. Courtesy of Aziza Hussein.

the most striking things about Hussein was his ability to get men like Sidqi, an extremely conservative politician, and even the king to support his programs. In 1946, when the committee was debating the proposals of various ministries and hence was determining the future of the social centers program, Hussein hit upon the idea of organizing a crafts exhibit. He thought that such an exhibit would demonstrate the tangible results of the social centers and emphasize to the conservatives who might oppose the expansion of the RSC project that his programs were designed not as political efforts to foment peasant uprisings but rather as practical efforts to improve the standard of living of the people of the countryside. Hussein developed a souvenir booklet on the crafts exhibit for general distribution, as a means of explaining his project, its ideas, and its tangible results.[71]

Hussein's crafts exhibit, souvenir booklets, and lobbying efforts succeeded in generating further support for his programs. It was after the 1946 establishment of the Committee to Combat Poverty, Ignorance, and Disease that the Rural Social Centers program began receiving serious attention. One of the first actions of the committee was to allocate LE 3 million to various projects, including "plans for 1200 social centers into which existing health and agricultural units will be merged, a scheme of workers' insurance, six recreational, health, and feeding centers for industrial workers, new hospitals for workers, workers' restaurants and reformatories for the training of vagrants."[72] By 1950, the number of centers had increased from 11 to 125.

After the Fellah Department, under Hussein's leadership, began the governmental social centers project in 1942, its goals were announced to be threefold. First, it was to integrate, coordinate, and unify all efforts at social reform in the villages in order to address all social problems simultaneously. Second, it aimed to actively involve the people of the villages in the project, its planning, its implementation, its financial obligations, its administration, and its evaluation, and to minimize the involvement of the government in the project in order to make the people of the village feel that the center and its projects belonged to them and to ensure their continuing commitment to the project. Finally, it wanted to ensure that the project would be simple to maintain and costs kept to a minimum so that the people of the village would be able to continue to fund and run the center after its establishment and so that the project could be replicated in other villages.

The first six locations[73] for social centers were chosen by the Fellah Department, with each center serving a population of approximately 10,000 people. The first six centers were as follows: the Abu al-Numrus center, serving the villages of Abu al-Numrus and Tirsa, located in Markaz al-Giza in the governorate of Giza; the Hala center, serving the villages of Hala, Qaitun, and Kafr al-Shaykh, located in Markaz Mit Ghamr, in the governorate of Daqahliyah; the Birma center, serving the villages of Birma and Hissat Birma, located in Markaz Tanta, in the governorate of Gharbiyah; the Mahallat Zayyad center, serving the villages of Mahallat Zayyad and Megoul, located in Markaz Samanud, in the governorate of Gharbiyah; the al-'Alaqimah center, serving the villages of al-'Alaqimah and Musa Umran, located in Markaz Hihya, in the governorate of Sharqiyah; and the Minyat al-Hayt center, serving the village of Minyat al-Hayt, located in Markaz Itsa, in the governorate of Fayyum.

Although the rationale for choosing locations for the first six centers was never elucidated by Hussein or by the ministry, an analysis of the social and economic conditions of these villages indicates the reasons they were selected.

Census data from 1937 show that these villages were overwhelmingly Muslim with the one exception of the village of Hissat Birma, which had a significant Coptic minority of 41.6 percent. The percentage of the working population engaged in agriculture, fishing, or hunting was over 50 percent in all but the village of Abu al-Numrus, where a significant number of citizens were engaged in commerce. All villages had extremely low literacy rates, although the village of Kafr al-Shaykh boasted a literacy rate of 33.8 percent, far higher than the other ten villages. The average village that received a social center in 1942 had the following characteristics: 64.3 percent of its working population was engaged in agriculture, hunting, or fishing, 95.2 percent of its population was Muslim, and 16.5 percent of its population over the age of five was literate.

None of these six centers is located in Upper Egypt; all are near Cairo in the provinces of Giza, Daqahliyah, Gharbiyah, Sharqiyah, and Fayyum. One obvious reason for locating the first centers near Cairo is that they could be supervised more closely. Also, their proximity to the capital made the villages more attractive to potential center personnel than villages in southern Egypt would have been. Unfortunately, the 1939 agricultural census of Egypt gives data only according to province; the data are not given by village or by *markaz,* making it difficult to determine whether factors such as the number of large landowners and the types of crops cultivated in the area had an influence on these villages being chosen as sites for the centers.

After the establishment of these initial six centers, subsequent RSCs were established only at the request of the villagers. Hussein personally publicized the social centers throughout the countryside, traveling between villages to tell villagers about the new project. He explained the procedures for requesting a social center from the government, and the people then decided whether to apply for a center in their village.[74] Before a center could be built, the people of the village had to raise LE 1,500 (approximately 15 piasters per person). The people also had to provide a 2-*feddan* plot of land and three houses to be used as temporary headquarters before they could request a center officially. Table 1 shows the cost of the construction and operation of a rural social center in 1950. The total estimated cost of each center was LE 9,958, with an estimated annual maintenance cost of LE 3,000. Hussein noted in another publication that the annual maintenance cost would be LE 3,000 for the first year of operation only; after that, he estimated that it would fall to LE 1,000, an average of ten piasters per person per year.[75] It should be stressed that Hussein was opposed to soliciting or accepting foreign aid for this program. All financial contributions to the program came from Egyptian government allocations and the funds raised by the villagers themselves.[76] This emphasis on Egyptian funds had both a practical and a political dimension. Hussein did not want his projects subject to the vagaries of international politics, nor did he want strings attached to funds. More significantly, he believed Egyptian funding to be philosophically consistent with the project's guiding principle of self-help.

Once appropriations were made for more centers, the Fellah Department reviewed the requests for centers, giving priority to the areas most in need of social reform and areas with the highest population density.[77] See table 2 for a list of the names and locations of social centers established by 1948. Hussein took care not to locate new centers close to existing centers. Requests for centers in areas where productive land was owned by a single landowner were categorically turned down because it was held that in such situations the center would be dominated by the landowner and would be unable to function democratically. Offers by large landowners to contribute all the land or all the money for the centers were likewise refused. Hussein explained that "on many occasions some wealthy people came forward expressing their willingness to contribute the whole amount required from the village, but the *Fellaheen* Service Department, in order to realise the desired object, namely, of making the inhabitants feel that the centre is an institution set up for all of them—did not accept these offers."[78] The eventual goal was to have centers in all provinces,

TABLE I

Cost of Construction and Operation of a Rural Social Center

Construction and grants-in-aid to the center during the first year, including permanent furniture	LE 7,150
Staff (salaries, remunerations, etc.) during the first year (architect, foreman, and watchman included)	LE 1,032
General expenses, transport, medicines, equipment, furniture, repairs, telephone, telegraphs, stationery, grants-in-aid to committees, etc.	LE 1,626
Fodder for stud animals, wages for animal caretaker, rent for barn, etc.	LE 150
TOTAL	LE 9,958[a]

Source: Ministry of Social Affairs, The Fellah Department, Cairo: Société Orientale de Publicité, 1950, 28.

[a]Annual maintenance costs after the first year estimated at LE 3000.

TABLE 2

Rural Social Centers in Egypt, 1948

Name of Center	*Province*	*Year Established*	*Name of Center*	*Province*	*Year Established*
Abu al-Numrus	Giza	1940	Bihwash	Minufiyah	1946
Birma	Daqahliyah	1941	Fisha al-Kubra	Minufiyah	1946
Hala	Daqahliyah	1941	Shubra Bilulah	Minufiyah	1946
al-'Alaqimah	Sharqiyah	1941	Shubra Zangi	Minufiyah	1946
Bahnay	Minufiyah	1941	Garawan	Minufiyah	1946
Minyat al-Hayt	Fayyum	1941	al-Baghur	Minufiyah	1946
Mahallet Zayyad	Gharbiyah	1942	Manawahlah	Minufiyah	1946
Saft al-'Inab	Buhayrah	1943	Kafr al-Qarinayn	Minufiyah	1946
Tilwanah	Minufiyah	1943	Bay al-Arab	Minufiyah	1946
al-Nukhaylah	Assiout	1943	Qashtukh	Minufiyah	1946
Tandah	Assiout	1945	Sindiyun	Qalyubiyah	1946
Nuqaytah	Daqahliyah	1946	Gamgara	Qalyubiyah	1946
al-Gamaliya	Daqahliyah	1946	Dahshur	Giza	1946
Mit al-'Amil	Daqahliyah	1946	Tubhar	Fayyum	1946
Mit al-Khawli	Daqahliyah	1946	Saft Rashin	Bani Suwayf	1946
Sa al-Hagar	Gharbiyah	1946	Infast	Bani Suwayf	1946
Shubra al-Namlah	Gharbiyah	1946	Bani Samit	Minya	1946
Shabshir al-Hissah	Gharbiyah	1946	Ibwan	Minya	1946
Shabur	Buhayrah	1946	Dayr Mawas	Assiout	1945
Shisht al-An'am	Buhayrah	1946	Dayrut	Assiout	1946
Sanhut al-Birak	Sharqiyah	1946	al-Hawawish	Sawhag	1946
Kafr Ibrash	Sharqiyah	1946	Fa'w Qibli	Qina	1946
Shaybat al-Nakkariyah	Sharqiyah	1946	al-Qal'ah	Aswan	1946
al-Hagarisah	Sharqiyah	1946	al-Busayli	Aswan	1947
Tamalay	Minufiyah	1946	al-Bayyadiyah	Qina	1947
Barhim	Minufiyah	1946	Armant al-Hayt	Qina	1947
Zawiyat Razin	Minufiyah	1946	Banga	Sawhag	1947
Minshat Sultan	Minufiyah	1946	al-Sal'a	Sawhag	1947
Dibirki	Minufiyah	1946	Durunkah	Assiout	1947
Sangirg	Minufiyah	1946	Rifah	Assiout	1947

serving the entire rural population of Egypt. Hussein envisioned establishing a total of 1,200 centers at the rate of 30 to 40 new centers per year.[79]

This method for creating new centers was important in that the impetus for each RSC after the initial six had to come from the people themselves. The required financial contribution of the people also ensured that their request for a center was genuine and, more importantly, gave the people a sense of owning the center. The people requested the center, the people raised the initial funds for the center, and the people provided the labor to construct the buildings of the center. In that way, the villagers felt that the center was truly

TABLE 2 (*cont.*)

Rural Social Centers in Egypt, 1948

Name of Center	*Province*	*Year Established*	*Name of Center*	*Province*	*Year Established*
Sudud	Minufiyah	1946	Sanabu	Assiout	1947
Bani Ahmad	Minya	1947	Mahallat Abu 'Ali	Gharbiyah	1948
al-Bayahu	Minya	1947	Hurayn	Gharbiyah	1948
Kiman al-Arus	Bani Suwayf	1947	Sigin al-Kawm	Gharbiyah	1948
Hawwarat al-Maqta	Fayyum	1947	al-Dahriyah	Buhayrah	1948
Abu Ganzir	Fayyum	1947	Zawiyat Saqr	Buhayrah	1948
Umm Khunan	Giza	1947	Minshat Balbaa	Buhayrah	1948
al-Qibabat	Giza	1947	al-Haswah	Sharqiyah	1948
al-Shawbak	Giza	1947	al-Rubimaya	Sharqiyah	1948
al-Marg	Qalyubiyah	1947	Kafr al-Hamam	Sharqiyah	1948
Mubashir	Sharqiyah	1947	Garris	Minufiyah	1948
Awlad Saqr	Sharqiyah	1947	Shanawan	Minufiyah	1948
Bisintaway	Buhayrah	1947	Tahlah	Qalyubiyah	1948
Armaniyah	Buhayrah	1947	Siryaqus	Qalyubiyah	1948
Dayout Buhayrah	Buhayrah	1947	al-Ga'afirah	Qalyubiyah	1948
Mit Garrah	Gharbiyah	1947	al-Qalag	Qalyubiyah	1948
Nawasa	Daqahliyah	1947	Karr al-Basil	Fayyum	1948
al-'Attawi	Daqahliyah	1947	Naqalifah	Fayyum	1948
al-Hayatim	Gharbiyah	1947	Ibshanna	Bani Suwayf	1948
al-Khadimiyah	Kafr al-Shaykh	1947	Abu Girg	Minya	1948
Mit Ya'ish	Daqahliyah	1947	Nazlat al-Falabayn	Minya	1948
Dundit	Daqahliyah	1948	Manqabad	Assiout	1948
al-Muqata'ah	Daqahliyah	1948	Musha	Assiout	1948
Ginazit Bani Ammar	Daqahliyah	1948	al-Dauwer	Assiout	1948
Kafr Sa'd	Gharbiyah	1948	Bandar al-Qaraminah	Sawhag	1948
Shubra Babil	Gharbiyah	1948	al-Kilh	Aswan	1948

Source: Hassan Dawood.

theirs and not a project imposed upon them by the government. Hussein insisted on the active participation of the villagers in the project, saying:

> Any projects charted for these people without their desire, consent, and participation, any projects imposed upon them from the armchairs of the country's capital, may draw their rejection and non-cooperation. On the other hand, if we were to capture their great abilities and resources, and work *for* them through working *with* them, we are sure to harness great powers of self help, which when aided technically and financially, and coordinated with government efforts in overall plans for social reform, will produce maximum results and bring us closer to success.[80]

Once a center was established, the Fellah Department provided two permanent staff members: a social-agricultural specialist and a health visitor. The department also required that the villagers choose a doctor and make arrangements for him to visit the village a minimum of three times per week. The doctor's fees were to be paid by the villagers themselves.[81] More personnel were added to centers as necessary at later dates. These additional personnel included a laboratory assistant, a club leader, a male nurse and a female nurse, three to five midwives, a messenger, an orderly, and a servant.[82]

The social-agricultural specialist was the key staff member, and his duties were widely varied. This person had to be a graduate of the Faculty of Agriculture[83] and had to have successfully completed a four-month course in rural social work and two months' on-the-job training at an established social center.[84] The selection process also included a lengthy series of interviews aimed at selecting a person who was educated yet still able to relate to and understand the villagers.[85] Men from rural backgrounds were often preferred for this position, on the theory that they would be better able to deal with the conditions of village life. Yet at the same time, Hussein made certain to instill a sense of professionalism and duty in the men. One social-agricultural specialist once asked Hussein why he insisted upon using college-educated men as specialists in the villages rather than using men who were high school graduates, since the latter would be closer to the level of the villagers and better able to understand them. Hussein replied that a high school graduate, when sent to the village, would only end up sitting in the coffee shop, smoking a water pipe and gossiping with the villagers, and would not be able to get any work done, whereas a university graduate would be prevented from doing this by notions of status. He would be more respected by the villagers and, because of the prestige attached to a university degree, would not be tempted to spend all his time in the coffee shop.[86] In other words, while the specialist was to be someone who could relate to the villagers, he was not to feel so comfortable in the village that he assimilated completely to village culture. This specialist was to look after the economic, social, physical, mental, and moral situations in the village. His duties included helping villagers obtain select seeds from the government, introducing new crops, maintaining a demonstration plot, teaching the villagers how to combat agricultural pests, assisting farmers with the marketing of their products, organizing night classes for village adults to combat illiteracy, encouraging cottage industries to increase the farmers' incomes, organizing sports and athletics during leisure times, helping settle disputes in the villages, organizing village charity, spreading popular culture by means of the radio, setting up a village library, and supervising the cleanliness of the village, its people, and its roads.

The doctor assigned to the social center had a similarly broad range of duties. His first obligation was to make a thorough physical examination of each villager and to compile a complete medical survey of the village. He also was to treat the sick, perform minor operations, transfer serious cases to the main hospital of the area, distribute medicine at no charge to the villagers, teach the villagers about disease prevention and hygiene, inspect the food supplies in the local markets, instruct the people how to keep the food supplies clean and safe, work with the social-agricultural specialist to fill up stagnant ponds, and combat unhealthy and superstitious practices.

The health visitor was always a woman. She had to be a graduate of a technical training program in nursing at Cairo's Qasr al-Aini Hospital and also had to have completed a course in rural social service. Young women of rural backgrounds were preferred for this position because they were more familiar with village life and practices.[87] The health visitor's duties centered on the women and children in the village. Her main duty was to take care of pregnant women and newborns. Her other duties included visiting each home regularly and teaching the village women proper housekeeping methods, general cleanliness, and ways to supplement their families' incomes through needlepoint, dressmaking, and other cottage industries, overseeing the cleanliness of the children, visiting the village school and teaching the children basic hygiene, cutting the boys' hair, brushing the girls' hair, trimming the children's nails, sending sick children to the doctor, giving health lectures to village women, training several young village women in nursing and midwifery, and organizing groups of village girls for courses in needlework, knitting, and first aid.

In order to facilitate the work of these three specialists, each rural social center was initially composed of three buildings: the social center building, which included a large meeting hall, a library with a reading room, a small museum, and a radio; the clinic, which included an examination room, a waiting room, a treatment room, an isolation ward, a dispensary, and a laboratory; and the maternity and child welfare center, which consisted of a waiting room, an examination room, a room for sterilizing equipment, and an eight-bed maternity ward. Other buildings that were subsequently added to the centers included a "hall for rural industries," which housed looms, spinning materials, and materials for other handicrafts, public baths and washing troughs, and a water supply unit to store clean water. The villagers often added other services and buildings that they desired. The social-agricultural specialist lived in a three-room residence attached to the RSC building, the health visitor lived in a small apartment attached to the maternity clinic, and the doctor lived in his own private residence. Hussein himself would have preferred to base the social center in people's homes, thereby emphasizing the informal, grassroots nature of the program. However, he decided that buildings were a necessary component of the program because they would be a visible base for the centers that could not easily be abolished should local or national political currents threaten the centers.[88]

Once the village met the preliminary requirements of the program, the real work of the social center started. All adult residents, regardless of gender, were members of the general assembly of the social center.[89] Each RSC also had a board of directors that was to "collect donations and arrange the building site and the execution of the building programme under the technical supervision of the [center staff] . . . This Board generally supervises all the work of the Center."[90] In order to encourage villager participation and to undertake the work of the center, the social-agricultural specialist established five committees (the health committee, the social and cultural committee, the agricultural and economic committee, the charity and public assistance committee, and the conciliation committee), all of whose members served voluntarily, and all of which reported to the center's board of directors.

These committees were in charge of planning, implementing, and evaluating new projects in the village with the aid of the social center staff, who also served as liaisons between the villagers and the national government in Cairo. Hussein explained the importance of citizen participation in the centers in the following way: "The Social Centre may be briefly described as similar to a national local government set up by the inhabitants themselves to look after their affairs and carry out improvements in their village in a democratic way by which they are trained to understand their rights and obligations as useful citizens, and by means of which they can prove, in a practical way, that they are able to use their own efforts in serving themselves and in raising the standard of their village."[91]

A program that developed alongside the Rural Social Centers project and had similar goals was the Rural Reconstruction Societies program (RRSs). These societies were formed by the villagers in areas that did not have enough funding for a full-blown social center. Table 3 lists villages with RRSs established by 1948. Hussein reported in 1950:

> The success of the Rural Welfare Centers [RSCs] had a beneficial effect on other villages resulting in numerous applications for the establishment of Centres. As financial provisions were limited, and the [Fellah] Department did not want to deprive those villages of the various services, it decided instead on the formation of rural reform societies [RRSs], the work of which is conducted through committees similar to those of the Centres, with the continuous supervision, financial assistance and guidance of the Welfare Specialists to supplement the contributions collected by the members of the community. These societies began operating in 1944. Their number has increased steadily and has reached 23, all of which are registered and receive both financial assistance and guidance, serving about 150,000 people.[92]

In the RRS villages, the same five committees as in RSC villages were formed, and they undertook projects of the people's choosing. The only significant difference between the RRSs and the RSCs was that the RRSs did not have any paid specialists. A special department within the Social Unit of the Fellah Department was in charge of the RRSs. This department provided technical advice and assistance to RRS villages and asked RSC staff in nearby villages to visit occasionally. RSC staff volunteered their time and expertise in RRS villages.[93] The ministry also provided limited subsidies to the RRSs. Writing in 1944, Hussein described the progress of the RRSs as follows:

> Many of these societies have actually succeeded in rendering various services to village dwellers such as the installation of drinking-water pumps, the improvement of mosque lavatories, the filling in of pools, the introduction of rural industries and the proper organization of charity funds. Two of these societies have created a dispensary and a clinic run by a nurse lent to it by the *Fellah* Department and a special doctor who visits the village two or three

> times a week in return for a fixed salary which the Society collects from the inhabitants. Twenty-three of these societies have already been registered and two more are under way.[94]

By 1950, the number of RRSs had grown to thirty.[95] Many people, including some RSC staffers like Salah al-Nimaky, considered the RRSs to be superior to the RSCs because they were more participatory. In the RRSs, there was less government involvement, and the people had to play an even larger role than in the RSCs. All meetings were held in village homes, and the RRS was therefore more integrated into village life. However, despite the good points of this more grassroots approach, al-Nimaky concedes that the RRSs were dependent on the RSCs for support and assistance and therefore could not have succeeded in a vacuum.[96]

TABLE 3

Rural Reconstruction Societies in Egypt, 1948

Name of Village(s)	*Province*
Shifa and Qarun[a]	Gharbiyah
Kafr Belshay	Gharbiyah
Kawm al-Tawil	Kafr al-Shaykh
al-Dahrah	Daqahliyah
Sahragat al-Kubra	Daqahliyah
Awish al-Hagar	Daqahliyah
al-Bagalat	Daqahliyah
Mit Salsil	Daqahliyah
al-Mamarna	Daqahliyah
al-Tawabra	Daqahliyah
al-Zarqa	Daqahliyah
Rahaminah	Daqahliyah
Barriyat	Buhayrah
Mashtul al-Qadi	Sharqiyah
Banayus	Sharqiyah
Sharwidah	Sharqiyah
al-'Awasigah	Sharqiyah
Umm Khunan	Minufiyah
al-Mu'tamadiyah	Giza
Nahya	Giza
Tetwan	Fayyum
Tahnasha	Minya
Dar al-Salam	Aswan

Source: Dr. Hassan Dawood.

Note: Total number of rural reconstruction societies by 1948: 23.

[a]The two villages share an RRS.

The results of the RSC project were spectacular. General health levels increased in villages where centers were located, sanitary conditions improved, illiteracy decreased, education levels increased, agricultural yields and farmers' income rose, and handicrafts produced by the centers' members generated added income. Hussein summarized the positive results of the centers in a 1955 speech in Washington, D.C., saying:

> The success of the social center as an institution most suited to serve the civic, economic, cultural, and social needs of the Egyptian village is now fully recognized. It is living proof that sincere cooperation between government and people can do much to bring about a real uplift in the social standards of rural areas. The enthusiasm of the people in some of these centers is very gratifying. With a little financial help and technical guidance from the Government, they were able to fill swamps, construct roads, build schools, introduce playgrounds and public parks. In a democratic fashion, they discuss their needs and plan their course of action. They volunteer their varied abilities to serve their communities. They have been able to improve agricultural production and to introduce certain cottage industries. They formed drama groups and sports teams. In one village I visited . . . the people's center had organized 18 evening classes to combat illiteracy.[97]

In the following sections, the results of the centers will be reviewed in the areas of agricultural and economic services, health services, social, cultural, and educational services, and women's services. It should be emphasized that the results presented in this section are largely from government sources; the statistics kept were assembled by social center staffers, who were employees of the Ministry of Social Affairs. These staffers made thorough surveys of their villages upon arrival in the villages, and thereafter most statistics were kept on an annual basis. Clearly, the government had an interest in presenting this project in the best possible light. However, there are no indications that these statistics are unreliable or that they were in any way altered to improve the project's image. Indeed, the reactions of government personnel, independent researchers, and international observers who visited the social centers and the overall reaction to the program from various quarters indicate that the centers did achieve significant positive results.

Agricultural and Economic Services

The goals of the economic services provided by the centers were to increase the income of the villagers, to improve agricultural production, and to provide nonagricultural sources of income for the population. Table 4 gives an overview of the main economic services provided at sixty-two social centers from 1949 to 1950. The main economic service provided by the centers was helping the villagers acquire the means to improve crop yields. The centers helped the farmers obtain superior cotton and wheat seeds, which resulted in yields higher than those on neighboring farms. These seeds were acquired through the social centers from the Ministry of Agriculture, the Agricultural Credit and Cooperative Bank, and the Royal Agricultural Society (RAS).[98] Table 4 shows that cotton yields in areas with social centers were approximately 50 percent higher than those on neighboring farms, while wheat yields were approximately 33 percent higher.

The acquisition of superior seed coupled with the adoption of updated agricultural techniques resulted in increased yields for other crops as well. Hussein gave several examples of these improved yields in a 1950 Ministry of Social Affairs publication in which he reported, "At Abu El Numros, the yield [of maize] rose from 9 to 12 *ardebs* per *feddan* as a result of improved seed and planting in rows as advised by the Social Welfare Agricultural Specialist. Another example of the activities of the Centre at Abu el-Numros was its purchase of 21 *ardebs* of *birsim* seed a few months before sowing time at LE 4 per *ardeb*. The price of seed later soared [and] was sold at LE 50 per *ardeb*, whereby the villagers profited considerably."[99]

Fertilizers were also acquired by the centers, as were fruit and wood trees and vegetable seeds. Crop diversification was emphasized as a way both to improve the nutrition of the villagers and to supplement their income by providing products to sell in the markets. Specific examples of crop diversification were cited by Hussein in 1950: "The farmers were also persuaded to plant an area of 15 *feddans* to plums at Hala village; Valencia orange cultivation was introduced at Mahallet Ziyad; five hundred grape vines were planted at Alaqma in addition to one *feddan* of good variety mangoes and date palms where none existed previously. At Burma, $^{2}/_{3}$ of a *feddan* were planted to grafted mangoes." Different varieties of trees were introduced as well. By 1950, 10,403 eucalyptus, 10,100 casuarina, 120 cypress, 120 acacia, 400 bougainvillea, and 750 poinciana trees had been distributed to the social centers.[100]

Pest control methods also were taught at the social centers with good results. The Giza Agricultural College furnished the centers with insect collections for use in educational campaigns in the villages, and particular attention was paid to eradicating cotton leaf worm in areas served by the centers. Examples of other pest control efforts included "control of aphis through spraying at Miniat Al Heyt, and the treatment of mole crickets with bait containing barium fluosilicate at Burma and Abu El Numros; control of grasshoppers by poison bait at Mahallat Ziyad, control of mildew on cucurbits; [and] eradication of loose smut on wheat in the field by collecting infected ears [of wheat] and destroying them by fire at Miniat El Heyt."[101]

Animal husbandry was taught, and chickens, rabbits, and calves were acquired with the help of the centers. Like the new vegetables and fruits introduced in the villages, these animals provided a varied diet and extra income. Each social center was loaned two seed bulls by the Ministry of Agriculture, and farmers were taught not to slaughter female calves. Table 4 gives statistics on the number of buffalo and calves distributed. An idea of the amount of profit realized from these livestock-breeding ventures was given by Hussein in 1950: "At Alaqma three farmers reared and fattened 20 calves between them during the spring season on *berseem,* which yielded when sold an average profit of LE 7–8 per steer. At Burma 30 calves were reared during the same season, netting LE 9 profit per steer."[102]

Beekeeping and silkworm raising also were popular means of increasing village income, as table 4 shows. Beekeeping was taught to children as well as to adults, and the use of modern hives was encouraged. In 1950, Hussein estimated that "the average crop per [modern] hive amounted to 50 pounds of excellent honey from the first extraction. The honey crop is extracted twice a year. [In contrast,] the average honey crop from local hives is 10 pounds per annum." The social centers at Bahnay, Saft al-'Inab, Tilwaneh, Kafr Ibrash, Gamaliyah, Hala, Dayrut al-Sharif, Kafr al-Qarinayn, and Sindiyun all became centers of honey production as a result of this program. Silkworm raising also helped the villagers supplement their incomes on a modest scale. Since mulberry trees were necessary to this industry, the project began on a small scale and included the provision of mulberry saplings. Hussein summarized this project in 1950:

TABLE 4

Economic Services Provided by 62 Rural Social Centers, 1949–1950

1. Seeds and Fertilizers Provided

	Quantity Provided	*Number of Beneficiaries*
Cotton seeds	5,165 *ardebs*	4,056
Wheat seeds	1,430 *ardebs*	902
Vegetable seeds	3,086 kilos & 18,850 saplings	193
Other seeds	14,630 *ardebs*	66
Fertilizers	9,711 sacks	3,801

2. Demonstration Plot Yields

	Average Production of Demonstration Plot	*Average Production of Neighboring Farms*
Cotton yields	6 *qantars*	4 1/2 *qantars*
Wheat yields	8 *ardebs*	6 *ardebs*

3. Trees Provided to Residents

	Number of Trees Provided	*Number of Beneficiaries*
Wood trees	16,617	1,553
Fruit trees	36,407	73

4. Other Agricultural Services Provided

	Size in feddans	*Number*
Plant nursery	1 1/4	14,517 saplings
Pest combating	2,601	15,730 beneficiaries

5. Handicraft Services Provided

	Number Employed	*Number of Looms*	*Production*
Wool handicrafts	173 boys	35	872 coup.
Weaving handicrafts	107 boys	48	4,494 coup.
Spinning handicrafts	17 boys	7	964 pounds
Palm tree products	139 boys	13	783 pieces
Needlework handicrafts	1,174 girls	—	1,588 pieces

At the beginning, every Centre received 12 boxes containing silk-worm eggs. These eggs were distributed among 28 *fellahin* mostly of the poorer class. These farmers realised LE 21.338 milliemes for the catgut [silk cord] produced which was a fair income considering that they had no previous experience. The best farmers at Alaqma made LE 3.339 each. One poor farmer

TABLE 4 (*cont.*)

Economic Services Provided by 62 Rural Social Centers, 1949–1950

6. Livestock Services Provided

	Number Distributed	*Number of Beneficiaries*
Calves	252	41
Chickens	11,758	609
Rabbits	26	5

Also: 100 male buffalo were selected for breeding, producing 1,916 male offspring and 1,416 female offspring (727 of the female offspring were kept).

7. Other Animal-Based Services and Industries Provided

A. Veterinary Services
Cattle in the villages: 12,863
Cattle treated: 1,880
Chickens vaccinated: 5,568

B. Beekeeping
Beekeepers: 71
Modern hives: 347
Average annual honey production (lbs.): 60

C. Silkworms
Silkworm seeds distributed: 2 boxes
Breeders: 85
Silk production: 45 kilos
Gut production: 2,575 kilos

Source: Ministry of Social Affairs, *The Fellah Department,* Cairo: Société Orientale de Publicité, 1950, Annex 1.

> at Burma received 1.5 boxes of eggs, which produced 2050 grams of catgut bringing him LE 5.991 in two months. In an effort to extend this work, the Centres obtained from the Ministry of Agriculture 9520 mulberry seedlings, 500 cuttings and 157 boxes of eggs which were distributed among the *fellahin.*[103]

The villagers also began handicraft industries, as table 4 shows. Wool spinning and weaving, needlework, and palm tree products all became part of the social centers' economic services. These rural industries provided a means of increasing the income of the villagers, and they also provided a productive outlet for energies of the boys and girls of the community. Hussein reported that "fifteen farmers in Behnay, 12 in Minia El-Heyt, 16 in Hala, 7 at Saft El

Enab, and 5 in Tanda were taught to weave. They are all working on their own. The average monthly production of cloth per loom is 250 metres." The introduction of palm leaf doormat production in the centers had an even more significant effect. Before the social centers began this rural industry, doormats had been manufactured in urban areas from imported coconut fibers. The centers used native leaves and produced the products in the villages, and "some areas supplied Government Departments and commercial firms in 1945 with big quantities of these products of the date palm leaf industry."[104]

Date drying and packing projects began at Abu al-Numrus, and the center at al-'Alaqimah began producing and bottling fruit juice and fruit syrups. The products produced by these local industries were marketed in Egypt and abroad. Hussein noted: "The *Fellah* Department organised an exhibition of these industries in 1946 which received considerable attention. All exhibits were sold in a very short time realising LE 1,303.468 milliemes which sum was distributed among the producers. The rugs and carpets were sold on the US market at LE 5.500 per square metre. They were very well received by the Americans."[105]

Finally, each center encouraged the formation of agricultural cooperative societies. Agricultural cooperatives attached to RSCs began providing social as well as economic services to their members. In addition, various local agricultural cooperative societies also undertook several health-related projects. The cooperative societies of Bani Ahmad and Nahya began programs of filling in stagnant water pools in their areas. These cooperative societies also helped fund the establishment of rural social centers in some communities; in others, they contributed funds to establish medical clinics or mother-and-child-welfare clinics, or they simply gave money to purchase first-aid boxes for their area. Hussein argued that the cooperative societies provided a framework for action during the cholera epidemic of 1947, installing 207 hand pumps for water and several larger mechanical water pumps as well.[106]

The cooperative societies also undertook a number of civic projects designed to improve infrastructure in the villages. For instance, the al-Allaqi cooperative funded an extension of postal services to its village, and the Hawamshed, Kafr al-Khadra, Naqeetah, al-'Alaqimah, and al-Bahw Furayk societies began programs of road and bridge repair and construction, filling of stagnant ponds, and viaduct construction in their villages. The Tura al-Faruqiyah society began construction of bathhouses and laundry sheds in its village, while the societies of Damas, Kafr Shukr, Fassna, Daynouna, and Naqeetah built mosques for their villages. Other civic projects included forming village councils, creating village parks and playgrounds, and providing street lamps.[107]

Relief work was also begun by several cooperative societies, including the societies of Alexandria, Kafr al-Dawwar, Isma'iliyah, and Bahtim. These societies were among the ones that began programs of distributing meat, clothes, and money to the less fortunate members of their communities on feast days. Additional relief projects included the encouragement of home industries such as rug making and knitting. Various other charity programs were also begun in many communities.[108]

Finally, some societies also formed conciliation committees, like those of the RSCs, in order to mediate disputes in their communities. The conciliation committees were closely supervised by the Cooperative Department, and their members were chosen by the society's board of directors from the socially prominent members of the community. Hussein explained the function of the conciliation committee as follows:

> One of its main duties is to settle tribal feuds which mar Egyptian rural life and are the cause of much crime; cooperative societies which include many of the prominent members of the rural community are most suited to remedy this disease to bring about social peace and tranquility all over the country. . . . It settles old as well as new disputes and enmities between families, thus averting further complications and crimes.[109]

Health Services

The fight to improve health conditions in rural areas was, at best, an uphill battle. The biggest problem faced by the program was the lack of trained doctors and nurses. Enticing trained medical personnel to work in remote rural areas was also difficult. In 1944, the total number of physicians in Egypt was 4,032. There were 637 dentists, 1,053 pharmacists, 333 assistant pharmacists, and 751 midwives. The total population of Egypt was some 19 million. Even assuming equal distribution of medical personnel in all areas, this means that each doctor would have had to serve a population of 4,713 people, each dentist a population of 29,828, each pharmacist or assistant pharmacist a population of 17,496, and each midwife a population of 25,300. The centers also faced a lack of health care facilities and supplies, an endemic problem in rural Egypt. Shalaby estimated in 1950 that the urban areas of the country contained some 20 percent of the total population of Egypt and 80 percent of its medical facilities.[110] This left 80 percent of the population with only 20 percent of the already inadequate medical resources.

Health services provided in social centers included free medical treatment, preventive health care, and distribution of free medicine. Table 5 shows some of the health care statistics recorded in eighty-one RSCs for 1949–50. The statistics kept on health matters show only the number of new patients in different areas of medical care; as such they do not indicate how effective the services provided by the centers were. Nonetheless, the numbers do indicate that the villagers used the medical services provided. Particularly encouraging were the numbers of pregnant women receiving prenatal care and attending lectures on child care and the numbers of women who either delivered their children in the health center or had health center personnel attending their deliveries. In 1950, Hussein reported, "The average number of women and children who frequent the Centres daily is 70. The number of confinements [due to childbirth] per week ranges from 10 to 15 and the number of difficult cases of birth which are referred to the nearest hospital [is] 7 per annum."[111] Women were given inducements to deliver their children in the maternity clinic; the provision of two sets of baby clothes, a week's free food in the clinic after birth, and guaranteed medical care for the child for two years after birth all served to raise the number of women giving birth under medical supervision.[112]

Vaccination campaigns played a major role in reducing mortality among young children. In 1950, overall child mortality, defined as the percentage of children who die before age five, was 34 percent.[113] Mattison reported that the centers were instrumental in reducing these rates. She remarked that "by vaccinations and inoculations of children, death rates in some of the older centers have dropped by almost two-thirds and the number of young men accepted for military service has doubled."[114]

The centers also proved useful in combating three major epidemics that swept through Egypt in the 1940s, the first of which was the typhus epidemic

TABLE 5

Health Statistics of 81 Rural Service Centers, 1949–1950

1. Total New Outpatients

Internal Diseases	*Surgical Cases*	*Skin Cases*	*Ophthalmia Cases*	*V.D. Cases Tested*	*V.D. Cases Treated*	*Other Cases*	*Total Cases Treated*
122,929	9,260	16,267	176,970	1,065	78	34,151	259,645

2. Cases of Endemic Diseases Diagnosed and Treated

	Urine Analysis	*Fecal Analysis*	*Number of Injections Given*
Bilharzia	19,414	13,827	70,953
Ankylostoma		1,795	
Ascaris		3,512	
Amoeba		1,332	
Other parasites		2,020	
Total examined	35,669	22,016	

3. Pregnant Women Attending Clinics

Total Attendance	*Deliveries in the Center*	*Assisted Deliveries in Homes*	*Total Assisted Deliveries*	*Number of Prenatal Visits*	*Number of Lectures Given*
21,550	7,806	10,266	18,072	38,122	3,337

4. Minor Public Utilities for General Cleanliness

Number of Artesian Pumps	*Number of Public Baths*	*Number of Street Lamps*	*Houses Sprayed with DDT*
808	604	6,480	9,303

Source: Ministry of Social Affairs, The Fellah Department, Cairo: Société Orientale de Publicité, 1950, Annex 1.

of 1943. Hussein reported that in one center situated near the area of the epidemic, the center's personnel began instructing the villagers in proper methods of hygiene, and "the people continued as a result of this campaign to boil their clothes and shave their hair or treat it with kerosene until the village was free from the disease for three successive years, 1943, 1944, and 1945." During the relapsing fever epidemic, "the Centres were active in fighting this epidemic free of charge in addition to free spraying of homes with D.D.T. The result was that the villages served by Centres had the lowest infection rates." Finally, during the cholera epidemic, the centers

> formed committees which undertook disinfecting and spraying houses and water closets and the removal of manure heaps, [and] the placing of barrels of disinfectant at the entrance to villages to treat all vegetables and fruit. They checked all movements into the villages and gave immediate notification of cases [of cholera]. They provided at a very short notice sufficient quantities of suitable drinking water by the installation of 272 pumps. They also undertook the inoculation of all the inhabitants of their areas. The results of these efforts were discernable by the very few cases [of cholera] in villages served by Centres as compared with neighbouring villages.[115]

Social, Cultural, and Educational Services

Other services provided by the centers included charitable services, educational services, leisure time activities, and conciliation. Table 6 provides a summary of the social, educational, and cultural services offered by sixty-two social centers in 1949–50. Of 14,779 families surveyed in sixty-two villages with rural social centers in 1949–50, 8,043 (54 percent) responded that they had benefited from the center's charity work. Statistics from the first eleven centers give more details about the types of charitable services provided:

> 1. The committees in three Centers purchased 40 female goats and 32 ewes and distributed them among 62 poor families with the right to its milk and progeny and half of its other products (wool hair and droppings). This has a beneficial effect in increasing family income. 2. Five of the Centers made a gratis distribution of 84 *ardebs* of wheat, maize, and rice while five other centres distributed 3917 pounds of meat among 4278 persons on feast [days] and other holidays. 3. They organized the collection of *"Al Zaka"* (almsgiving) [the religiously mandated charitable contribution in Islam] in 4 Centres, collecting LE 462.078 milliemes from a few well-to-do farmers. This was distributed among needy families; in six other centres LE 146.720 milliemes was collected and distributed among needly [*sic*] *fellahin* in emergency cases, such as chronic sickness, and collapse of houses due to the floods, etc. 4. These committees also undertook the ritual clothing of corpses of deceased poor people to the number of 73, in an other [*sic*] center 890 metres of cloth were distributed for this purpose, valued at LE 6.585 milliemes.

TABLE 6

Social Services Provided by 62 Rural Social Centers, 1949–1950

1. Public Assistance and Charity Provided

	Aid (in LE)	*Beneficiaries*
Aid based on self-help	1,803.570	1,198
Temporary aid	4,278.528	23,306
Total families surveyed	14,779	
Total families aided	8,043	
Total individuals aided	20,793	

2. Educational Services Provided

	Number Given	*Individuals Participating*
Public lectures	385	40,967
Evening classes for adults	107	3,817
Educational trips	267	166,736
Library visitors and borrowers	—	22,441
3. Rural Clubs and Scouting Activities:		
Adult members	1,490	
Young members	1,875	
4. Conciliation Committee Activities		
Cases presented for conciliation	160	
Disputes settled	137	
Success rate	85.63%	

Source: Ministry of Social Affairs, *The Fellah Department,* Cairo: Société Orientale de Publicité, 1950, Annex 1.

> 5. The Social Welfare Centers also distributed 5660 pairs of sandals in the drive against bare-footedness. School children received the greatest share of this distribution.[116]

As table 6 shows, the number of people benefiting from lectures, adult evening classes, educational trips, scouting activities, and library services was high. Activities such as team sports (including basketball, soccer, and table tennis) were begun in many villages, and competitions were arranged between villages.[117] Village women also participated in athletic competitions—a very unusual activity for rural females at the time. As 'Ali Hassan al-Haggagi, one of the social-agricultural specialists, observed, "These were women who carried pots on their heads and who never left their homes, but they participated in the races because of the rural social centers."[118] Scouting activities also proved very popular. In 1950, Hussein reported that "48 packs of cubs containing 1277 boys and 13 troops of boy scouts with 329 members have been started. A pack of Brownies (known as Flowers) was set up for the first time in rural Egypt."[119] In addition, the Ministry of Social Affairs provided educational films, traveling theater troupes, and radios to the centers.[120]

The success rate of the conciliation committees (85.63 percent) is also an indication of the ability of the centers to serve their people effectively. Hussein reported, "The Conciliation Committees have succeeded in settling many disputes without reference to Government or Court authorities; they have in addition been able to settle cases that have been before the Courts for years. The success achieved by these Committees has made the authorities in a number of areas refer cases to these Committees in the first instance."[121]

The results in elementary education were also positive. Although elementary education had been compulsory and free in Egypt since 1924,[122] absenteeism rates were higher than 70 percent in some areas, and schools in rural areas were administered like their urban counterparts with the same curriculum and the same penalties for truancy. Hussein explained the need for a system of schooling adapted to the conditions and realities of rural life, saying that "because of their meager resources, the peasants could not afford to spare child labor from the fields. Yet they were required by law to send their children to school, subject to punishment in case of failure to comply. This was certain to arouse much anger against the Government." In addition to high rates of absenteeism, the type of schooling provided in rural areas often only served to increase rural-urban migration. In Hussein's view, "The boys who attended became unhappy with village life. They looked down on farming and thought they were entitled by their limited education to get white collar jobs in the cities where they were not needed."[123]

Recognizing that rural students needed instruction in practical as well as academic subjects, the social centers encouraged rural schools to alter their curriculum. As a result of the success of the al-Manayil village school, the Ministry of Education and the Fellah Department agreed to cooperate in setting up schools based on the al-Manayil model in all villages with rural social centers.[124] Subjects such as modern agricultural methods, animal husbandry, needlework, and carpet making were introduced into the rural schools by the Ministry of Education, beginning in 1942.[125] Hussein explained that "this catered to the interests of both parents and children. It meant to them preparation for a better livelihood. It also produced better elements that were more in harmony with their environment and capable of serving their communities." The introduction of practical subjects, along with the medical services offered to schoolchildren by the social centers and the provision of a free daily meal to students, resulted in increased school attendance.[126] Both parents and students were able to see tangible benefits from school attendance as a result of the changes introduced by the social centers.

The Fellah Department and the Ministry of Education also reached an agreement that gave the Fellah Department responsibility for combating illiteracy in rural areas. The Ministry of Education agreed to provide the Fellah Department with funds and equipment for literacy education, and the Fellah Department, for its part, agreed to provide basic literacy classes for males between 12 and 25 years of age and for females between 12 and 15 years of age.[127] In addition, evening classes were organized to teach adult villagers reading, writing, basic religion, arithmetic, and general knowledge.[128] These supplementary classes were in addition to the provision of education for children through the new village schools.

Other services were also provided in various villages, and projects that may not have been seen by center staff as essential were carried out if the people decided upon them. Ahmad Fathi al-Difrawy, one of the social-agricultural specialists in the RSC program, recalled that the people of one of the villages where he worked decided that they wanted to build a minaret for the local mosque. Although it did not bring tangible benefits to the people, the project was carried out because it was a project the people wanted.[129] Another example is the issuance of health cards to villagers in some social centers. The villagers wanted to make health identification cards with their names, ages, the number of visits to the clinic, and their health condition printed on the card. The villagers felt more secure in their rights to health care once these cards were created, although there was no tangible benefit to issuing the cards, and the cards were not required for access to health care.[130] These two examples were characteristic of the program; the villagers set their own priorities, and it was the projects they wanted for themselves that were carried out.

Women's Services

Another example of the setting of priorities by the villagers themselves was evident in the provision of women's services. The services already discussed served women as well as men, but occasionally initiatives were taken that exclusively targeted the women of a particular village.[131] One such project, on which Hussein and his wife Aziza collaborated, was the establishment of a program to aid the women in the village of Sindiyun, near Cairo. Sindiyun had a rural social center complete with a maternity and child welfare clinic, and the women of the village had been generating extra income by doing embroidery and sewing projects and selling these items at local bazaars. Yet Hussein believed that the women of Sindiyun needed more, and he encouraged Aziza Hussein and her colleagues from the Cairo Women's Club (CWC) to get involved in the project and help meet the needs of the village women.

The CWC was enthusiastic about the project and began by establishing the CWC Village Committee in 1950. Working in conjunction with an established rural social center seemed ideal to the women of the CWC, who had been looking for ways to aid village women. Yet, as Aziza Hussein stated, "It had been inconceivable that women who lived away from a village and were too busy to make daily trips to it could have been expected to do any worthwhile work along any social welfare lines."[132] Hussein's encouragement to work within the framework of the existing RSC made it possible for these urban women to begin such a program.

Yet the invitation to become involved in the project was prefaced with a caution to adhere to the principles set down in the social centers project. Hussein asked the women to visit the village three times a week for three months, and during this time they were to act only as friends to the village women. They were not to suggest projects nor were they to say they had come to help the village. After befriending the women of the village and demonstrating to them that they were serious in their friendship and goodwill, the Cairo women felt that a good rapport had been established. Aziza Hussein described the process as follows:

> We started working slowly and carefully. We followed conscientiously all the instructions of the social experts concerning the democratic approach, and

> the patience and time to be taken in establishing friendships with the village women before involving them in any project. We would pay weekly visits to several homes, visit socially with the women, and listen to what they had to say without trying to project our own ideas. Most of them, especially those whose husbands were active in committees in the [rural social] center, expressed their enthusiasm and gratitude for what the social center had enabled them to do for their community in the short period of three years. Then they talked of what they, as women could also do for themselves. At that point, we immediately offered our services to help them in whatever projects they would like to undertake.

As the village women began to talk to the Cairo women about their needs and their hopes for their community, the two groups began to work together to plan projects for Sindiyun. The time taken by the Cairo women to establish friendships with and gain the trust of the village women proved worthwhile. Aziza Hussein recalled that "at the end of one year, Sandyun had its first Village Women's Committee which took up various organized activities such as sewing and knitting, the preparation of jams and preserves, etc."[133]

Yet the activities of the newly established Sindiyun Women's Committee were not limited to small-scale rural industries. What the women of Sindiyun really wanted was a day care center for their children. The village women asked the Cairo women about this project and whether it could be done in Sindiyun. In coordination with the Ministry of Social Affairs, the Cairo Women's Club and the women of Sindiyun set up the first village day care center in Egypt. Children from the ages of three to six attended the center, where they played in a clean environment and ate healthy food. Aziza Hussein recalled a follow-up study done on the children who attended the day care center in Sindiyun, and the results of the study showed that these children had higher IQs and higher grades than other children in the village. She attributed their success to the nutritional and health services given to them at the day care centers.[134]

Aziza Hussein remembered that the project not only helped the children of the village but also became a focal point for the expansion of women's activities within the village:

> Our nursery school was a simple and economical project, adapted to the conditions of the village people. It offered the minimum services required for these youngsters, such as food, clothing, daily bathing, and recreation. . . . This nursery school soon became the center of gravity for women's participation. It proved to be an effective means of reaching the mother and the family through the child. It became very easy through it to organize the mothers into groups to participate in adult education classes, in child care and in hygienic habits.

The village day care center at Sindiyun helped the children and the mothers, and it did so at a very low cost. According to Aziza Hussein, "This program cost only fifteen dollars per child a year for food and clothing plus a maximum of another fifteen dollars for supervision expenses. . . . The principle of financial participation by the villagers was also taken into consideration."[135]

The program of day care centers quickly expanded and was praised as a model project. Not only was it economical, but it also filled a real need in many villages. Women in nearby villages began to ask for advice in setting up day care centers in their own villages. Aziza Hussein remembered that "Sandyun's name rapidly rose to fame in the surrounding villages. One after the other representatives from different villages came pleading with us to start the same project in their respective communities. We seemed to have hit on the practical approach to meet an acute basic need."[136] The second village day care center was set up in the village of Tirsa, ten miles from Sindiyun. Like the center in Sindiyun, this day care center was set up with the help of the CWC and was administered in conjunction with the local rural social center.

Shortly thereafter, in 1953, the Egyptian government took the Sindiyun day care project as a model for the establishment of day care centers at all government social welfare centers in rural areas. By June 1954, six more day care centers had been established, some by groups of women within a village and some in cooperation with the health visitor of the village's RSC. But the governmental recognition of the success of these day care centers was not limited merely to encouraging their spread throughout the country. In a 1954 speech in Washington, D.C., Aziza Hussein reported on the progress of the project started by the CWC in Sindiyun, saying:

Ahmed and Aziza Hussein opening a social center. Courtesy of Aziza Hussein.

> More promising still is the fact that in a conference recently organized by the Health Administration of the *Fellah* Department, the Cairo Women's Club, as well as the other agencies which subsequently worked on nursery schools in villages were called upon to pool all the information they had gained in their respective experiences, with a view to formulating a basic program for the rapid spread of nursery schools all over Egypt. The United Nations World Health Organization's regional office was so favorably impressed that they decided to adopt this movement, and assumed the initial responsibility for establishing, as a first installment in Egypt, thirteen nursery schools in one province.[137]

The government's commitment to expanding the program of rural day care centers culminated in the 1954 decision to provide "200 more nursery-equipped rural social centers."[138]

The interest of the World Health Organization (WHO) in the day care centers established at Sindiyun and Tirsa stemmed from the ability of the centers to reduce the incidence of bilharzia, a parasitic disease endemic to Egypt.

Speaking in 1954, Aziza Hussein recalled asking WHO officials about the reason for their commitment to the day care project:

> They found out, they explained, that the village youngsters who were 3 to 6 years old were the most vulnerable group to the Bilharzia worm, and that the nursery schools, by caring for them and teaching them and their mothers hygienic habits, have reduced the incidence considerably. In other words, unintentionally, and as a by-product of our nursery schools, we furnished the WHO and the country with a positive program that may finally check and eliminate a grave public health problem that has damaged the peasants' productivity and cost us incalculable sums of money for many, many years.[139]

The success of the day care center project serves as another example of the overall success of aided self-help projects in prerevolutionary Egypt. Like the rural social centers to which they were attached, the day care centers were established to help the villagers carry out projects they wanted for themselves. As the projects provided tangible benefits, more and more villages clamored for help in founding their own centers. As the number of centers grew, the United Nations began to recognize them as being worthy of international support and emulation.

The day care centers were not the only popular component of the program. As the benefits accruing to villages where social centers were located became more and more apparent, the demand for new centers skyrocketed. Villages strove to raise the necessary LE 1,500 and locate suitable plots of land so that their village would be able to participate in the program as well. Hussein, writing in 1950, remarked: "They [the villagers] are now all anxious for the establishment of centres in their areas. They all take their share; some contributing funds, others contributing land; while others give building materials and finally the labour required; they all believe that they have an interest in this scheme and hence no canvassing is necessary."[140]

As noted earlier, it was not until after World War II and the 1946 establishment of the Committee to Combat Poverty, Ignorance, and Disease that the Rural Social Centers program began expanding rapidly. The Rural Social Centers program began in 1941, with 6 centers serving only 50,000 people.[141] By 1950 there were centers in 126 villages across Egypt, serving 1.5 million people; by 1951, there were 141 centers. Table 7 shows the annual increase in the number of rural social centers in Egypt. While the number served by the social centers represented only about one-tenth of the rural population (a fraction of those in need of services), the program's benefits, its popularity with the people, and its constant expansion are testimony to its effectiveness. Had the program been left intact after the 1952 revolution and had it expanded along the same lines and according to the model developed by Hussein, it could have brought substantial benefits to the entire nation, perhaps radically altering Egyptian politics and rural society.

Problems, Competition, and Reactions to the RSC Project

Despite the successes of Hussein's rural social centers, the program did face several challenges. The lack of equitable land distribution in Egypt, the country's rapidly growing population, and the lack of coordination of the various social reform projects of the era were serious obstacles. The Ministry of Social Affairs also faced competition in social service provision from other governmental bodies that officials feared would jeopardize project funding.

TABLE 7

Annual Increase in the Number of Rural Social Centers in Egypt and Number of People Served

Year	*Rural Social Centers in Egypt*	*People Served by the Rural Social Centers*
1941	5	50,000
1942	5	50,000
1943	11	122,000
1944	11	122,000
1945	11	122,000
1946	11	122,000
1947	51	480,000
1948[a]	81	780,000
1949	111	1,250,000
1950	126	1,500,000

Source: Ministry of Social Affairs, *The Fellah Department,* Cairo: Société Orientale de Publicité, 1950, p. 28.

[a] There is a discrepancy between the number of centers in Egypt in 1948 reported above (81) and the number reported in table 2 (114). This table shows the number of centers up and running in 1948; table 2 reports the number of centers formally approved by the Ministry.

Additionally, competition from nongovernmental bodies provided services in order to attract adherents to their political views. Hussein and his colleagues were aware of these problems and sought to address them. Though their attempts were not always successful, the program nonetheless received favorable review from all quarters prior to the 1952 revolution.

Hussein and his coterie recognized that the lack of equitable land distribution in Egypt was one of the principal problems faced by the RSC program. Mohamed Shalaby, the social-agricultural specialist in the experiment at al-Manayil, summed up the problem, saying, "The problem of land tenure in Egypt can be shown by the fact that 0.4 percent of the landowners hold more than one-third of all cultivated land, while more than two-thirds of the landowners hold less than one-eighth of the land." He stressed the necessity of structural change without which, he believed, the best social reform measures would not succeed entirely. He remarked, "We [the EASS] believe that solving these [economic] problems will not be determined by the improvement in agriculture practice alone. Considerable changes in tenancy and [the] tax system as well as improvement in transportation must be brought about."[142]

Hussein was well aware of the problem of inequitable distribution of land, knew that the social centers would not achieve substantial results without changes in the land tenure system, and was himself a proponent of land reform.[143] In Hussein's view, the social centers were just one part of his plan for the reconstruction of rural Egypt. They were designed to provide integrated services but, more important, to empower the peasants and to get them to participate in setting their own reformist agenda and in participating in local and national politics. While he knew how difficult it would be to get elite support for changes in the land tenure system, Hussein believed that a slow, gradual approach to the plan of land reform would succeed, just as his slow, gradual social centers program had succeeded. He viewed land reform as a crucial element in reconstructing rural Egypt, and as minister he formulated a plan to address this issue.

Speaking after the revolution, Hussein praised the new regime for its program of land reform, saying that the "semi-feudal conditions" in Egypt before the revolution "were responsible for arresting progress and development, and for the plight of the bulk of the population." He praised the new measure extensively, saying, "This one action surpasses all others as a true and long overdue step towards the emancipation of the Egyptian peasant, raising his morale and social status and improving his lot. Its psychological impact is immense. It created the prerequisite for the success of measures of social and economic reform that the country will launch."[144] It is true that one might expect a government employee to praise ʿAbd al-Nasir's plan lavishly. Hussein, though, was no yes-man for the regime and frequently criticized the new government. Comments such as these, then, can be taken as representative of Hussein's true attitude toward changes in the land tenure system, supported as they are by the testimony of his colleagues about his views.

The project planners also recognized Egypt's rapidly growing population as a problem that might easily overtake their efforts at reform. Shalaby again summarized the views of the EASS members on this topic, saying,

> The population question in Egypt is a very important social problem to be realized as [with] any decrease in the high infant mortality with the advent of modern medical care and the improvement of sanitation conditions in the rural areas, one can reasonably expect an acceleration of population growth. The main problem of Egypt is essentially one of fully utilizing available resources in order to meet the requirements for livelihood of a rapidly increasing population.[145]

Though recognizing rapid population growth as a serous problem, neither the initial EASS-sponsored centers nor the ministry-sponsored centers attempted to address the problem directly or to promote family planning actively. Instead, the centers focused on increasing crop yields and arable land, improving animal husbandry, and fostering the development of rural industries in order to improve the standard of living for the existing population. These efforts were based on the arguments of experts who believed that "to increase the income of the *fellaheen* is . . . the only way to elevate the standard of living, both economically and socially."[146] Given the cultural difficulties attendant upon instituting a comprehensive family planning campaign at that time, increasing rural incomes was a sensible approach to rural reform. However, one might reasonably argue that without slowing the rate of population growth in the country, these efforts would not have been sufficient to increase the standard of living for more than a fraction of the rural population in the long term. On the other hand, had the RSC program continued after 1952, it might well have proved a useful framework within which to organize population control efforts.

Hussein himself was well aware of this problem and viewed population control as an essential element of rural development. In a 1950 speech, Hussein remarked, "It is nothing new to state that the first problem facing the Egyptian rural districts is the continuous increase in the number of the population as compared with the small area of cultivated land."[147] However, he knew that without the support of the religious establishment and the government (support that did not come until well after the revolution), overt attempts to address the problem would not succeed. Instead, discreet attempts were made through the centers to promote smaller families. Efforts were made by the centers' health visitors, by doctors, and by volunteer organizations such as the Cairo Women's Club, working on a one-to-one basis with the village women, to emphasize the benefits of fewer children.[148]

Another serious problem was the overlapping jurisdictions and projects of different ministries. Radi Bey, the undersecretary of the Ministry of Social Affairs, acknowledged this problem in 1946 when discussing the Committee to Combat Poverty, Ignorance, and Disease with American diplomatic officials.[149] This overlap was also noted by Shalaby in his evaluation of the project in 1950. Although he was careful to note the need for reform projects in rural areas, he argued that the result of several ministries attempting to address the same problems in rural areas would only lead to lack of accountability, poor-quality service provision, and a feeling of competition.

Speaking for the EASS, Shalaby, perhaps predictably, praised the work of the Ministry of Social Affairs, saying, "The effectiveness of the Rural Welfare Centers . . . has been shown. The scheme shows its usefulness, simpleness, and adaptability to the village community." He then added,

> We have one remark which we consider of great value. The function of the rural welfare center is a duplication of the functions and services of different ministries and departments. Its concern is the improvement of health, which is the function of the Ministry of Public Health. It deals with agriculture and cooperation problems and development which are the services of the Min-

> istry of Agriculture and the Cooperative Department. It encourages the home industries which are part of the program of the Ministry of Commerce and Industry. It covers a wide program in education, especially for adults, which is the concern of the Ministry of Education. The results of this overlapping of function is that in some villages different projects of different departments are carried out with different philosophies although all projects are aiming to improve the conditions in village life. Many other villages lack any of these services. We also find items in the budgets of the different departments of the same nature—health, education, etc. According to this we find an administrative office for health in the Ministry of Public Health, another in the Ministry of Education, and a third in the Ministry of Social Affairs. This is a division of services between many hands which results in a loose feeling of responsibility. The quality of work will be very low and ineffective.

Shalaby continued in the same vein, remarking that the frequent cabinet changes in the prerevolutionary period contributed to the problem and that "in certain number of cases, a project is buried, whatever its value, the day the minister who presented it leaves the seat." He called for more coordination between the ministries, more cooperation between government personnel belonging to the different ministries, and an end to the duplication of services and competition among various government branches.[150]

The problem of coordinating services in the villages was one with which Hussein and his staff were familiar. When the Committee to Combat Poverty, Ignorance, and Disease was formed in 1946, the subject of overlapping ministerial jurisdictions and overall lack of service coordination was discussed at length. The committee decided to found a new body, the Higher Council for Workers and Peasants Affairs, to deal with coordination and to begin an experiment at Sirs al-Layyan in Minufiyah to ensure cooperation and coordination of the programs of the various ministries in rural areas.[151] Actually begun in 1950, the Sirs al-Layyan regional council center was to serve as a prototype unit, and similar units were to be built in each village, with the goal of "coordinating the technical activities of the Ministries concerned: Education, Social Affairs, Health, and Agriculture. Such units will serve at the same time as a technical headquarters for social welfare centres."[152]

Unfortunately, this coordination program did not bear fruit. Despite the goal of using the Sirs al-Layyan center as a headquarters for coordinating projects, rivalries between the various ministries, coupled with an unresolved debate over who would have the final word on coordination issues, sounded the death knell for the experiment. Although buildings were constructed in the village and the regional council was formed, no work was ever undertaken. The Ministry of Finance refused to recognize the council as an official government body and therefore allocated no funding to it. The buildings at Sirs al-Layyan remained empty until taken over by UNESCO as the headquarters for their project, Fundamental Education for the Arab States.[153] The episode provides a concrete example of the problems of competition and overlapping jurisdiction Shalaby and the EASS criticized.

In addition to the problems posed by the land tenure system, Egypt's burgeoning population, and the overall lack of coordination and communication between ministries, the Ministry of Social Affairs also faced the related problem of competition from other bodies. Making use of the currency of reformist ideas, both nongovernmental and governmental agencies strove to implement their own schemes of social reform and service provision, sometimes complementing the efforts of the Ministry of Social Affairs and sometimes conflicting with them.

The Muslim Brotherhood was one organization that used social service provision as a means to attract political supporters; as an opposition group, its activities can be seen as competing with the governmentally sponsored RSC program. The Brotherhood opposed both external and internal imperialism, which it defined as the domestic forces that served the interests of the occupying foreign powers and "diverted Egyptians from their traditional faith to a dead pacifism, lowly humiliation, and acceptance of the status quo." It opposed political parties, which it viewed as servants of the capitalist class, exploiting the majority of the population for the parties' own personal gain. The Brotherhood viewed party leaders as corrupt, incompetent, and oppressive, and the bureaucracy as the means by which party leaders perpetuated their tyrannical misrule of the country:

> The hallmarks of the bureaucracy had been inefficiency, muddle, corruption, abuse of authority, and personal power; appointments had been made

> without regard to the qualifications of the appointee. . . . [The results were] (1) a loss of confidence in the law and respect for it as it had been administered by "corrupt officials"; and (2) the centralization of authority in the hands of the "powerful leaders" to the point where subordinates dared not take upon themselves responsibility and had become "tools with neither will nor opinions."[154]

The Brotherhood was particularly vocal in its support of the peasants against the large landowners, whom they saw as the root of Egyptian capitalism and hence, in conjunction with foreign capitalist domination, of all society's evils. The Brotherhood argued that by controlling the government apparatus these landowners neglected their social and national responsibilities, focused only on personal gain, and maintained the woefully inadequate distribution of land and wealth through the tax laws that required the poorer classes to pay all the taxes, while denying them true representation. The Brotherhood argued that this situation was intolerable and that:

> it leads to many evils: (1) it "paralyzes the strength of the nation in work and production"; (2) it "destroys human dignity and rights"; (3) it "corrupts the character and the conscience"; (4) "it denies individual security"; (5) it "pushes people into the arms of the communists"; (6) it "violates the spirit of religion".[155]

In order to provide an alternative to government oppression and its lack of social reform in the 1930s, the group began organizing its own social services. Originally a social movement, the Brotherhood began combining social and political activities at the start of the strikes in Palestine in 1936; it was not until 1939, however, that the Brotherhood officially defined itself as, among other things, a political organization. In 1945 Law no. 49 was passed concerning social work and organized charity. This law required all charitable organizations to register with and be supervised by the Ministry of Social Affairs, thus necessitating the Brotherhood's formal division into two sections, one of which was a section of welfare and social services. Although this section was secondary to the political activities of the Brotherhood in the post–World War II period, it nonetheless represented a nongovernmental approach to social service provision. As Richard Mitchell reported in his groundbreaking study of the group:

> The creation of the new section reflected a great upsurge in the activity of the organization in this as well as all other fields to which the movement dedicated itself in its effort to exemplify its belief in the totality and applicability of Islamic teachings. Night and day schools and institutes, which offered both technical and academic programmes, were established for boys, girls, and adults. Some small industries were founded, both to relieve post-war unemployment and to dramatize the viability of "Islamic economics." Welfare activity was supplemented by social work, largely in rural areas, and medical work in the form of hospitals, clinics, and dispensaries.[156]

The Brotherhood's own service provision focused on efforts to reintroduce religious education into the schools, to recruit teachers and students to its cause, to oppose foreign missionary schools, to argue for a blend of scientific and religious training for students, to found its own schools and adult education programs, to give agricultural instruction to farmers, and to encourage its members to help in the battle against illiteracy by volunteering in adult literacy classes.[157]

The group also was concerned with health service activities. Beginning with informational campaigns, the Brotherhood began including medical service provision as part of its "rover units," units that traveled throughout the countryside giving information and providing services. Established in 1943, these units "undertook the actual work of cleaning up the streets and alleys of the villages, encouraged villagers to use hospitals and clinics, and provided simple first aid." These roving units were soon supplemented by an official Brotherhood medical section, established in 1944 by doctors who were Brotherhood members. The goals of this new section were "the establishment of dispensaries, clinics, and hospitals, the intensification of the programme for 'spreading the message of hygiene' and the 'raising of the health level of all classes' by all means available." The Brotherhood continued to expand its health programs, and by 1953, "it was claimed that each province of Egypt had at least one dispensary and that sixteen clinics in Cairo had treated over 100,000 patients." The society also provided many charitable services to the poor, including "help in money or in kind to poor families, especially those without breadwinners, the aged, the homeless, and the orphaned." Its branches also distributed food, clothing, and soap on various religious holidays.[158]

The Brotherhood blueprint for village reform was another of its attempts to give the people an alternative to what it saw as governmental indifference and inaction. Although the rural reform plan remained only a plan and was never implemented by the Brotherhood, the group's focus on both tangible aid and future plans for development highlight its position as a potential nongovernmental competitor in the arena of social service provision. The Brotherhood plan for village reform was remarkably similar to the social centers project. Al-Banna argued that the reform of Egyptian villages should be given considerable attention by government authorities, and the initial orientation of the organization was toward the rural areas. The Brotherhood believed that medical services should be provided to the villages, that charity should be organized in the villages, and that issues such as clean water, well-constructed roads and houses, proper lighting, and the establishment of village industries should be part of any village reform project. The Rural Social Centers project included all of these things. In a 1946 article in one of its dailies, the Brotherhood argued that each village should have a leader who was a responsible civil servant with an agricultural education and knowledge of sociology and administration. The Brotherhood also argued that this leader should be supervised to ensure that he met the needs of the community and that village councils should be established to help him govern wisely.[159] Interestingly, the Brotherhood's description of a proper village leader sounds almost exactly like a description of the social centers' social-agricultural specialist. The parallels between the Brotherhood's plans for rural reform and Hussein's own projects are striking. Both programs stressed the need for a new type of Egyptian village and a new spirit among the people, and both the Brotherhood and Hussein himself advocated land reform. The organization had little official reaction to Hussein's programs, however (nor is there any record of criticism of Brotherhood social service activities by Hussein and his staff), and continued its social service activities as a means of both expressing its discontent with governmental programs and attracting adherents to its political views.[160]

The competition faced by the Ministry of Social Affairs was not restricted to nongovernmental organizations. The Ministry of Health also envied the authority given to the Ministry of Social Affairs in the RSCs, perceiving it as an encroachment on its own sphere of health service provision. Prior to creation of the RSC project, the Ministry of Health, like the Muslim Brotherhood, had begun its own rural medical units. Though offering neither effective nor comprehensive health care, this ministry nonetheless did not care to see its units replaced nor, even worse from a bureaucratic standpoint, improved upon by another ministry.[161]

At the beginning of the twentieth century, the Department of Public Health in Egypt began a program of traveling medical units and tent hospitals for rural areas. These units "carried out programs for smallpox vaccination and campaigns against the eye diseases that affected so many Egyptians." In 1939, at the same time that the Ministry of Social Affairs was founded, the Ministry of Health added a Rural Health section "to supervise rural health services." In 1942, the minister of health, Abd al-Wahid al-Wakil,[162] got the government to pass the Improvement of Village Health Law, "which called for the creation of a health unit for every thirty thousand people. The initial plan was for 850 units."[163] Each health unit was to have an outpatient clinic, an endemic disease clinic, and a hospital unit for inpatient and maternity care.[164] In the 1943–44 budget, the health centers were given an allocation of LE 2.5 million (more than half of the LE 4.5 million Ministry of Health budget, the largest budget ever given to that ministry).[165] By 1950, however, there were only 203 of the planned 850 units in operation.[166]

The units established by the Ministry of Health, Aziza Hussein recalled, were the fruit of a political battle between Health and Social Affairs concerning who should have jurisdiction over health-related programs. She argues that "the Ministry of Health was the biggest opponent [of the RSCs], and it developed its own health units all over the country in a clear challenge to the social centers."[167] In fact, in 1946, when the various ministries were submitting proposals to Sidqi's new Committee to Combat Poverty, Ignorance, and Disease, the Ministry of Health's proposals centered on the provision of a new type of health unit. These health units were similar to the RSCs, although more limited in scope. They were each to serve 15,000 people and were to begin projects to improve village dwellings, plan and improve streets, provide area for village expansion, provide clean water systems, provide public baths, repair mosque lavatories, and provide every sort of health service to the villagers.[168] Shalaby, writing in 1950, praised the Ministry of Health for attempting to address rural health problems but added that the ministry's rural health units "are still limited in number and lacking adequate service because of the shortage of technical personnel—doctors, laboratorians, and nurses. . . . They need much development to meet all the needs."[169] Hussein, remarking in 1950 on this competition between the two ministries, politely noted that "the efforts of the Ministry of Social Affairs which have been directed towards the rural districts [since] 1941, had a good effect in increasing the interest of the various Ministries in these aspects."[170]

The unresolved political battles between the Ministries of Social Affairs and Health were doubtless part of what Shalaby, Hussein, and others were criticizing when referring to overlapping jurisdictions and duplication of efforts in the countryside. Not all governmental and nongovernmental organizations tried to compete with the RSC program, however. Some attempted to work with the program, complementing and augmenting its efforts at reform rather than duplicating them. The Ministries of Agriculture, Education, Public Affairs, and Commerce and Industry all began projects in the same era that served to facilitate the efforts made by Hussein's social centers project. The efforts of many independent organizations helped as well.[171]

The Ministry of Agriculture was especially supportive. In addition to helping the RSCs maintain demonstration plots, the ministry was also involved in "valuable scientific research and important practical improvements in connection with the application of chemical fertilizer, cotton seed selection, control of pests and diseases, animal husbandry, and fruit and vegetable culture".[172] The social-agricultural specialists of the RSCs served as the liaisons between the villagers and the Ministry of Agriculture, helping the villagers obtain improved seed, fertilizers, and stud animals from the ministry. This cooperation between Agriculture and Social Affairs personnel resulted in tangible improvements in agriculture in the villages where RSCs were located. In addition to these efforts, the Ministry of Agriculture also prepared literature on agriculture and used lectures, posters, films, and radio broadcasts to "popularize agricultural knowledge." In 1944, the Ministry of Agriculture began a program of agricultural units designed to support, not duplicate, existing RSC activities.[173]

The Ministry of Education also attempted to increase educational services in rural areas. The curriculum changes introduced in rural schools certainly helped make education more popular in the countryside. The drive to build more schools in rural areas gained momentum in the 1940s, although the actual establishment of new schools was a slow process. Shalaby praised the Ministry of Public Affairs' management of irrigation and drainage, noting that irrigation was an "essential matter for the cultivation of the land of Egypt" and saying that thanks to the efforts of this ministry, the irrigation system in Egypt "can be considered one of the best systems in the world. It enables the *fellaheen* in many parts of Egypt to cultivate two or three crops a year on the same land."[174] The Ministry of Commerce and Industry also got involved in rural social service, beginning a program for rural industries in 1946.[175] The Royal Agricultural Society, the Egyptian Association for Social Studies, and various other institutions also contributed to the RSC project.[176] These activities, in providing infrastructure, materials, and networks for the RSCs, served to augment the work the RSCs had begun.

While the Ministry of Social Affairs did face competition from nongovernmental groups and from other government departments, the programs of the ministry, particularly the RSC program, were unique in their approach to development. Charity organizations such as the *awqaf,* the Red Crescent Society, and Mubarrat Muhammad 'Ali had been in existence in Egypt since the late nineteenth century and early twentieth century. Such groups confined themselves to offering charitable contributions and philanthropic services, rather than attempting to draw up a comprehensive, integrated development plan. The activities of the Brotherhood (with the exception of its plan for rural development) and the health units of the Ministry of Health continued this pattern of providing services without encouraging integrated development or citizen participation, and other small-scale independent organizations did the same.

Aside from the competition described above, the Rural Social Centers project encountered almost no opposition. Varied sources, including the Egyptian government, the American government, the United Nations, the local village leadership, and the Free Officers, all either openly supported or did not oppose the project. One of the most unusual features of this program is the almost total lack of documented opposition to it. The activities of government departments notwithstanding, the program received the full support of the Egyptian government. Despite the numerous cabinet changes between 1939 and 1951, the number of centers steadily increased, and there was no noticeable Palace or party opposition. U.S. diplomatic sources attributed Palace support of the program to its limited scope, saying that "it may be expected that the program [of Rural Social Centers] will continue to receive the full support of the government, especially since it does not touch on fundamental questions of taxation or land tenure."[177] Hussein's own standing as a nonpartisan expert also contributed to the ability of the program to flourish in the turbulent political period after the Second World War. Since the project was the outcome of a pilot project initiated by a nongovernmental organization and run by the apolitical Hussein, it was not identified as a project of a particular party or government and hence was not targeted for elimination or reduction when the cabinet changed.

American diplomatic sources also championed the project and, while calling it "a diminutive effort . . . compared with the magnitude of Egypt's social problems," also believed that the program was a step in the right direction, remarking, "The program is well planned and well administered and each center is a real and growing contribution to social improvement."[178] The United Nations agreed with this assessment and, in 1951, the Economic and Social Committee of the UN adopted a resolution stating that the Egyptian Rural Social Centers project should be used as a model for village reform on an international level.[179]

Further international recognition was also forthcoming from a variety of sources. In a 1950 ministry publication, Hussein cited numerous letters from international bodies and politicians praising the social centers program. The Regional International Labor Organization (ILO) Conference for the Far East, at its meeting in New Delhi in 1946, praised the Egyptian program and recommended that other agricultural countries adopt similar schemes. The Permanent Agricultural Committee of the ILO made the same recommendation during the Geneva conference in 1947. Hussein also cited correspondence from a Professor Spon of Columbia University, the former director general of the FAO, Sir John Boyd Orr, and American philanthropist Hamilton Wright, praising the work of the centers and recommending that other countries follow Egypt's example.[180]

On the local level, the majority of large landowners accepted the program

Hussein and Dawood showing M. Vincenau the RSCs. Vincenau was a French financier associated with the Agricultural Credit Bank and the Crédit Foncier Egyptien. Courtesy of Aziza Hussein.

as well. Often, landowning families tried to take an active role in service provision. Omar Rashed al-Mikawy, who served as the social-agricultural specialist in Gamgara in Markaz Banha in the province of Qalyubiyah, recalled two of the wealthy landowning families in Gamgara vying with each other to provide the most support for the social center in that area. Al-Mikawy says that it was a matter of family prestige for each to be known as the family who contributed the most to the center. The land for centers was often donated by wealthy landowning families, although financial contributions were made by all villagers. Although there were isolated instances of the wealthy rural elite opposing the program, most large landowners accepted and encouraged the social centers as a good alternative to a popular, communist-inspired uprising of the peasantry.[181]

Most village leaders also accepted the program. There are no published records of local opposition to the program. It must be acknowledged, however, that the lack of documented opposition does not necessarily mean that no opposition existed. Those who may have objected to or opposed the program in the villages are not likely to have left records, nor was the government likely to have publicized any incidents. However, Hassan Dawood, one of the social-agricultural specialists in the first series of RSCs begun by the Ministry of Social Affairs, recalls an incident in Assiout, where the social-agricultural specialist was physically attacked in broad daylight because wealthy members of the community thought the project a threat to their own status. However, Dawood noted that "this opposition faded in front of the support and enthusiasm of the majority of the rural people."[182]

Others who worked as social-agricultural specialists in the villages agreed with Dawood's assessment. The consensus of those who worked in the centers is that although there was some local opposition, it was usually very minor and confined to one or two notables who feared their own position would be undermined in the village. In most cases this opposition was overcome by popular support for the program and by the consensus-building efforts of the centers' staff. In other cases, opposition to the centers occurred for personal reasons that were divorced from the project itself. For instance, in one village two feuding brothers each offered to donate land for a basketball court for the center. When the social-agricultural specialist accepted the offer of land from one brother, the other brother was incensed and attacked the specialist. Anwar al-'Abd, who served as social-agricultural specialist at Tirsa in Giza, recounted an incident that happened during his tenure when one of the loom instructors hit a student. The boy's family was outraged and came to kill the teacher, whereupon al-'Abd stepped in and hit the loom instructor himself, thus satisfying the family's desire for retribution and forestalling a potentially devastating series of events.[183] Incidents such as these, however, were rare and cannot be taken as representative of local response to the project.

Indeed, the rapid increase in villagers' demands for new centers supports Dawood's observation that the good results of the centers and the people's enthusiasm outweighed potential opposition. Writing in 1950, Hussein argued, "Nothing is more indicative of the success of these Centres than the enthusiasm met with from the public who clamour for the establishment of Centres in these villages. We quote as an example the following: In 1947 it was decided to construct 40 Centres. Applications were submitted for 123 centres with undertakings to furnish the land and subscribe LE 1500 for each. Applications submitted in 1948/49 were for 260 centres while the number approved by the Government was 30 only."[184]

The continual popular demand for more centers also indicates that despite occasional personality conflicts, the program was able to function effectively without significantly challenging the village leadership. The *'umda* of each village was incorporated into the conciliation committee of the center, which allowed him to continue to help resolve disputes, one of his traditional tasks. The structure of the program, which emphasized responding to the requests of the villagers, was largely responsible for the relative lack of friction with the traditional village leadership. The training of center staff in consensus building, diplomacy, and crisis management was also useful in diffusing problematic situations.[185]

Finally, the Free Officers also seemed to support the program immediately after the 1952 revolution. Although the program was changed substantially after 1952, all available evidence suggests that the changes made to the program that eventually resulted in its destruction were made in ignorance, with the goal of expanding and enhancing the project.[186] While postrevolutionary literature and programs on social and economic reform all made vague references to the pitiable state of the Egyptian peasant and his oppression at the hands of the corrupt and money-grubbing pasha class, every specific reference made to the Rural Social Centers project was favorable. As chapter 5 will demonstrate, the project was treated as a potentially great idea whose main flaws were its small scale and slow progress.

4

Gaining International Recognition

In January 1950, elections were held in Egypt. The Wafd Party was the overwhelming victor, and Mustafa Nahas Pasha came to power for the seventh time. Since the previous Wafdist government was dismissed in 1944, eight minority governments had come and gone. All of these governments had been largely unsuccessful in controlling the escalating political violence and the increasing social and economic problems of Egypt. The 1950 elections brought a new era of hope to the nation. These elections were considered to be free and fair,[1] and many believed that they heralded a new era in Egypt. As Joel Gordon wrote:

> The assumption of power by the Wafd in 1950 sparked renewed hope that the parliamentary order might right itself. Majority rule, many felt, would bring a welcome degree of political stability, the restoration of civil liberties, and, it was hoped, produce an agreement with Great Britain that would end the occupation. The emergence of new, fresh faces in the Wafd's leadership ranks engendered hopes that the majority party would initiate a program of social and administrative reform and rise above the traditional political bickering that brought so many into the streets denouncing political parties.[2]

The new cabinet appointed by Nahas included the Wafdist ministers who, like himself, had been dismissed by the king in 1944. The cabinet also included a number of technocrats and reformers, including Ahmed Hussein and three other ministers (Taha Hussein, minister of education, Zaki 'Abd al-Mut'al, minister of finance, and Hamid Zaki, minister of state) who had few or no ties to the Wafd Party and were known for their experience and expertise

Mustafa al-Nahas (on left), Hussein, and Dr. Edith Summerskill, Britain's Minister of National Insurance, ca. 1950. Courtesy of Aziza Hussein.

in their respective fields. Calling these men "the professors," Gordon says that their appointment was seen as a sign that the new Wafd government would stick to its promises and not fall prey to nepotism, inertia, and corruption.[3]

But why were "the professors" selected to head their respective ministries? Was the Wafd truly committed to an agenda of substantive social and economic reform? Gordon argues that these four reformers were chosen on the recommendation of Wafd executive committee member Ahmad Nagib al-Hilali. Al-Hilali had been a founding member of the EASS and was a close associate of Hussein. He also had a reputation as a reformer within the Wafdist party:

> Despite his aloofness from party affairs, Hilali wielded considerable influence in the formation of the 1950 government. A professor of civil law who had served in a minority government from 1934 to 1936, Hilali joined the Wafd in 1938. Close to Makram 'Ubayd, Hilali chose to remain with the Wafd after the former's ouster in 1942 and came closest in the public eye to

Hussein and Wafdist cabinet during meeting. Courtesy of Aziza Hussein.

> replacing him as the conscience of the party. Dedicated to administrative reform and bitterly opposed to party patronage networks, Hilali gathered around himself a coterie of young academics and technocrats through whom he hoped to impress a reform agenda on the Wafd. He had become increasingly disillusioned with Wafdist leadership and withdrew from active participation in party matters. He refused to run for parliament in 1950, and Nahas could not entice him to join the cabinet. Hilali did suggest alternative candidates; that four posts went to men who received his blessing underlines the grudging respect with which his colleagues held him.[4]

Two of the four "professors" were somewhat unlikely candidates for their jobs. Zaki 'Abd al-Mut'al's appointment as minister of finance was a surprise to some observers because that portfolio had traditionally gone to a staunch party supporter, which 'Abd al-Mut'al was not. He was, however, a respected professor of economics and finance "and a former legal adviser to the commerce and finance ministries." Hamid Zaki was a professor of international and civil law, and many wondered at Nahas's choice of him as minister of state. Although al-Hilali suggested Zaki to Nahas for the post of private secretary, the prime minister "named him as minister of state, intending him to serve as his right-hand man and political troubleshooter." The two Husseins (no relation) were both considered expert in their field. Taha Hussein, a well-known intellectual and writer, "had earned a reputation as a progressive spokesman for educational reform."[5]

Ahmed Hussein was already a well-established expert on social issues, owing to his myriad successful programs throughout his career in lower levels of service in the Ministries of Agriculture and Social Affairs. British ambassador Campbell praised Hussein's appointment, reporting that Hussein "is young and keen and has a good grip of the work of his department which in the past has suffered too much from having been in charge of unimaginative politicians."[6] Remarking on Hussein's appointment as minister, Gordon notes that Hussein "brought considerable expertise to his post. A shining star in reformist circles, he had already made a name for himself as an energetic and ethical undersecretary in the ministry he now headed."[7] For his part, Hussein agreed to join Nahas's ministry for several reasons: the recommendation of al-Hilali (an old friend and dedicated reformer whom Hussein admired very much), cautious optimism that the Wafd would fulfill its promises on the economic and social fronts, and a belief that as minister he would be able to broaden the scope of his successful reform initiatives.

The appointment of these four respected professionals was not the only thing that raised hopes of a new era of change in Egypt. In his inaugural speech, Nahas,

> [whose government] had already lifted censorship of the press, promised to take immediate steps to end martial law. The new government would initiate measures "for the good of all classes, especially underprivileged peasants and workers." Nahas pledged steps to lower the cost of living. The government proclaimed primary, secondary, and technical education to be free. A social security bill was in the works. Nahas promised legislation to mandate a reorganization of the government bureaucracy. Civil service would be based solely on merit; government employees would no longer fear a loss of post to political appointees.[8]

Some of these initial promises were acted upon, and several substantive reforms were made fairly quickly after the new government assumed power. The government began "legislating wage raises and subsidizing basic foodstuffs; it also allocated significant increases in funding for education and social services, undertook the building of new schools and hospitals, and passed a social security bill which provided old-age and disability benefits for families without a breadwinner."[9] Ahmed Hussein was a prime mover behind many of these reforms.

Reconstructing Rural Egypt

The RSC program was without question the centerpiece of Hussein's reform efforts, yet his plans for reform had a much broader scope. Hussein envisioned nothing short of the wholesale reconstruction of rural Egypt, and as minister, his reform plans were geared toward achieving this goal. Hussein was well aware of the need for gradual change—experience in the Cooperative Department had shown the importance of citizen participation in reform initiatives and the dangers of pushing for the rapid expansion of reform programs. Under Hussein's guidance, the RSC program was started slowly, and although he anticipated the program's eventual expansion to cover all rural Egypt, Hussein's own annual goals for the project were modest. The RSC program was designed to improve the standard of living in the countryside, but, more broadly, it was designed to accustom the peasants to participating in reform programs, to speaking out and setting their own priorities, and to dealing with government officials as equals. With the success of this program well established, with its slow but sure expansion ensured, and with himself in a position to direct future reforms personally, Hussein turned his attention to developing his other plans for the reconstruction of rural Egypt. The three main components of Hussein's plan were a program of limited land reform and reclamation, the establishment of a minimum agricultural wage, and the regulation of the relationship between landowners and their tenant farmers.

During the prerevolutionary period, two methods were proposed for alleviating the problem of inequitable land distribution: either create more arable land through reclamation efforts or redistribute already arable land. Like most reformers of his era, Hussein was well aware that inequitable distribution of land was a major problem in attempting to reform the Egyptian countryside: some two-thirds of the land was owned by approximately 6 percent of the population, with the remaining 94 percent of the population owning less than 5 *feddans* each. Hussein himself favored widespread land reform legislation, and when the land reform law was finally passed after the 1952 revolution, he praised it lavishly.

However, he did not limit himself to simply wishing for land reform. Instead he devised a plan to distribute reclaimed lands to landless peasants. Hussein, writing in 1950, described the plan (nicknamed the "Five Feddans Scheme")[10] as follows: "This policy aims at establishing holdings of an optimum size for a farming family, and it enables landless cultivators to become owners of adequate size. It also aims at switching manpower from densely populated areas to newly developed agricultural areas."[11] Hussein's plan reprioritized the list of those eligible for settlement on reclaimed lands. Previously, government policy had stated that reclaimed land would first be given to large landowners, with second priority given to graduates of the Faculty of Agriculture, and landless peasants a distant third. The result was that during the period 1935–49, 90.7 percent of the total area of newly reclaimed state land was sold to large landowners, 7.6 percent to graduates, and only 1.7 percent to small tenants and landless workers, a group that represented nearly half the total agricultural population and whose average annual earnings were only LE 14–15.[12] In 1949, as undersecretary of the Ministry of Social Affairs, Hussein reached an agreement with the Council of Ministers to distribute state-owned reclaimed land in the Delta regions of Kafr Sa'd, Ibshan, and Fuwah to landless peasants in the area.[13] The Kafr Sa'd reclamation area contained approximately 6,000 *feddans*, and Hussein's plan was to distribute this land to peasants in parcels of approximately 5 *feddans* each.[14] He intended to start with this small redistribution project, garner the support of prominent politicians, landowners, and members of the royal family for the project, and gradually expand the program, much in the same way he was able to gradually expand the Rural Social Centers project.

These allotments of reclaimed land were made on the following terms: Each family received a plot of 5 *feddans*, with the price "being payable in installments over a period of 30 years. Monthly subsidies [were] also granted during the first year of settlement to enable families to live until the crop is gathered. Credits [were] given, not in cash, but in the form of livestock, agricultural implements and dwellings. . . . Social services [were] rendered to the settlers and their children by specialised workers. Cooperative societies [were] formed, and cooperative marketing [was] followed whenever possible."[15] By 1951, 597 of the 5–*feddan* units had been distributed to landless families, and there were 583 more such units awaiting redistribution.[16]

Hussein's plan for land reform and redistribution did not end with advocating the sale of limited amounts of reclaimed land to landless peasants. Under Hussein's guidance, the Fellah Department also proposed that the government sell to landless peasants all reclaimed lands, all excess agricultural lands not needed by the Ministry of Agriculture for research and experiments, all *waqf* agricultural lands (using the money raised by the sale for charitable purposes), all land seized for nonpayment of taxes, and a portion of land owned by agricultural societies. In addition, the department also advocated "the levying of a progressive taxation on arable lands" in order to "limit the expansion of vast ownerships" and to direct "the wealth and efforts of well-to-do people towards industry, commerce, and other construction schemes." The department also argued for blanket tax exemptions for small farmers whose income did not exceed a specified amount. Although Hussein himself favored limits on the size of agricultural holdings, many believed that this new tax scheme was preferable to and less disruptive than wholesale land reform would be.[17] Finally, the department argued that ceding a certain portion of land to the landless should be a condition in all settlements of land debts, that the expropriation of a certain percentage of land from large landowners should be carried out, and that the spread of cooperative societies to help these newly landed peasants function effectively in the economy should be undertaken.[18] When all facets of these proposals are taken into account, Hussein's plan for land redistribution was really quite ambitious. It was, however, modeled on his success in the RSC program in that it was a gradual plan and relied upon winning the acceptance of the economic and political elite by degrees.

Having addressed social services and participatory education in the RSC program and having begun to address the inequitable distribution of land through various plans for land reform and reclamation, Hussein turned his attention to another serious issue confronting the fellahin: the problem of low agricultural wages. Industrial and commercial workers in Egypt had enjoyed a certain degree of legislative protection for decades, yet agricultural workers had received no similar legislative attention. Hussein believed that economic security in the form of a minimum agricultural wage should be extended to rural workers, particularly in light of their importance to the national economy and the fact that they comprised the vast majority of the nation's population—the rural poor. While serving as minister of social affairs, Hussein drafted a law to establish a minimum wage for agricultural workers.

In this law, Hussein proposed that local committees be set up to decide the amount of the minimum wage for agricultural workers. These committees would be composed of landowners representing themselves as employers of agricultural laborers and officials of the Ministry of Social Affairs representing the interests of the agricultural laborers, who were not represented by unions. The draft law stipulated that the committees could not set a wage that would result in the agricultural worker being paid less than a subsistence wage, an amount that would presumably be calculated by the ministry. Hussein also argued that the purchasing power of the agricultural laborers should be increased. He thought minimum wages were a first step toward this goal, but he also argued that "the system of direct and indirect taxation should be reconsidered with a view to reducing the tax on consumption commodities whose whole burden falls on these poorer classes. These taxes may be replaced by others payable by richer classes." He also believed that tenancy rates should be "compatible with the production and price of crops" and that supply and demand of agricultural labor should be regulated by providing employment for surplus agricultural workers in industry and in rural building projects.[19]

Although this law was never passed by the Egyptian parliament, it was nonetheless another indication of Hussein's desire to improve the standard of living in the Egyptian countryside. Writing in 1950, Hussein justified his minimum wage plan, saying:

> This draft law is one of the most important means of raising the standard of living among the rural population in particular and among the working classes in general in addition to extending the principles of social justice between rural and urban labour. Industrial wages are higher than agricultural wages, and the country's interest as an economic unit is that a balance should

> prevail as far as possible between the income of the rural and industrial wage-earner. Every increase in rural wages is in the interest of local industry as an increase in the purchasing power of the millions of farmworkers will increase their consumption of local industries.[20]

The defeat of this law in the Egyptian parliament was a deep disappointment to Hussein and was a factor in his later withdrawal from government service.[21] Nonetheless, his attempts to establish a minimum agricultural wage and the importance he attached to the opposition his draft law encountered testify to the central role wages played in his plan to reconstruct rural Egypt. As discussed later in this chapter, the land reform law of the revolutionary government did include the establishment of a minimum wage for agricultural labor. Hussein's efforts to pass such legislation before the revolution and the studies he made of the subject no doubt influenced this aspect of 'Abd al-Nasir's land reform law.

Though the minimum wage plan failed, Hussein did succeed in implementing a law requiring large landowners to provide certain social and health services to the workers on their estates. By regulating the treatment of tenants by the landowners, Hussein was addressing another central element in his plan for reconstructing rural Egypt. In August 1950, Law no. 118 was passed. Known as the Estates Act, one of the provisions of this law was to require large landowners to supply workers with clean drinking water, a storage facility for manure and another for fuel, a first-aid box complete with bandages and disinfectants, and a meeting hall for prayers. The law also regulated construction on the estates, specifying the minimum size of buildings to be used as living quarters for the agricultural workers and requiring that the buildings for workers be made of limestone or fired brick, as opposed to sun-dried bricks. It mandated that enclosures for animals be kept separate from the workers' living quarters and that a water closet be part of every residential building. Finally, it required the landowner to provide to the workers, free of charge, small plots for growing vegetables.

Penalties for noncompliance with this law ranged from LE 5 to LE 20, and landowners not complying with the law were given a period of time within which to bring facilities on their estate up to code. If the landowners still refused to make the necessary changes, the government then had the authority under the law to make the changes and bill the landowner for the cost of the improvements. This law was significant because it was a serious attempt by Hussein and his ministry to hold landowners accountable for the health and safety of their fellahin. After securing passage of this law and beginning his other plans of rural reform, Hussein turned his attention to broader reforms for both rural and urban areas.

Beginning Broader Reforms

Despite his own interest in rural areas, Hussein's projects were not limited to rural social reforms. Although Hussein succeeded in instituting a number of new programs of social service provision in rural areas, he also was aware of the need for more extensive development measures. During his brief tenure as minister of social affairs, Hussein was able to address two broader reform issues: the need for affordable public housing in both urban and rural areas and the need for a comprehensive system of social security for all Egyptians.

Governmental concern with the poor housing facilities in Egypt began long before the Ministry of Social Affairs was founded in 1939. Projects to build model urban and rural homes had been tried and had failed, largely due to the high expense involved. Because the model homes were too expensive, the experiments were not reproducible on a large scale. Recognizing the failure of such projects, the government changed its policy from building model dwellings to offering assistance to those who asked. Speaking in 1953, Hussein recalled,

> Assistance then was given in the form of guidance, tax exemptions, as well as initial loans at easy interest terms. Whenever possible, the Government provided the land necessary for building. One major aspect of this change was that it resulted in the organization by the people themselves of cooperative housing societies. It is a matter of satisfaction for me to remember that ten months ago I was honored by being invited to lay the cornerstone of the first of these cooperative housing projects.[22]

In 1949, while serving as undersecretary of state for social affairs, Hussein prepared a lengthy report on the housing problem in Egypt, complete with his own ten-year plan for addressing the problem. In this report, Hussein began by calculating the number of new houses that would be required in Egypt between 1950 and 1960. He based his calculations on the annual increase in population, the building rates of new houses (taking into account the changes in these rates during World War II), and rural-urban migration rates. He calculated that Egypt would require 140,000 new houses (each house to be occupied by a family of five) in the following ten years, 100,000 of which should be located in rural areas, with the remainder in urban areas.[23]

He argued, in the best-case scenario, that the construction of each new house and its provision with services such as streets, drainage, lighting, and other public utilities, would cost LE 150. Hussein estimated that the Egyptian family should spend one-sixth of its income on rent. He calculated that rent of each house at LE 1, a rate that would provide an 8 percent annual revenue, would be enough to maintain the property and pay for its taxes and management. However, as he noted, each family would have to earn LE 6 per month in order to be able to afford this new housing. The crux of the problem lay in the fact that the average monthly income of industrial and commercial workers was LE 2.68, while the monthly income for agricultural workers was significantly less.[24]

To address this problem, Hussein formulated a comprehensive program of construction, land reclamation, financing, and changes in building materials. He recommended the following steps:

> 1. Government construction of offices so as to free up space in residential buildings [many offices were located in apartment buildings during this era, and there were few office buildings as such]; 2. Government construction of housing for government officials in areas where no suitable housing existed; 3. Government provision of financial assistance, either in the form of a subsidy or a loan, to individuals and organizations interested in constructing affordable housing; 4. The leasing or ceding of government-owned land suitable for housing construction to organizations wishing to use the land for the construction of popular housing; 5. The substitution of locally pro-

> duced building materials for imported ones, the intensification of the production of such local materials, government control of their distribution, standardization of the quality and dimensions of the materials, an exemption from customs and excise taxes for all building materials and machinery, a reduction of the freight charges for building materials and machinery, and an increase in mechanization of construction by contractors; 6. The taking of steps to increase the number of architects and technical workers in the building industry and the formation of a board of technical advisers for the construction of popular housing; and 7. Encouragement in every way possible of the total reconstruction of all villages.[25]

Hussein's recommendations highlight the depth of the housing problem in the country. They were also an early indication of the priority he would attach to improving public housing while minister.

Providing healthy, affordable housing for all Egyptians was a goal of Hussein's ministry. During his tenure as minister, a special department for housing was created within the Ministry of Social Affairs. Its duties were "to see that popular healthy homes are made available to the greatest number of people; to assist individuals, through cooperatives and credits, to build their homes, and to effect considerable rebates on custom duties imposed on building materials."[26] This department was concerned with both urban and rural housing problems and their solutions.

In urban areas, housing requirements were addressed by the ministry within the context of factory employee housing. The Law on the Individual Contract of Employment[27] imposed upon factory owners the duty of providing housing and meals for employees in areas not in urban centers. Many industrial and commercial firms in this category began building "workers' cities" in response to the law. In these cities, workers were housed according to age, gender, and marital status. In addition, the government began construction of 6,000 houses near Cairo on the western side of the Nile River; 1,100 of these houses were completed by 1950. The houses were designed to provide homes for skilled government employees with large families.[28]

The government also dealt with housing conditions in rural areas. Land reclamation projects in the area north of the Nile Delta had already begun by 1950. This new land was distributed in smallholdings to landless peasants, and the government built homes for the new landowners. It was hoped that the housing situation would be improved both by building new homes on the newly created small farms and by alleviating the overcrowding of already populated areas.[29] The rural social centers were also engaged in improving housing and living conditions in the villages where they were located. This combination of urban and rural housing programs was to serve as a first step in addressing the problem of affordable public housing in Egypt.

One of the most important projects to Hussein, after the Rural Social Centers project, was enactment of Egypt's first comprehensive social security measure, the Social Security Act of 1950, passed while Hussein was minister of social affairs.[30] Hussein personally worked to establish this program, and he was deservedly proud of the law. Although some efforts had been made to establish a social security program before Hussein introduced his scheme, they were minor and generally limited in scope.[31] The ability of Hussein to succeed in securing passage of a social security plan in prerevolutionary Egypt, a monarchy whose political and economic systems were dominated by a few wealthy landowners and elites, was historic.

There were two primary schools of thought on the issue of social security in Egypt. The first was articulated in 1949 in a plan that was devised in cooperation with the International Labor Organization (ILO) to provide coverage for industrial and commercial workers in urban areas.[32] Those who favored this plan believed that the focus in new legislation should be on providing for urban workers. The thinking of this group was that since low wages and seasonal work would make implementing a contributory pension system almost impossible in rural Egypt, the government should direct its attention to commercial and industrial workers. It was believed that social services in rural areas should continue to be provided by existing social centers, health units, and local educational initiatives.[33]

The second school of thought (the one to which Hussein belonged) believed that social security was a protection that should extend to all workers, not just those in commerce and industry. Since Egypt was predominantly an agricultural society, the ILO plan would address the needs of a mere third of the country's population.[34] Therefore, as Hussein noted in 1950, a system of noncontributory pensions was essential in Egypt because "a scheme based on contributions from workers and employers would not be applicable outside industry and commerce, partly due to the low incomes and instability of work among the majority of the rural population."[35] As a result, Hussein and others in the ministry set about drawing up a social security plan to cover all workers, including those in agriculture.

Before drafting the plan, a thorough survey of low-income urban and rural families was carried out with the assistance of the ILO and the Statistical Department of the Egyptian government. Using a system of sample towns and villages, officials worked with 191 social workers to complete the survey, which Hussein termed "one of the most extensive surveys ever carried out in a rural country."[36] This emphasis on surveying and planning reflects Hussein's adherence to modern methods of social research. In all the projects begun by Hussein, the emphasis placed on thorough study and planning of projects is evident and is one reason why his projects succeeded where previous ones had failed.

When drafted in 1950, Hussein's plan aimed at providing coverage for all people living in Egypt. He explained the differences between his plan and the previously proposed scheme in 1950, saying:

> The new scheme, therefore, covers all groups of the population irrespective of their location or occupation. A scheme based on contributions from workers and employers would not be applicable outside industry and commerce, partly for administrative reasons, and partly due to the low incomes and instability of work among the majority of the rural population. The new social security scheme, therefore, does not impose any direct contributions but is financed exclusively through government funds. The estimated cost of the scheme is 6 million pounds a year.

Hussein saw this program as "a new departure in the history of social service in Egypt" and as a "major component of the national social legislation program which is steadily being carried out in Egypt." Hussein also argued for the generalizability of his plan, saying, "The Egyptian Social Security Plan . . . is important from an international point of view as many of its aspects may set a pattern for countries with traditions and social conditions similar to those of Egypt."[37] It is clear from his remarks that Hussein believed that his ministry could and would, under his leadership, address the real economic and social problems of his country. It is also clear that on a larger scale, he viewed his programs as models to be replicated in other developing nations. That he saw the social security plan as a major part of his reform program is evident from the emphasis he gave it in his speeches and writings, and it was conflict with Wafdist politicians over this program that eventually led to his resignation as minister.

The immediate goal of the program was "to cover the needs of destitute families caused by the death of the breadwinner, disability, and old age."[38] Accordingly, these were the groups targeted for coverage in the initial phase of the program. Karl de Schweinitz, who worked with the program in 1951, described the Egyptian plan as "a system of noncontributory pensions" similar to public assistance programs in the United States.[39] Hussein summarized provisions of the law in a 1953 speech, saying:

> Under that legislation [the Social Security Act of 1950], and to start with, four major groups were entitled to pensions, namely, the aged, the disabled, the widowed, and the orphaned. Other groups, such as the unemployed and the sick were considered as entitled to assistance. . . . the objective of the law was not to simply distribute benefits and relief. More constructive measures were envisaged, as for instance, rehabilitation of the disabled and education for the orphaned, with a view to making them self-sufficient and useful citizens. Moreover, the law, stressing the principle of social solidarity, granted full coverage for the urban and rural population, on a non-contributory basis. The law also provided for assistance to foreigners residing in Egypt. This law was praised by international experts as a very sound and progressive social reform legislation.[40]

Although the annual benefits for pensioners were acknowledged to be below the cost of living, the plan was nonetheless a step in the right direction.[41]

The social security law comprised seven parts and is divided into a total of forty-seven articles. The first part discusses the general applicability of the law (it applies to both Egyptians and foreign residents), defines the technical terms used in the law, explains how to apply for a pension, states the role various government offices play in the application procedure, and sets up a process for registering complaints and submitting appeals. Part 2 covers in detail the qualifications for receipt of pensions, establishes the maximum number of beneficiaries in each family unit, and sets minimum and maximum age limits for pensions. The third part sets the rate of pensions, which differ according to whether the pensioner lives in an urban or a rural area, establishes family bonuses, and discusses conditions of amendment and suspension of pension funds. Part 4 is devoted to matters related to financing the pension scheme. It sets up a system of financial control and allows for cooperation with governmental and nongovernmental bodies. Part 5 commits the Ministry of Social Affairs to setting up centers to rehabilitate the disabled, and part 6 creates a social security department within the Ministry of Social Affairs to carry out the new law, enumerates the functions of the department, and establishes a Higher Council for Social Security within the same ministry where both governmental and nongovernmental bodies will be represented. Part 7 sets maximum penalties for the attempted and actual illegal receipt of pension funds.[42] One particularly striking feature of this law is that it establishes social security as the *right* of those who fit the categories of pensioners detailed in part 2.[43]

Efforts were made to explain the new scheme to the public and to employees of the new Social Security Agency. One of the most widely distributed brochures was one published in Arabic, *Social Security in Ten Questions.* This seven-page booklet attempted to answer the most frequently asked questions about social security in clear, simple language. It addressed issues such as who is entitled to a pension, what the monthly amount of each pension is, whether receipt of a pension affects one's right to other assistance, whether information given to the Social Security Agency would be kept private, and what duties a pensioner must fulfill.[44]

After the social security law was passed in 1950, Egypt sought technical assistance for implementing the law from the United States's Point Four program. Previous Point Four international aid programs had focused on technical cooperation in the sciences, public health, forestry, agriculture, and biochemistry; this project was the first Point Four social service project.[45] The result of this technical aid project was the publication of a booklet, *Social Security for Egypt,* written by Karl de Schweinitz, chief of the Point Four Social Security Mission to the Ministry of Social Affairs. The booklet was published in both English and Arabic in 1952 and was based on the findings of de Schweinitz and his team after they spent approximately three months in Egypt during 1951. It was designed as a training manual for social security program staffers and stressed ideas like professionalism, the importance of training for staff members, and establishing relationships of mutual trust between social workers and potential pensioners. The emphasis placed on the proper conduct of staff members in de Schweinitz's manual is reminiscent of the emphasis placed by Hussein on the proper conduct of staffers in the social centers.[46]

It is particularly important to recognize the relationship between the social security scheme and the other social reform programs begun by Hussein. Hussein had in mind a plan for the complete reconstruction of rural Egypt, one of the key elements of which was local participation in reform programs. The structure of the social security program likewise emphasized decentralization and local participation and was based on the success of the social centers model. Hussein himself explained the similarities in the programs after the passage of the social security law in 1950:

> The administration of the [social security] scheme is highly decentralised. The execution of the law will be in the hands of district and regional offices and only appeals will be referred to the Department of Social Security in Cairo. The law furthermore calls for the co-operation of local voluntary bodies to secure local participation in the administration as well as to develop the trend toward local self-government, which has helped so much in the success of the Rural Social Centres in Egypt.

He continued, saying that the social security scheme "is intended to be a part of a comprehensive programme for further social progress in Egypt. Other parallel schemes, promoting employment and social housing, are already prepared."[47]

In addition to the programs already discussed, Hussein succeeded in securing the passage of a number of new labor laws[48] during his brief tenure as minister of social affairs.[49] Some of the most notable of these were the 1950 law on compensation for vocational diseases, which "expands the principle of workmen's compensation to cases of vocational diseases, classifies dangerous trades and operations, medical supervision and lays down protective procedures"; the 1950 law on collective agreements, which regulated collective contracts between unions and employers; and the Workmen's Compensation Act of 1950, which updated and replaced the older, 1936 law.[50]

Writing in 1950, Hussein listed a number of programs he hoped would be part of the Fellah Department's future. His hoped-for programs included regulation of migrant agricultural labor, further reclamation of wastelands and their redistribution to small landowners, further development of rural industries and crafts, further extension of potable-water projects in the countryside, reform of village planning and buildings, extension of firefighting services to villages, further adoption of modern agricultural methods by farmers, programs to improve nutrition in rural areas, livestock insurance, reduction of taxes for small landowners, an expanded role for village councils, and an increase in funding for social reform programs.[51] It is significant that the rural social centers were expected to play a key role in virtually all of these new programs. Hussein clearly intended that all rural reform would revolve around the centers. Expanding the program of rural social centers was his top priority when he was appointed minister of social affairs in 1950. These plans for future reforms as well as the actual reforms Hussein succeeded in making are evidence of his continuing pursuit of social justice for all Egyptians.

Of course, not everyone appreciated Hussein's crusade. In addition to competition from other governmental bodies, opposition sometimes took a more personal form. Minister of Agriculture 'Abd al-Latif Mahmoud expressed his disapproval of Hussein's programs in 1951 by calling Hussein "the Red [communist] Minister" *(al-wazir al-ahmar).* Though Hussein was anything but a communist, he responded in typical fashion, humorously quipping, *"Mafish had ahmar minak"* ("No one is a bigger jackass than you," a play on the Arabic word *ahmar*).[52]

The International Dimension

As Hussein continued to expand his social reform projects in Egypt and as his programs continued to succeed in improving the standard of living of the Egyptian poor, he began to gain further domestic and international acclaim for his expertise. As minister, Hussein organized and chaired the United Nations-sponsored Second Social Welfare Seminar for Arab States of the Middle East, at which his programs were recognized by experts worldwide as models to be followed.

International interest in rural reform and, more broadly, in the economic

Hussein speaking to closing session of Social Welfare Seminar in Cairo Opera House. Courtesy of Aziza Hussein.

development of underdeveloped countries had been growing since the end of World War II. Although European and American organizations had been involved in international social service since the early part of the twentieth century (primarily providing educational and health services), it was not until the late 1940s that rural reform and economic development became subjects of international interest. Evidence of this growing interest in development comes from many sources. In 1949, U.S. president Harry Truman delivered his inaugural address in which he listed "a bold new program for making the benefits of our scientific advances and industrial progress available for the improvement and growth of underdeveloped areas" as the fourth point of American foreign policy.[53] The resulting American aid program, named the Point Four program, became an ambitious program of technical assistance to numerous foreign countries; Hussein's social security law was developed with the help of Point Four advisers. The American public reacted favorably to programs of technical aid to other countries for several reasons: "First, it seemed intuitive. . . . Second, agricultural extension was something Americans already understood. . . . Third, technical assistance seemed to fulfill Americans' altruistic impulses for a very small price. . . . Finally, technical assistance seemed the perfect antidote to resurgent Communism in the late 1940s."[54]

In addition, many American aid programs already had rural community development as their focus. The rural community development program in Etawah, India, that began in the 1940s was taken as a model for Point Four programs. This program, like Hussein's RSC program, had as its goals "to enlist the peasants in improving their environment, to instill a belief in democratic processes, and to begin to bridge the chasm between rich and poor that was characteristic of developing societies."[55] Community development was seen both as a way to improve living conditions in underdeveloped nations and also as a bulwark against communist influence in the developing world.

In 1950, the United Nations commissioned a report on how to develop the so-called underdeveloped areas. The resulting report, written by five economists, addressed both domestic and international solutions to poverty and underdevelopment. The authors advocated "the creation of an urban consumer class which would monetize poor economies, reward entrepreneurship and relieve overcrowding in the countryside"; argued that the World Bank would not be able to meet the aid requirements of all underdeveloped nations; and criticized the upper classes in underdeveloped nations who "hoarded" their profits. Agricultural extension services were recommended, as were thorough resource surveys and better economic planning. This UN report was a turning point in international aid thinking because "it presented an integrated plan for the development of poor countries based on the coordinated and integrated efforts of those countries themselves, wealthy countries, and international organizations."[56]

Both international organizations such as the United Nations and the governments of individual states began to take an interest in developing the underdeveloped countries for both altruistic reasons and geopolitical considerations. The expansion of aid programs from such sources testifies to this growing concern with living conditions in developing countries. In addition, the emerging cold war and the resulting politicization of foreign aid in this period often led to increased attention from donor countries. Within this framework of growing international interest in development programs, local experts like Hussein were often called upon to contribute their ideas to a broader audience.

By the time of his appointment as minister of social affairs, Hussein had already made a name for himself internationally as an expert on rural reform. Previously, Hussein had represented Egypt in the organizing conference for the United Nations Food and Agriculture Organization (FAO), held in the United States in 1943. He had represented his country in regional ILO and FAO conferences, held in Istanbul in 1947 and Cairo in 1946, respectively. He was elected to the Middle East section of the Permanent Committee of the ILO and to UNESCO as one of that body's nine experts on fundamental education, and he served as head of the Egyptian delegation to the ILO conference in Geneva in 1950. In addition to these activities, Hussein also received international recognition as a result of his role in organizing the Middle East's first conference devoted entirely to issues of rural social reform.[57]

The Second Social Welfare Seminar for Arab States of the Middle East, held in Cairo from November 22 to December 14, 1950, was sponsored by the UN. Under the patronage of King Faruq, and with Hussein serving as president and organizer, the conference was attended by representatives from all Arab states, as well as experts and observers from several European countries, Australia, New Zealand, the United States, and various international organizations.[58] The purpose of the seminar was to discuss and make recommendations regarding village welfare. In Hussein's words:

> The selection of this subject was based on the firm belief that we in the East cannot possibly achieve our aims for a decent social life and keep pace with other nations in their onward march towards real happiness unless we turn—first and foremost—to our less-developed countryside and provide for its inhabitants the essential amenities of a decent life: raising their general standard of living, improving their sanitary conditions, affording them opportunities for the adequate employment of their mental and physical resources and securing their spontaneous co-operation in achieving common interests and public utility schemes.[59]

Topics addressed by the conference committees included basic education in rural areas, village planning, agricultural and industrial development, training of rural project staff members, nutrition, social security for rural areas, rural social welfare, health and hygiene, maternal and child health, sanitation, and cooperative associations. Many of the committees' recommendations included aspects of rural social welfare that had already been instituted in Hussein's reform projects.[60] Perhaps even more significant, experts from several countries and organizations (including Iraq, Egypt, Australia, Syria, Lebanon, and UNRWA, the UN Relief and Works Agency) cited Hussein's Rural Social Centers project as a model for other nations' social reform projects, and, as already noted, the UN Economic and Social Council passed a resolution stating that Hussein's program of rural social centers should be used as a model for rural social reform on an international level.

Hussein also organized an exhibit of handicrafts from villages of participating nations. This exhibit was held in conjunction with the conference and had the dual purpose of calling attention to rural industry projects already begun in the participant countries and encouraging their further development. Crafts on exhibit included pottery, lace, cloth products, embroidery, carpets, woodwork, and palm tree, copper, brass, silver, and leather goods. This exhibition, like its 1946 counterpart, proved to be a resounding success and generated further enthusiasm for rural industries.[61]

Hussein published the proceedings of the conference in both Arabic and English as soon as possible after the conclusion of the conference, "so as to give these proceedings the widest possible publicity in the hope that they may arouse due interest in the countryside and its problems and create an enlightened public opinion that will lend its support to social reform and give willing and intelligent response to its programmes."[62] The success of this conference as well as the publication of its proceedings for an international audience did indeed help generate further interest in rural social reform, as well as interest in Hussein's own expertise on the topic.

Hussein's Resignation

Despite Hussein's successes and growing regional and international recognition, however, his tenure as minister of social affairs was short lived. Political differences with the Wafd Party led to Hussein's resignation as minister of social affairs in 1951. The initial reforms of the Wafd soon tapered off, and the hopes so many had pinned on the party to restore political stability and improve living conditions were largely disappointed. "Soon after the government's inauguration . . . it became apparent that the presence of reformers and technocrats in the cabinet would prove to be largely a facade. Party elders continued to practice politics as usual. Patronage was rampant, and one scandal followed another. The Wafd had no monopoly on corruption, but public patience grew thin. Too many works projects seemed to benefit government officials, their business associates, and relatives."[63]

The promise of the Wafd to put an end to nepotism and to base appointments to government service solely on merit was another promise the party failed to keep. The Wafd, in Gordon's words, "did what all ruling parties do; it initiated a full-scale purge of civil servants." The government also "adopted a conciliatory stand towards the Palace. Banished to the political wilderness for five years, the Wafd now resolved to avoid any confrontation with the King that would give him any excuse to dismiss the government. Almost immediately the public perceived the Wafd's primary goal to be the retention of power at all costs. . . . The Wafd's policy of political servility was deliberate and cynical, and, coming at a time when the behavior of Faruq and his coterie threatened to undermine the legitimacy of the monarchy as an institution, it undercut the Wafd's claim to popular support."[64] Gordon adds an interesting anecdote on the Wafd's policy of appeasing the Palace: the refusal of three of the "professors" (Hussein, 'Abd al-Mut'al, and Zaki) to kiss the king's hand during the official inauguration ceremonies.

The failure of the Wafd to commit fully to a social reform agenda was especially frustrating for Hussein, who had spent his career working for the goals to which the Wafd merely paid lip service. Yet Hussein was not the only one annoyed at the direction the Wafd was taking. The lack of commitment of the party leadership to substantive reform was increasingly frustrating to all the professors. Three of the four left the government before the end of 1951: "Zaki 'Abd al-Mut'al and Ahmad Husayn collided head-on with party patronage. 'Abd al-Mut'al was fired outright in November 1950; Ahmad Husayn resigned nine months later. Hamid Zaki, who found himself increasingly isolated within the cabinet and shunted from one ministry to another, broke with the government in December 1951. When the reformers left the cabinet, old-line party loyalists filled their shoes, and business resumed as usual."[65]

Gordon claims that the historians of this period have largely written from a Wafdist point of view by arguing that the four reformers were a renegade faction within the Wafd—more part of the problem than a solution. Yet this Wafd-centered view is a distorted one. These men (Hussein in particular) were never traditional party loyalists and never professed to be such. Instead, they were just what they purported to be: reformers and technocrats, not politicians. As Gordon succinctly put it:

> To them, the Wafd was simply . . . political party. Like other factions, they hoped to influence government policy and strove for a greater say in internal party affairs. They were not radicals, but proponents of an activist government role in promoting social welfare and in raising the standard of living in rural areas and among the growing industrial working class. They were technocrats and academics, and they scorned the inefficiency of the government bureaucracy. Their disregard for party patronage, in particular, alienated old-line Wafdists, both elders and second generation. To the veterans, the Wafd represented a sacred ideal: to speak of it as a mere political party smacked of insolence; to interfere with party patronage smacked of treason.[66]

Hussein's resignation was in keeping with his apolitical character. Perhaps more than any of the other three, he was committed to a program of action rather than playing political games. Gordon argues that Hussein's resignation was the most significant, saying that "Husayn stood much farther from the center of political battles for supremacy within the Wafd. Yet, because of his reputation as an achiever, his failure produced the most resounding repercussions."[67]

The immediate catalyst for Hussein's resignation from his post as minister of social affairs was Wafdist meddling in his ministry.[68] Soon after the social security plan (a plan to which Hussein was personally committed and very concerned that it be carried out properly) was approved by parliament and signed into law by the king, Hussein went abroad, traveling to Geneva for a meeting of the ILO and then to West Germany for a review of German public housing projects. Before leaving on this journey, Hussein made a series of appointments to the administration of the new program, including a new undersecretary of the ministry who was to be in charge of the program. In addition, the cabinet met to discuss who would be in charge of the Ministry of Social Affairs in Hussein's absence. Hussein agreed with the other members of the cabinet that the then minister of justice, Muhammad al-Wakil, would serve as acting minister of social affairs.[69]

Hussein and Hassan Dawood and the ministerial officials who accompanied them left for Europe thinking all would be well in the ministry during their absence and the new social security program would be in good hands. Unfortunately, things did not go as planned. During the return journey, Dawood's assistant telephoned Dawood in Rome to inform him that after Hussein and his colleagues left Egypt, the cabinet reneged on its decision to appoint al-Wakil as acting minister. Instead, 'Abd al-Latif Mahmoud, then minister of agriculture, was appointed by Nahas as acting minister of social affairs. Mahmoud promptly reversed Hussein's appointments to the social security administration and replaced the newly appointed undersecretary of the Ministry of Social Affairs who was to be in charge of the new social security law. Dawood attributes this to the government's desire to have party loyalists in key positions, particularly in the new social security administration.[70]

Hussein became extremely upset when he heard the news. Since the group was traveling by sea, their ship had to go from Rome to Beirut and thence to Alexandria, where the Egyptian cabinet conducted affairs of government during the summer months. Upon arriving in Beirut, however, their return was delayed for several days by widespread strikes following the recent assassination of the Lebanese prime minister. During the wait, Hussein decided to resign from his post. Hussein discussed the matter at length with his colleagues, particularly with Dawood, who recalled that "all the day and all the night, he did not let us sleep at all. He was thinking whether it was good to resign or not to resign." Dawood advised against resignation, telling Hussein that this problem could be solved and that Hussein would be free to reverse the appointments and transfers made in his absence.[71]

However, by the time the ship reached Alexandria, Hussein had rejected Dawood's advice and informed him that in spite of his recommendation to continue as minister, Hussein would resign. When Dawood asked why he made this decision, Hussein replied, "Because I cannot work. I am trying to help the poor people here and I am begging Cabinet Ministers to approve projects, as if we are the people who are going to benefit from such things. We are working and killing ourselves because of the people, the poor, [and these

Ministers are preventing us from helping them]."[72] His wife remembers that Hussein "was mad because he had such a passion for what he was doing and really these [other ministers] were just being jealous of what he was doing and wanted to destroy it and interfere in his work."[73] Aziza Hussein argued that other government officials envied the success of Hussein's programs and his growing international stature. She recalled that "wherever he succeeded, there was competition."[74] Hussein deputed Dawood to carry the resignation to Nahas's staff, and Dawood did so.

When Nahas read Hussein's letter of resignation, he personally went to persuade Hussein not to resign and informed Hussein that his resignation was not accepted.[75] An article in the independent newspaper *Ruz al-Yusuf* reported the conversation between Hussein and Nahas in some detail and stressed Nahas's objections to Hussein's appointments in the Ministry of Social Affairs. According to the reportage, Nahas expressed his displeasure at the lack of appointments of Wafd loyalists to the new social security department, telling Hussein that he was taking important opportunities for advancement away from the Wafdists. Nahas also criticized Hussein's guidelines for choosing new appointees for the program, saying that a Wafdist would never meet his qualifications for appointment. Hussein replied that he chose the appropriate people for the appropriate jobs and that party loyalty was not a factor in these decisions. After this remark, Nahas gave up trying to convince Hussein to remain in the ministry.[76]

Aziza Hussein recalled that the Wafdist government did not want Hussein to resign, in part because of his family's ties to the party; after all, his father was one of the founders of the Wafd Party, and other members of his family were prominent Wafdists.[77] After the meeting between Nahas and Hussein, numerous other prominent politicians also met with Hussein to try to influence his decision. Osman Muharram, minister of public works and Hussein's uncle, spoke to Hussein, as did Mahmoud Suleiman Ghanam, minister of communications, and Mahmoud Kamal Abu al-Nasr, the deputy minister of social affairs.[78] None of these attempts at mediation succeeded. This was in keeping with Hussein's character. A stubborn man, never one to keep silent about issues he believed were important, and not one to tolerate working under someone else's rules, Hussein rejected compromise in matters of principle, and so he viewed this issue.[79]

Hussein believed that Nahas was personally responsible for nullifying the appointments made by Hussein prior to his trip to Europe, and he also believed that Nahas himself made the decision to replace al-Wakil with Mahmoud.[80] Whether or not Nahas was directly responsible for the shenanigans in Hussein's ministry during his absence is not clear from the documentary evidence. However, as Gordon noted, "If Nahas did not meddle directly in the social affairs ministry while Husayn was abroad, he nonetheless appointed a colleague hostile to Husayn as acting minister and sanctioned the interim minister's meddling."[81] Because of Hussein's belief that Nahas was responsible for the personnel changes and despite the intercession of these prominent figures, Hussein refused to reconsider his position and rebuffed all attempts at mediation, including Nahas's offer to reverse the changes made in his ministry.[82] Hussein told Dawood, "No, I am fed up. This is the end of it. I cannot struggle more than that."[83] As Aziza Hussein recalled, "He resigned because he couldn't complete his mission and nobody understood him."[84]

Another possible reason for Hussein's resignation was mentioned prominently in an article in the newspaper *al-Asas.* This article claimed that the real reasons for Hussein's decision lay not in the shuffling of ministerial personnel during Hussein's absence but rather in the desire of the Wafd Party to manipulate the Rural Social Centers project. The article argued that a prominent Wafdist had proposed that funds allocated for RSCs be turned over to the Wafd Party, which would then use the money to pay for all social services for the inhabitants of the villages and also use the centers to spread party propaganda. The article tied the meddling with ministerial appointments to this alleged plot, saying that after Hussein refused to use the RSCs for any party activities, Mahmoud was put in charge of the ministry, and personnel transfers were made to get the appropriate party loyalists into positions where they could influence this new funding proposal.[85]

In any event, Hussein never regretted his decision to resign.[86] He became known as the first man in Egypt to resign from the government on a matter of principle.[87] Press reports about the resignation were either neutral or tended to side with Hussein. An editorial written by Bint al-Shati about the resignation was published in *al-Ahram* in July 1951. The editorial praised Hussein as one of the few decent officials and called him a good son of Egypt and a noble person. The author argued that, unlike his colleagues in the cabinet, Hussein cared not for high position but rather for honor and right, and she lamented the government's loss of one of the few remaining men of morals.[88]

A French-language cartoon in the Egyptian newspaper *Akher Lahza* depicted Hussein surrounded by sweating government ministers all wearing heavy coats. Hussein is shown removing his coat while the ministers ask him, "Are you not afraid that you will die of cold outside?" to which Hussein responds, "I would rather die than suffocate in the atmosphere of the government."[89] An article in the same newspaper on August 1, 1951, reviewed the praise of international experts for Hussein's methods of selecting personnel for the new social security administration and concluded that, following Hussein's departure and the personnel changes made during his absence, there was not a single staffer in the new department with any expertise whatsoever in the field of social insurance.[90]

Articles in the socialist publication *al-Ishtiraki* expressed the same views. An article published in July began by wondering why Hussein had been part of the Wafdist government in the first place since he clearly lacked the necessary qualifications for the post, which the author listed as a willingness to embezzle state funds, punish effective and honorable employees, reward thieves and corrupt men with promotions and raises, embrace corruption, and abide by the law of patronage. Unfortunately, continued the article, Hussein met none of these qualifications and, in his innocence, did not understand that the government ministers ought to serve the prominent and the wealthy. Instead, Hussein thought that the purpose of the ministry was to work for the people and for their interests. So, concluded the author, Hussein insisted on dignity and honesty like a discordant note that causes a musical piece to lose its harmony.[91]

The English-language *Egyptian Gazette* also sided with Hussein, calling his resignation a "severe loss" and saying that "Hussein Pasha has acquired a reputation stretching well beyond the borders of Egypt for single-minded devotion to the welfare of the people and for determination and efficiency in carrying out his schemes of social reform. Without him, the Cabinet will be a weaker team and its prestige will be diminished." The article went on to note that "public sympathy has undoubtedly lain with Hussein Pasha" and Hussein did the right thing to resign, since "considerations of self-respect and responsibility allowed of no alternative."[92]

British and American reactions to the resignation were also part of Egyptian news stories. *Al-Ahram* carried articles detailing British expressions of regret that the Egyptian government had lost such a competent and successful minister and British hopes that Hussein's accomplishments would not be lost.[93] The comments of American officials, particularly Point Four experts such as Karl de Schweinitz, who had worked closely with Hussein on the social security program, were also reproduced. American officials expressed their appreciation for Hussein's pioneering works, their sorrow at his resignation, and their hopes that those trained by him would continue to carry out his projects.[94] The royal decree accepting Hussein's resignation was signed by Faruq on August 1, 1951.

Hussein's resignation was a clear sign of the failure of the Wafdist government to fulfill its campaign promises. After Hussein's resignation, little progress was made on his projects because of "inefficient administration and a lack of morale among the staff he had groomed."[95] Lack of morale was not unique to Hussein's staff, however. The Wafd's reversal of its promises and the resignation of Hussein and the other professors engendered widespread public frustration with the party as well. Gordon argues that even more significantly:

> The Wafd's failure to meet the challenge it faced shattered public confidence in its ability to lead the nation and further undermined the legitimacy of the liberal order. In July 1951, a disgruntled Ihsan 'Abd al-Quddus, editor-in-chief of the influential independent *Ruz al-Yusuf*, proclaimed Egypt a "country of failure." "We in Egypt believe in failure and worship those who fail," he wrote, pointing specifically to Nahas and his chief ministers. "Woe to the man of talent who looks at matters with a serious eye and works with determination to succeed. . . . Woe to him, for the doors are shut in front and in back of him, oppressive power pursues him wherever he settles and false charges follow him every day."[96]

Furthering Nongovernmental Reforms

Hussein's resignation from the Ministry of Social Affairs in 1951 did not mark the end of his interest in and commitment to social reform. Following his resignation he began to address social reform issues within a nongovernmental framework. Hussein continued to push for projects he thought would benefit the nation. One of the projects started by Hussein to advance his ideas of social welfare and to generate further support for the programs of the Fellah Department was the Fellah Association, or Jam'iyat al-Fellah. In 1951, after his resignation from the Ministry of Social Affairs, Hussein founded this organization to serve as a forum for discussion of various issues related to rural social welfare and broader social reform. Its members included many prominent citizens and politicians of the era, including Hassan Dawood (Hussein's lifelong colleague and friend in the Ministry of Social Affairs, later Egyptian ambassador to Romania), Fu'ad Galal (later minister of social affairs under 'Abd al-Nasir), Sayed Marei (later minister of agriculture and agrarian reform), and Hosni Sayeed (head of the Department of Agricultural Economics in the Faculty of Agriculture of Cairo University).[97]

Headquartered at 17 Abu al-Saba'a (Tala'at Harb) Street in downtown Cairo, the association held weekly meetings to discuss methods of improving the standard of living in the countryside and ways to mobilize the fellahin to help themselves. The constitution of the association defined the group as a social reform organization whose basic goals were the "realization of the power of the nation," furthering social, economic, health, cultural, and labor reform and establishing social justice. The constitution further defined the goals of the group as including the spread of basic education in the countryside and the cities in order to increase professional competence, to improve levels of health, and to help form good, enlightened citizens who are aware of their rights and duties. However, the association was never concerned with devising and implementing its own projects of social reform. Instead, it limited its activities to discussions, debates, and cooperation with existing reform projects. The constitution stated that each member's first priority should be to make himself a practical model by helping others, influencing public opinion in favor of complete social reform, and educating the public about the importance of cooperation, by means of personal connections, lectures, study groups, conferences, and publications.[98] In this sense, it was very similar to the Pioneers.

The document also stated that the association should cooperate with governmental and civil groups who shared similar goals, and it stressed the importance of cooperating with practical experiments in social reform in order to determine the most effective means of promoting total integrated reform, or reform encompassing all aspects of life—economic, health, cultural, social, spiritual, and moral. The importance of molding children into good citizens was also emphasized. Declaring that "the youth are the support of the future," the association encouraged support of projects that were geared toward children, including camps, clubs, trips, lectures, discussion groups, and athletic activities, all of which it believed would help create a "physically, mentally, and spiritually sound generation" of enlightened young citizens.[99]

The association, like Hussein himself, was careful to state its opposition to party politics and its complete unwillingness to become involved in the struggles of political parties or religious sects. Given the events surrounding Hussein's resignation, the inclusion of such language is not surprising. It argued that serving the nation as a whole by working to increase national pride, national rights, and national security was the most important duty of every proper citizen, and political and religious differences had to be put aside in favor of concentrating on social reform efforts. Composed of a president, a treasurer, a secretariat, and a general assembly, the association sold subscriptions of membership in order to raise funds to support projects it deemed worthy. One could join the group as a working member by paying a joining fee of 100 milliemes and an annual subscription of 100 milliemes or as an associate member by paying only 25 milliemes as an annual subscription. The association also raised funds through gifts and *waqfs*, income from its activities, and voluntary contributions from its members and others. The ultimate goal of the association was to have branches throughout the kingdom. It encouraged the formation of independent women's branches to help with reform projects related to women's activities. It also envisioned a group of advisers and friends of the association who would not be members but who would support materially and morally the goals of the association and from whose expertise and consultation the association would benefit.[100]

The association continued into the beginning of the 'Abd al-Nasir era, and one of its postrevolutionary sessions included a discussion led by Dawood and Marei on the proposed land reform law of the revolutionary government. Other social reform laws introduced by the new regime, including the new labor law, were also discussed and analyzed by the association.[101] Membership in the association was one of the key links between pre-and postrevolutionary reform, as many of those who worked on 'Abd al-Nasir's projects either were associated with or benefited from this group of intellectuals. Although 'Abd al-Nasir's overall program of reform was a disappointment to Hussein and his coterie, the importance of the association specifically and, more broadly, of Hussein's other reformist groups, programs, and ideas as a sort of "reform bridge" between the prerevolutionary and revolutionary eras, should be noted.

Despite the number of prominent figures associated with this organization, the association was short lived. After the revolution, as the group's "founding fathers," Hussein and Dawood included, were sent to other countries and as the group's enthusiasm for the revolution began to wane, the association was dissolved. Although Dawood does not recall the immediate reason for dissolution, he does attribute it in part to the new government's utter lack of interest in informal policy advisory groups such as the association.[102]

Achieving Further International Recognition

Although Hussein's resignation meant an end to his career in governmental reform projects in Egypt, it did not mean an end to his career in social reform, and he continued to receive international recognition for his efforts. In 1951, while still minister of social affairs, Hussein had been asked by UN secretary-

Hussein in Puerto Rico, with unidentified Puerto Rican official.
Courtesy of Aziza Hussein.

general Trygve Lie to accept the post of assistant secretary-general of that organization. Hussein declined the offer, preferring to stay and complete his reform projects in Egypt. In 1952, following his resignation, Hussein was asked, along with Carl C. Taylor of the U.S. Department of Agriculture, to head a group of UN experts on a ten-month mission to Mexico and the nations of the Caribbean, and this he agreed to do. The purpose of the mission was to examine Mexican and Caribbean schemes of community development and rural welfare and to provide technical assistance to area nations. Although the political climate in Egypt was not conducive to further reform efforts, Hussein believed that he could continue to advocate reform for Egypt and for other primarily rural countries in this new, international forum. Under the auspices of the Technical Assistance Administration, and as a result of Resolution 390D (XIII) of the Economic and Social Council (adopted August 9, 1951), the group of experts was charged with studying the "use of Community Welfare Centers as effective instruments to provide economic and social progress throughout the world."[103] The mission visited Mexico, Haiti, Jamaica, Trinidad, and Puerto Rico.

According to its literature, the project was based on the assumption that "it is possible and practicable to transfer knowledge and techniques from one area to another for the purpose of advancing the economic and social development of the people of the world." Despite this statement, however, the mission did recognize that methods of reform and community development that are successful in one area "frequently require drastic modification before they can be adapted to the needs of the people of [other countries]." It urged its members to be careful to "distinguish between those elements [of reform projects] that have universal application and those that were appropriate only in [your own] environment."[104] The parallels between the 1951 UN mission and Hussein's own role in the transfer of technical knowledge and application of ideas from Germany to Egypt are obvious.

In addition to the assumption that knowledge is transferable, the mission was founded on two other beliefs: first, that the primary goal of community organization "should be to make the population of a fairly limited area conscious of the improvements possible in its standard of living, and to help it take advantage of the means of improving social conditions by improving self-organization," and second, that "governments have an important part to play [in community organization and development] by creating pre-conditions and affording assistance in conformity with community needs."[105] Thus, the mission was conceived as a means of using experts from other countries to recommend ways in which their knowledge could be applied to further community organization and development and to bolster aided self-help programs.

The mission was charged with observing community development projects and means of community organization, determining the goals and scope of the various projects they observed, determining the methods used to achieve these goals, and determining what successes and what failures resulted from these methods. After these determinations were made, the mission staff were to "formulate recommendations with regard to possible future international action to be taken in the field of community organization and development," to prepare a report for submission to the secretary-general of the United Nations, "to advise governments concerned on problems related to community organization and development, on their request," and to inform them of the resources available to them through the United Nations.[106] The mission staff were instructed specifically not to include "national or agency programs" in their study (although community projects receiving national or agency aid were included), and to include only multipurpose projects in their report.[107]

The mission spent a total of ten months in the five nations. During this time, the group traveled to thirty communities and evaluated their organization and development projects. Of the thirty communities studied by the mission, "twenty-nine were definitely rural or open-country communities,"[108] although there were significant differences among the rural areas studied. It is interesting that although the UN instruction manual uses only the terms "community welfare centers" and "community development," the report written jointly by Hussein and Taylor uses the terms "rural welfare center" and "community welfare center" interchangeably; "rural welfare center" was one of the names given to the rural social centers in Egypt.

The mission began with meetings between Hussein and his colleagues and the directors of national programs to explain the purpose of the UN mission and to select jointly the areas that would be included in the mission's study. The second phase of the mission consisted of traveling to selected communities and meeting with "members of local project staffs, local functionaries, non-paid local leaders, and members of the community." Following these two series of meetings, the mission staff recorded their observations and conclusions about the projects in question, and "thorough discussions [about the mission's conclusions] were held with the staff of each agency whose work had been observed in one or more communities." The final stage of the mission included finding local experts to participate in and validate the results of the UN mission. The mission report stated that "one or more persons were sought out in each country who were either outstanding intellectuals or national figures, not at the present attached to any of the programmes or projects studied, the objectives of the mission were explained to them and they were challenged to assist in the final analysis and validation of observations."[109]

Several of the projects studied by the mission included features similar to the Egyptian rural social centers. In Trinidad, the group studied an agency called the Extension Education Service (EES), whose stated purpose was "to promote social change through adult education of an informal type, to foster community self-help and mutual aid and to assist voluntary agencies to carry out programmes of community development." The mission report explained the activities of the EES as follows: "Most of the attention of the staff, the majority of whom are normal school graduates, is devoted to helping rural communities organize voluntary associations and to advising such groups as to the activities they can undertake, such as handicraft work, health campaigns, recreational activities and cooperative savings. A number of community councils and associations have also been organized."[110] The existing program in Trinidad thus used popular councils and educated leaders and attempted to organize many of the same programs the RSCs organized in Egypt.

In Haiti, the much-touted, UNESCO-led Marbial Valley project also shared some features of the Egyptian RSCs. Using this project as evidence that rural populations can be organized to help themselves, the report explained the Marbial Valley project as follows:

> The aim of the project is to use fundamental education as a means of bettering existing cultivation methods, furthering soil conservation, promoting the development of small industries and improving the health conditions in the overpopulated and mountainous Marbial Valley area devastated by soil

> erosion. The project headquarters, with a school, clinic, and cooperative, is located at Poste Pierre Louis. There is also a training centre for community leaders at Lafond near Jacmel as well as nineteen basic education centers scattered throughout the isolated area.[111]

This project resembled the RSCs even more closely than the project in Trinidad in that it included agricultural improvements, a school, and a clinic, as well as proper training for project leaders.

The Mexican Bureau of Cultural Missions, established in 1923, was another similar program. The program consisted of forty mission teams, each composed of eight to ten staff members, "including a doctor, a nurse, and agronomist, handicrafts teacher and recreation instructor, and [each mission team] serves an area which includes a number of different communities." The mission teams each spent one to three years in a given area. Their work began with a thorough survey of the village. After that, "an overall community organization is formed . . . and several sub-committees are also set up to deal with particular phases of the programme. These committees work with the mission while it is in the area with the hope that they will continue to function after the mission leaves." Although these missions were temporary in nature, and although the report criticized them as "by no means adequately financed or staffed,"[112] they did include a wide variety of specialists with a correspondingly wide range of duties. In this they were similar in scope to the Egyptian RSCs.

The Welfare Commission, a quasi-governmental organization in Jamaica, was also similar to the RSC project. The Jamaican project's description is strikingly similar to that of the RSCs, indicating again the potential applicability of such aided self-help programs on an international scale:

> The general aim of [the Welfare Commission] is to assist in the improvement of social and economic conditions in the island, particularly by stimulating among the villagers and peasants a desire for self-improvement and guiding them in their efforts. The senior field staff are trained in community organization and development techniques through special training courses. These District Welfare Officers are assisted by village instructors and handicraft and cooperative specialists. . . . Welfare officers are only sent to communities when the Commission is invited to do so, and homes, shops,

> schools, and meetings of different groups are visited until a simple social survey of the community has been completed. If sufficient interest is exhibited, a meeting is called to discuss general community needs and welfare and the organization of a Village Committee is encouraged to plan and promote a programme of action. No fixed pattern of community organization is conceived, but the people are stimulated to help themselves and are advised as to how to take advantage of the services available to them through the government or other agencies.[113]

The community survey, the invitation to the commission to send representatives to the village, the lack of a fixed agenda, and the encouragement of popular participation and agenda setting are all features the Jamaican program and the Egyptian program shared.

Despite a number of programs somewhat similar to the successful Egyptian project, Hussein and Taylor pointed out in their report that the agencies were not all successful nor did they all properly employ "the community approach." One of the mission's criticisms of such programs was that they often worked with a group that did not feel itself to be a community—a group that was a community only in terms of geographical proximity or similar occupation. The report also criticized some technical agencies for "using sub-groups, quite often groups which they themselves had promoted, and by this practice were segmenting communities rather than developing programmes in which all local residents were to some extent participating."[114]

In addition, the mission criticized what its members saw as a trend in some of the countries visited merely to build more infrastructure rather than to foster long-term, serious efforts aimed at developing a real sense of community. The report stated, "The mission . . . saw a number of situations in which special groups had attempted to develop community cohesion and pride by doing spectacular things, erecting a community center building or staging campaigns of one kind or another. In most of these cases, little or no progressive community development resulted, and in some instances, disappointment and frustration followed."[115] This criticism of the building projects in the Caribbean is remarkably similar to subsequent criticisms of 'Abd al-Nasir's Combined Units project in Egypt (see chapter 5).

The mission also criticized a lack of integration in several of the programs studied. The members of the mission saw the integration of social services as the most successful approach, and they were very critical of programs that were limited to economic services and did not have corresponding programs of social services. The report noted that in many areas, lack of integration negated the positive effects of the services provided. For example, it cited one agriculturally productive area that was unable to get its products to market for lack of an adequate road system, another area where schools existed but no qualified teachers were available, another where there was a surplus of agricultural products and adequate transport but "market outlets for farm products [had] not yet been developed," and another where there were schoolteachers available but not enough schoolhouses for more than a fraction of the population.[116] The mission attributed this failure to integrate services to "the fact that each programme is directed by a highly specialized technical agency . . . [In many cases], one agency did not know what other agencies were doing; each was insulated because of [its] own specialization or because of bureaucratic administrative practices."[117] This criticism of segmented service provision was also one that was to be heard in Egypt in later years with the replacement of the RSCs with the combined units.

Despite the criticisms, however, the mission did note several successful community development programs in the area. Concluding that "the programmes operating most effectively to accomplish [their] objectives were those which start by analyzing felt needs and which conclude with definite projects and programmes," the mission praised Puerto Rico's community education program, Mexico's cultural missions project, and the Jamaican Welfare Commission as prime examples of the correct approach to community development. In the mission's view, these three programs included "first, the involvement of residents of local communities in discussion of their needs; second, a selection of an activity to be undertaken which will yield benefits to the whole community; and, third, the planning and carrying out of a programme of activity which will meet specifically felt needs and bring early and obvious results."[118] The mission observed that all successful programs in the region had followed this pattern and concluded that as a result of the success of the communities in solving one local problem, "they developed a degree of group responsibility, pride and zest which led them to attack other community problems."[119]

Hussein and Taylor expanded on this theme and outlined five principles of community development that they believed were "valid and effective in all cases":

> 1. Maximum self-help effort must be developed, which requires the participation of a specialist in community organization. 2. This specialist must be trained and must know where the community can seek and find necessary technical and material assistance. 3. The specialist must reside in the community "for a substantial period of time." 4. Training must be initiated for locally-recruited technical assistants to assist in service provision. 5. There should always be at least one full-time, salaried specialist in the community "regardless of the adequacy that welfare centers and their services may achieve."[120]

The mission's report also stressed the importance of personnel properly trained in fostering community organization and initiating development projects. It praised a project in one country that it called "an outstanding example of the use of community development techniques and processes." In this program, the potential leaders were selected "on the basis of each having done some outstanding piece of community work and each having satisfied the selectors that he [could] work well with other people." After selection, the potential leaders enrolled in three months' intensive training, and those who completed the course successfully returned to their native area where their job was to

> guide the development of an average of 25 communities, and remain indefinitely in this area, working with its communities. . . . Their objectives are to help each local community to diagnose basic needs and problems, organize to solve community problems by maximum use of the efforts and talents of local residents, and learn when, how and where to request technical and material assistance from technical agencies, local and national governments which can render such assistance.[121]

The report expressed support for the practice of using personnel of rural backgrounds in project fieldwork, remarking that "such persons will have a great advantage over others, because they not only know the conditions of rural life, but above all they know the habits, attitudes and viewpoints of rural families." However, it cautioned against sending people to their native areas where they might be unduly influenced by previous friendships or rendered ineffective due to previous animosities or subordinate relationships with local leaders.[122]

The report argued that "an actively organized community can do much for its own economic and social improvement. It can do a great deal more if it has the help of the right technical agencies at the right time. A community organization and development specialist situated in a local community can do a great deal to assist in the development of this much-needed co-operation."[123] Hussein and Taylor stressed the necessity of locating such people to help organize and foster awareness among rural populations in all nations, concluding,

> It was the mission's repeated observation that the people living in isolated rural communities either were not aware of some of their basic needs, or if aware of them often lived in the belief that fate had destined them to continue to live with unsatisfied needs. In all cases where local communities were seen vigorously attacking their local problems in an organized way, some agent or agency from outside the community had stimulated the people to the new undertaking. In practically all cases, it was a person skilled in group organization who had provided the stimulation.[124]

Although some programs in some countries did provide specialized training to their staff, the mission called for further training of specialists in community development and for more training facilities for rural social workers. They observed that "there are many facilities in the world for the study of social welfare skills and techniques necessary for work with individual families or with institutions caring for individuals with special needs," but the mission also noted that "there are no equally good facilities for training persons to work with groups or communities, especially with rural communities. Rural communities differ from country to country but there are certain universal processes and techniques of which persons working with communities should be aware and in the application of which they should be trained. The more effective agencies whose programmes of training were observed provide this type of training."[125]

The report also decried governmental focus on providing services to urban populations and urged that more attention be paid on a national and international level to raising the standard of living of rural populations. The mission staff urged that these rural communities be given appropriate aid in developing programs to improve their living conditions, noting:

> In the economically under-developed countries of the world, the vast majority of the population is found in rural communities. As a rule, however, the people living in the towns, especially the large towns, of these countries are accorded better treatment by their governments than are the rural inhabitants. There are usually many more hospitals and schools, better facilities for communication, better water systems, etc. than are found in the rural areas. Thus the rural communities have many more unserved needs than the urban communities. Their own economic resources are practically always inadequate and the education of their residents less advanced. Furthermore, it is the general rule that the members of the rural population who do gain some degree of advanced education leave their rural communities for the greater advantages which prevail in towns and cities. Therefore, few, if any, rural communities in the economically under-developed areas of the world can be expected to improve themselves by their own efforts. They must have technical assistance, and frequently material assistance, from their governments.[126]

The mission staff was also quick to point out that national governments should not regard contributions to improving the standard of living in rural areas as charitable endeavors or minor attempts to improve conditions for only one sector of the population. Hussein and Taylor were quite emphatic that the improvement of rural areas needed to be a national priority, in large part because an improved standard of living for the rural population benefits the nation as a whole:

> The creativeness, power and enthusiasm of organized community effort, if skillfully guided, can be mobilized and harnessed not only for the economic and social improvement of any local community, but for the development of the whole economy of any country. The power and creativeness of the common people is often, if not always, the greatest undeveloped resource of economically under-developed areas. . . . When these programmes yield immediate and obvious results in better farm production, better home life,

> better education and better health in the local communities, their beneficial effects are felt not only at the community but on the national level as well.[127]

The report concluded on much the same note, with a reaffirmation of the value of aided self-help programs in all underdeveloped nations—a statement that seems to embody many of Hussein's lifelong beliefs concerning social welfare:

> It should once again be stressed that it is not believed that community self-help can of itself accomplish all that is needed to improve the level of living of local communities in the economically under-developed areas of the world. Community effort must be helped by both technical and material assistance. But if aided, it can provide greater power and enthusiasm for the solution of [the] problems of the masses of the people than can be mobilized from any other source. Only if this power and enthusiasm are harnessed and developed for the solution of the problems of the people who live in local communities will the human resources of under-developed areas be mobilized for the solution of economic and social problems of the nations concerned.[128]

This 1952 UN mission was the final official social reform effort in which Hussein took part. As the above excerpts suggest, Hussein believed his ideas of rural social reform were essentially universally applicable. After completing this mission, however, Hussein never again had the opportunity to present his views on the subject to such a wide audience.

Prelude to Revolution

While Hussein continued furthering his reformist agenda in a new environment, events in Egypt were quickly moving toward their denouement. Disgust at the Wafd's lack of action on any reform agenda ran deep. As in the past, the British military presence in Egypt again became the focus of much frustration as well. Britain had agreed to the evacuation of its troops from Egyptian soil in 1946. By 1951, however, British officials had reconsidered their position in light of the cold war and had declined to withdraw their troops from the Suez military base. In October of that year, clashes between Egyptian citizens and British forces grew increasingly severe:

> Nahas unilaterally abrogated the 1936 treaty and the Anglo-Egyptian Condominium over the Sudan and proclaimed Farouk king of "Egypt and Sudan." The government now encouraged guerilla fighting to harass the British in the canal zone. Cairo ordered some 25,000 Egyptian laborers to abandon British outposts; each side blockaded the other, and an Egyptian campaign of anti-British terror was instigated. The British retaliated by seizing Egyptian villages in the zone and placing them under martial law. By December 1951 battles between British troops and Egyptian auxiliary police had resulted in the destruction of a village and in the death of forty-three policemen in the province of Ismailia.[129]

The political situation in Egypt was deteriorating rapidly. In January 1952, a meeting to protest events in the canal zone the month before quickly turned into mob violence against British and foreign targets. January 26, 1952, became known as "Black Saturday." On that day,

> Nearly 500 shops and businesses were destroyed—including such landmarks as the Turf Club and the famous Shepheard's Hotel. The demonstrators began by methodically ravishing luxury installations such as liquor warehouses, cinemas, and department stores. By evening, most of Cairo's business center was destroyed, to say nothing of the incalculable harm done to commercial credit, currency exchange, and tourism. No accurate tabulation was ever made of the deaths and casualties that occurred, but almost 12,000 families were left homeless. Subsequent investigations of the riot indicated that it had been well planned, probably by [Ahmad Husayn's] pseudo-socialists and the Muslim Brotherhood. Some maintain that Farouk was forewarned, but that he had hoped to exploit the demonstrations to his own advantage before they got out of hand.[130]

In fact, the king used the occasion to dismiss the Wafdist government of Mustafa Nahas. Ahmed Maher and Negib al-Hilali followed as prime ministers, but the entire regime was essentially discredited. On July 23, 1952, a group of young army officers staged a rapid and bloodless coup against the now unpopular king. These "Free Officers" took control of the government, forced Faruq into exile, and embarked upon a plan of social and economic reform, drawing many of their plans from the programs, debates, and ideas discussed and practiced during the prerevolutionary years.

5

After 1952

Hussein and Gamal 'Abd al-Nasir

The new regime that took power in Egypt in July 1952 comprised a small group of army officers, primarily from middle- and lower-class backgrounds, led by Gamal 'Abd al-Nasir, with the popular and charismatic Major General Muhammad Neguib as their front man. Neguib was known for his integrity, courage, and intelligence, spoke four languages, held a degree in law, had some graduate training in economics, and had been decorated for being thrice wounded in the war in Palestine in 1948. However, 'Abd al-Nasir, a postman's son from Upper Egypt, was the real mastermind of the coup and was soon to replace Neguib as the country's leader. In a very short time and with almost no resistance, this group of army officers managed to seize the reins of government and force the king and his immediate family into Italian exile aboard the royal yacht *Mahroussa.*

Most Egyptians greeted the news of the coup with enthusiasm. For many, it offered the first real hope of change in years. The goals of the new government, which included the establishment of social justice and the liberation of Egypt from foreign domination, were goals that echoed the hopes of the majority of the population. The abolishment of the Palace-conferred titles of pasha and bey, symbols of social stratification in Egypt, was one of the new government's first moves. In articulating a program of land redistribution and industrialization domestically and insisting upon self-determination for the Sudan (nominally under joint Anglo-Egyptian rule) and the evacuation of

British troops from Egyptian soil, the Free Officers demonstrated their commitment to national freedom and independence.

Yet despite some positive programs, enthusiasm for the new regime soon began to wane. Hussein and his reformist colleagues, though initially supportive of the new regime, were quickly disillusioned by the direction the government's reforms took. This chapter begins with an account of 'Abd al-Nasir's more notable rural reforms, focusing on the changes made by the new government to Hussein's Rural Social Centers program. Despite Hussein's disagreements with 'Abd al-Nasir over rural policy, Hussein served the new government as its ambassador to the United States for five years. The remainder of the chapter analyzes Hussein's ambassadorship, presenting it as primarily an exercise in public relations and window dressing by 'Abd al-Nasir.

'Abd al-Nasir's Rural Reforms

On the domestic front, the first priority for the new government was land reform. Passed only a few months after the revolution, the land reform bill was the new government's decisive measure to improve the conditions of life in the countryside. Its main provision was a ceiling on landownership. The original reform bill stipulated that no individual could own more than 200 *feddans* of land (though later legislation capped the holdings at 50). Landowners holding more than 200 *feddans* were required to sell the excess acreage to the state, which was to reimburse the landowners for the seized land. The seized land was valued at seventy times its annual tax, and the landowners were paid in government bonds bearing an annual interest rate of 3 percent and redeemable after thirty years.

The seized land was then redistributed to the peasantry in parcels of not more than 5 *feddans* each. Peasants purchased the land at the same price the government had paid the former landowners. Payments for the land were to be made by the peasants in annual installments over thirty years, with a 3 percent annual interest rate. In these areas of redistributed land, the land reform law created new agricultural cooperatives to purchase agricultural inputs and market agricultural produce. The law also set a standard land rent (seven times the annual tax) and required that crops be shared between tenant and owner on a fifty-fifty basis. Finally, a minimum wage for agricultural labor, with a provision for annual review, was established by the new law, and farmers were given the right to form agricultural unions.

Unlike Hussein's Rural Social Centers project, which was substantially changed and in consequence effectively eliminated after the 1952 revolution, the cooperative movement in Egypt continued to expand despite the change in regime, in part because of its links to land reform.[1] The Cooperative Agricultural Bank changed its lending practices after the revolution. In the past, the bank had required the owner of the land on which a crop was grown to guarantee any loan made by the bank. After the revolution that policy changed, and for those owning 30 *feddans* or fewer, the crop became the guarantee of repayment.[2] After the revolution's program of land reform, agricultural cooperatives were expanded and became an important part of the redistribution plans.[3] Hussein el-Shafii, central minister for social affairs and labor, summarized the new laws dealing with cooperative societies and cooperation in a speech to the First Session of the National Union General Conference of the United Arab Republic in July 1960, saying:

> Several other ministries have issued a number of laws connected with the co-operative movement, such as Law No. 192 of 1959 governing the trading in forage and the processing thereof. This law gives the social societies a big role in the processing of cotton-seed cakes and trading therein. Law No. 8 of 1960 concerning new communities on reclaimed areas and their organization on cooperative lines. Presidential Decree No. 572 of 1959 creating the Deserts General Authority and empowering it to form cooperative organizations in keeping with its principles. Law No. 61 of 1959 governing the profession of pharmacy and providing room for cooperative pharmacies for the protection of consumers from the greediness of middlemen. Law No. 203 of 1959 on export, including cooperative societies and their federations among bodies permitted to take up export operations. Law No. 153 of 1958 on Chambers of Commerce and the representation of cooperative societies therein. Law No. 43 of 1959 modifying the law on wholesale commerce and including cooperatives, among bodies allowed to open and operate wholesale shops.[4]

A 1969 law on cooperative agriculture was "directed towards economic study of cooperative societies to determine the needs and set priorities to development projects from the economic and social angles, [and] to implement them." In addition, plans were drawn up for extending the cooperative marketing of agricultural produce, based on experiments with cooperative marketing of cotton in Gharbiyah and rice in Buhayrah.[5]

A report issued in 1965 by the Egyptian government documented the expansion of the cooperative movement after the revolution as follows: "Cooperation is the best way to spread agricultural services among the farmers and to liberate them from all forms of exploitation. Therefore the State has consolidated the agricultural cooperative movement. These societies numbered 40,078 in 1963, comprising 1,900,000 members; whereas the number of societies numbered 7,103 in 1952 with a membership of 400,000."[6] The new regime thus continued to develop the system of agricultural cooperatives along the same pattern Hussein and his colleagues had developed during Hussein's twenty years of service in the Cooperative Department.

These changes (land reform, a minimum agricultural wage, and further expansion of agricultural cooperatives) had been recommended by Hussein before the revolution. However, Hussein's most important contribution, the Rural Social Centers project, did not survive intact after his resignation from the ministry. After the 1952 revolution, Fu'ad Galal and subsequent ministers of social affairs attempted to develop a new approach to rural social reform.[7] The result was a gradual dismantling of Hussein's successful project. Before the end of the decade, the Rural Social Centers project had been almost thoroughly transformed, and its tattered remnants survive today in the Community Development Associations (CDAs), run by the Ministry of Social Affairs.[8]

'Abd al-Nasir envisioned a three-part revolution: he believed the first revolution to be a political revolution against imperialism, the second to be an Arab revolution to break through the barriers imposed by the imperialists, and the third to be a social revolution, to achieve social justice in the nation.[9] On October 17, 1953, a new organization called the Permanent Council for Public Welfare Services was created by the revolutionary government as a means of expressing the government's commitment to pursue social change and justice, thereby achieving the third revolution. The law creating this new body enumerated the four objectives of the council:

> a) To examine general policy and draw up the main plans for the promotion and coordination of education, health, construction, and social affairs in order to realise social development in conformity with the supreme policy of the state. b) To evaluate the services rendered by the state to the public and elevate them to the highest standard of efficiency and success by promoting technical training, organisation and orientation and securing the response and cooperation of the people in social activities. c) To follow-up the execution of various projects by charging individuals and committees to undertake particular studies and researches and submit regular reports to the Council thereon. d) To look into the activities of non-governmental bodies engaged in work connected with the work of the Council in order to coordinate mutual efforts and utilise them to the utmost.[10]

The council chose to achieve the first of these goals by inaugurating a "new" project for the rural areas, called the Units of Combined Services, or the Combined Units (CU) for short. Of course, the "new" project was not new at all. Instead, it was an expanded version of Hussein's prerevolutionary Rural Social Centers project, invested with a new name, bigger buildings, and more bureaucrats sent from Cairo.

The 1955 fiscal year budget included provision for 200 combined units. Each CU was to contain the following buildings:

> 1. A complete Health Centre, containing ten beds for internal patients, an operating room, an out-patient's section, one for general diagnosis, one for indigenous diseases, a child-welfare centre, a centre for expectant mothers, a dispensary and two waiting-rooms, one for men and the other for women. 2. A social service centre comprising an assembly hall to seat 150 persons, a library, a museum for health and agricultural extensions, as well as a room for the social expert. 3. A school containing twelve classrooms, a headmaster's room and a teacher's room. 4. A nursery for one hundred children. 5. Five villas, each consisting of four rooms for married officials. 6. Dwellings for twenty-four bachelor officials.[11]

In addition to including a nursery and expanded living quarters for the expanded staff of the CUs (to include a doctor, two nurses, two midwives, a laboratory technician, a public health officer, a clerk, six medical workers, a headmaster, twelve teachers, two agricultural-social workers, and three or four agricultural laborers),[12] the council claimed that its program would be a financial improvement on the RSCs. The council estimated the cost of each CU in Upper Egypt at LE 30,000 and the cost of each CU in Lower Egypt at LE 22,000.[13] Citing the prerevolutionary cost of each RSC (including a health center, a school building, and a social center building and excluding the villas and nursery) at LE 57,500,[14] the council believed that its new plan would save the government approximately LE 8 million per year, while expanding the number of buildings and personnel at each service unit.[15] The council believed that it would be able "to bring down the essential cost [of the program] to an incredible minimum":

> Credits for the construction of hospitals amounting to LE 350,000 have been reduced to a third and brought down to LE 117,000. It was possible to bring down the cost per bed from LE 1300 or LE 1000 to LE 300. It was at first thought that this estimate was imaginary and that it would crumble to pieces when the time came to put the operation to the tender. Yet in spite of the rising prices of materials and labour, these estimates have been confirmed by the tenders so far received. This was indeed a miracle, a miracle in construction and planning.[16]

These optimistic funding projections turned out to be gross miscalculations. The council had called the incredibly low projected costs of the new centers a "miracle," and indeed it would have been a miracle to get more services, a vastly expanded staff, and more buildings at half the prerevolutionary price. As it turned out, however, "pipe dream" would have been a more accurate description. Reliable data on the cost of the 250 CUs to be built by 1957 are hard to come by, yet even the most conservative estimate of LE 13 million (the figure announced by 'Abd al-Nasir before the National Assembly in 1957) boils down to almost double the predicted cost per combined unit, and this does not even take into account annual administrative costs or the costs of running the attached schools.[17]

Another change made in the program was the number of citizens served by each unit. Prior to the revolution, each RSC had been designed to serve a population of 10,000 people either in one village or in a cluster of smaller villages. However, the council changed this, declaring that each of the new CUs would serve a population of 15,000 rural citizens. The council justified this change on the basis of the boundaries of administrative centers, dividing each center, or *markaz,* into "service units" of 15,000 people. The council's criteria for choosing new sites included the accessibility of the village to roads and communication, the population of the village in comparison with the other villages in the service unit, its location relative to the other villages of the service unit, and its water supply, its existing services, and general fairness in unit distribution.[18]

The Combined Units program, as envisioned by the overly optimistic and extremely ambitious council, would expand to cover the entire rural population of Egypt within five years. In the view of the council,

> by executing the programme of Combined Units within five years all services will be available to every individual in the country on an equal footing. . . . [providing] in one year a sound foundation for the just distribution of health, cultural, and social services of a high standard. This is something never achieved in Egypt before. . . . Within five years all the 864 combined units needed for the whole country will be completed.[19]

Table 8 shows the distribution of the combined units throughout the country and those whose completion was anticipated as of the end of the 1955 expansion program. This ambitious but naive goal of providing complete, modern social, medical, cultural, agricultural, and educational services to the entire rural population within five years at bargain-basement prices was a contrast to the rather cautious and modest annual goals of the RSC program. As it turned out, it was also incredibly unrealistic.

On Wednesday, July 13, 1955, the first of the combined units was inaugurated by 'Abd al-Nasir at the village of Barnasht in the province of Giza. The president spoke of his great hopes for the program and said that the CU at Barnasht demonstrated that "results can be achieved through hard work from a contented group of citizens who do their best in order to enhance the dignity of their country."[20] Unfortunately, although the building of more and more units proceeded apace, the actual provision of services accomplished by the

TABLE 8

Distribution of Combined Units in Egypt in 1955 and the Number to Be Built in Each Province

Province	*Population Estimated in 1953*	*No. of Markazes*	*No. of Divisions*	*No. of Areas at Present Supplied w/Services*	*% of Areas at at Present Supplied w/Services*	*Areas Without Services*	*No. to Be Built in 1955*	*No. of Areas Served after 1955 Program*	*% of Areas Served after 1955 Program*
Buhayrah	1,445,000	11	69	26	38	43	17	43	61
Gharbiyah	1,857,000	11	88	39	43	50	17	56	63
Fuadiyah	878,000	7	41	17	42	24	8	25	61
Daqahliyah	1,659,000	8	83	32	39	50	18	50	61
Sharqiyah	1,485,000	9	75	35	46	40	12	47	63
Minufiyah	1,330,000	7	70	44	63	26	5	49	71
Qalyubiyah	804,000	5	41	19	46	22	7	26	63
Giza	980,000	5	44	14	31	30	13	27	61
Bani Suwayf	702,000	6	34	10	29	24	11	21	62
Fayyum	760,000	5	37	11	29	26	12	23	62
Minya	1,203,000	8	60	22	36	38	14	36	60
Assiout	1,549,000	10	71	24	34	47	20	44	62
Girga	1,440,000	10	69	17	24	52	23	40	60
Qina	1,238,000	8	65	21	32	44	18	39	60
Aswan	328,000	4	17	9	41	13	5	14	64
TOTAL[a]	17,658,000	114	864	340	39	529	200	540	62

Source: The Permanent Council for Public Welfare Services. Cairo: Société Orientale de Publicité, 1955, 100.

[a] The table lists only the provinces *(mudiriyat);* the governorates *(muhafazat)* (Cairo, Alexandria, Canal Zone, Suez, Damietta, the southern desert, Sinai, the western desert) are not listed. The totals include statistics from both the *mudiriyat* and the *muhafazat.*

program in no way matched the results achieved by the program's prerevolutionary counterpart, and the optimistic estimates made in 1955 were quickly abandoned. By the middle of 1956, fewer than 100 units had been completed, and even fewer had been fully staffed.[21] By May 1958, three years after inaugurating the Combined Units program, a mere 210 of the 864 to be completed by 1960 had been finished.[22] By August of 1958, the minister of social affairs, Hussein el-Shafii, called a halt to the building of new CUs and declared that the next step in rural reform would be the "expansion of existing pre-Revolution social and health centers so that they can provide the multiplex services offered by a Combined Unit."[23]

The Revolutionary Command Council (RCC)'s lack of a lasting commitment to social reform was one reason for the limited success of the Combined Units program, but other problems existed as well. In formulating its ambitious building spree, the council overlooked what should have been the obvious difficulty of finding the necessary number of qualified staff members in such a short period of time.

> According to Salah Ismail, assistant to the Council's chairman, it was difficult to obtain people to administer Combined Service Units, especially in Upper Egypt. A Council tender in the spring of 1956 for one hundred persons had brought only seventy responses; and the qualifications of many of the applicants were low. Moreover, it seemed that the more urbanized Delta area had received preferred treatment over Upper Egypt. . . . In August 1956, . . .not a single Combined Service Unit was functioning between Kena and Aswan in Upper Egypt, a distance of over 400 kilometers. And except for a few "display units" near Cairo, it was questionable as to how fully staffed the other centers were.[24]

Another problem with the CU program that should have been obvious to the planners of the program was the way in which the units were placed in the villages. Whereas the RSC program placed its primary emphasis on the staff members' relationships with the villagers and believed that reform projects would spring up naturally by popular initiative, the CU program placed its primary emphasis on infrastructure. Instead of responding to popular requests for services and centers and allowing the people to contribute financially, intellectually, and materially to the scheme, as the RSC program did, the CU program tended simply to construct a few buildings in a village, partially staff the unit with personnel of dubious qualifications and commitment, and let it go at that.

The CU program was essentially a well-intentioned but poorly planned and even more poorly understood attempt to expand and to improve the RSC program. In its haste to cover the entire country with infrastructure, it swept aside the very elements of the RSC program that had made it such a resounding success in the prerevolutionary era: popular participation and service integration. As Shalaby observed, "Before the Revolution, the government and the individual social worker sought to give confidence, then funds to local communities, but now they build a unit, then try to obtain the people's confidence."[25]

An example of this tendency is seen in government literature describing efforts at social reform in the countryside. In sharp contrast to the rhetoric of the RSC project, postrevolutionary pamphlets on social reform heavily emphasize the role of the government, relegating the people themselves to the status of beneficiaries of government charity. For instance, according to a pamphlet issued in the 1970s describing the history of rural reform efforts since the revolution, "The State uses the various means and organs to guide the farmer"; "it [the state] establishes the cooperative society premises to be used for meetings"; "the State has allocated the necessary funds"; and "the State works for realising agricultural-industrial integration by establishing the suitable rural industries."[26]

But what was the underlying reason for this change in approach to rural social reform? The answer is twofold. First, the consensus of those who worked on the RSC project (many of whom were later transferred to the Combined Units program) is that the leaders of the revolution wanted to sweep aside all elements of the old order, including the old order's social reform projects.[27] However, at the same time that the new government wanted to develop its own signature social reform project, it also recognized the accomplishments of the social centers. For this reason, the CUs were implicitly modeled on the RSCs. Put quite simply, although the new government recognized the success of the old program, the revolutionary leaders wanted their own project—a highly visible rural reform effort that they could point to as their own. Because of this desire for a "show project," there was a heavy emphasis on developing infrastructure. At the same time that they were using the RSCs as a model, a plan was also devised to destroy the old RSCs. One of the new leaders, ʿAbd al-Razzak ʿAbd al-Megid, believed that this would be best accomplished by transferring the most effective personnel in the RSC program into the new CU program. Accordingly, sixty-seven agricultural-social specialists from various RSCs were removed from that program and placed into the new CU program.[28] Stealing the most effective personnel away from the old program and placing them into the new program and launching a massive building project for the CUs were the two main methods of giving the new program legitimacy.

The second reason that the revolution's leaders changed Hussein's successful program was a political one: they wanted to placate the peasantry by providing services that were directly attributable to the new government. The funds for the new CU program were to be gotten from the sale of confiscated royal property. The decision to use these expropriated monies for the CU program was clearly political: by doing so, the revolutionary regime could say to the individual peasant, "You have these new buildings and new services because of us. *We* threw out the old order, *we* expropriated their lands and funds, and *we* gave them to you." The combined units were vigorously promoted as the fulfillment of the revolution's promises to the rural people.[29]

James Mayfield has accurately commented that most writers on postrevolutionary rural development have tended to accept blindly government statements and figures and laud the combined units as a potentially spectacular means of social reform in agricultural areas.[30] They have tended to attribute the problems of the CU scheme to a dearth of buildings and personnel. Yet Mayfield agrees with Shalaby that the real reasons for the failure of the program are intangible and that the real deficiencies in the program are more likely to be found in the "attitudes, values, and behavioral norms of the administrators or the villagers."[31] Writing in 1971, Mayfield stated that:

> After careful analysis of some 250 interviews with officials, *fellahin,* and private citizens, I have come to the conclusion that in the vast majority of the combined units, health units, social centers, and other government-sponsored rural development programs, their effectiveness, their ability to stimulate change, and their success in generating enthusiasm and commit-

> ment to the goals of development and modernization have largely failed to reach their stated aims. This rather harsh statement is substantiated by several Egyptian sources who have objectively analyzed the rural programs presently functioning in Egypt. Thus, most of the evaluation teams sent out to various governorates generally reached the same conclusion as Ahmad Tawfiq, who laments over the fact that the "combined unit, which is the center of all government services for the villagers, rarely has any peasants in it for they never go there unless it is absolutely necessary."[32]

The conclusion that the people in rural areas generally avoided the combined units and did not seek their services was corroborated by a study sponsored by the International Labor Organization in Geneva and conducted by the Institute for National Planning in Egypt. While the purpose of the study was to analyze employment in rural areas, one of the questions asked of the heads of households by the interviewers was "whether he or his family had received any benefits from administrative services available in their village."[33] The responses to these questions are summarized in table 9. As Mayfield remarked, the responses demonstrate that "aside from medical help and schools, over 75 percent of the families interviewed claimed they had not received any benefits from the other categories of government service available in the village. Even more dramatic is the fact that 34 percent of the women and 18 percent of the men claimed that their families had not even received medical or educational benefits from government-sponsored programs." He continued, lamenting that "the ineffectiveness of this institution [the combined unit] for rural development is largely due to the attitudes and assumptions that both the peasant and the village official have toward each other."[34]

Along with the spiraling costs of the Combined Units program and the lack of popular confidence, the program experienced another unanticipated difficulty. Initially, the sale of confiscated royal property was to finance a large portion of the new program's costs.[35] The council, counting on these anticipated funds, used the confiscated property as security on advances from the government. As it happened, however, the council received only a small portion of the revenue it had expected to receive and were thus forced to scale down "to the capacities of the responsible ministries: primarily the Ministries of Social Affairs, Municipal and Rural Affairs, Education, and Public Health.

TABLE 9

Services Received from Government Agencies in the Villages

Type of Service	*Male %*	*Female %*	*Total %*
Health	76	61	74
Education	29	12	27
Agricultural	26	13	24
Veterinary	20	6	18
Agricultural extension	18	9	17
Recreation	11	9	10
Vocational training	2	—	2
Industrial extension	1	1	1
Other services	2	5	3
No services used	18	34	20

Source: From *Rural Politics in Nasser's Egypt: A Quest for Legitimacy,* by James B. Mayfield, copyright © 1971, renewed 1999. By permission of the University of Texas Press, 1971.

The Combined Service Units became the responsibility of an under-secretary of state who reported directly to the Minister of Social Affairs. In January 1957, the Permanent Council for Public Welfare Services officially was dissolved."[36]

With the dissolution of the council, the rural reform projects of the revolutionary regime ran out of steam. The removal of prominent RCC member 'Abd al-Latif Baghdadi from his post as minister of municipal and rural affairs in July 1957 was seen by many as symbolic of the government's waning interest in and energy for social reform projects; the vacancy of this post for half a year following Baghdadi's removal furthered the popular notion that the government had simply ceased to care about the "third revolution."[37] Abu Nosair, who eventually replaced Baghdadi as minister, devoted himself to two projects: potable water and urban housing, relegating the ambitious rural reform projects of a few years earlier to the permanent back burner.[38]

Although no longer involved in governmental reform efforts after his 1951 resignation from the Ministry of Social Affairs, Hussein retained an interest in and a deep commitment to social reform. After the revolution in 1952, Hussein repeatedly expressed to 'Abd al-Nasir his displeasure at the direction the new government's reforms were taking, warning him that if the CU program abandoned the two guiding principles of the RSC program (popular participation and integrated service provision), the program would not succeed.[39] 'Abd al-Nasir chose to disregard Hussein's advice, with the result that with the exception of its land reform program, the revolutionary regime's program of rural social reform was largely a failure.

Accepting 'Abd al-Nasir's Nomination

When the 1952 revolution took place, Hussein was still abroad on the UN mission to the Caribbean and Mexico, and Aziza Hussein was speaking on a lecture tour in the United States. When news of the Free Officers' coup reached him, Hussein was hopeful. Like most Egyptians, Hussein and his colleagues were cautiously optimistic about the new government, particularly in light of the political scandals of the preceding years. Hussein hoped that the revolutionary government would breathe new life into Egypt's decaying political, economic, and social systems by putting an end to the corruption and dissipation of the old regime and by committing itself fully to broad reforms. Although Hussein, like many Egyptians, gradually lost enthusiasm for the revolution, in July 1952 the country's future could only look bright.

When the couple returned to Egypt, 'Abd al-Nasir and Neguib asked Hussein to serve as a minister in the new government. Aware of Hussein's reputation and his successful programs during his career in the Ministries of Agriculture and Social Affairs, 'Abd al-Nasir and his cohorts believed that Hussein would be an effective, progressive minister. The new leaders knew Hussein's reasons for resigning from the Wafdist cabinet, and they were impressed with his insistence on principles. But Hussein refused the offer. In his view, if a political party such as the Wafd would not allow him to conduct the affairs of his ministry without interference, the possibility that a military government would allow him the latitude to make his own decisions was slim at best. Aziza Hussein recalled that Hussein told 'Abd al-Nasir directly that he would not accept any ministerial appointment in the government, saying, "You are military people. You give orders, but I cannot be there to take responsibility without also having the authority [to do what I think is best]."[40]

Although Hussein declined the pressing invitation to join the new government, he did not lose interest in social affairs and still strove to influence the direction of 'Abd al-Nasir's social policies. Hussein continued to give lectures at Cairo University, at Fellah Association meetings, and in other venues as well, often speaking to those who would later hold positions in 'Abd al-Nasir's government and determine the revolution's policies of social reform. In these speeches, Hussein, as he had always done, emphasized that the primary role in social reform ought to be played by the people themselves.[41]

When Hussein refused the new government's repeated offers of a position as minister, 'Abd al-Nasir shifted direction and asked Hussein to serve his country as Egypt's ambassador to the United States. The leaders of the revolution believed that Hussein would be able to deal with American officials as an equal because he had considerable international expertise and was widely respected outside Egypt. Aziza Hussein remembered that prior to his selection for the ambassadorial post, 'Abd al-Nasir and Hussein both attended a meeting with a group of foreign officials, including the American ambassador to Egypt. She recalled that 'Abd al-Nasir was not able to speak with the foreign guests and felt uncomfortable in their presence. He noticed that Hussein was very much at ease dealing with the foreign officials, that he spoke openly and frankly with them, and that they responded to this in a positive manner.[42] Aziza Hussein's success during her American lecture tour also played a role in Hussein's nomination. 'Abd al-Nasir believed that as an educated, modern, active woman, Aziza Hussein would present a very positive view of Egyptian women to the American public.[43] 'Abd al-Nasir was also well aware of Hussein's reputation as a patriotic man who would not sacrifice the best interests of his country for personal gain.[44]

It is clear that 'Abd al-Nasir chose Hussein in part because Hussein fit the image 'Abd al-Nasir wanted to project to the outside world. Hussein was well educated, handsome, and comfortable dealing with foreigners. He had had a long and distinguished career in government service and had received international acclaim for his reform projects in Egypt. He would be taken seriously in the United States because of his previous experience, and his own political views were in consonance with American attitudes. Hussein was a liberal and a reformer, yet he was also staunchly anti-communist. At home, Hussein's lack of political affiliations meant he would not be seen as a leftover from the past but rather as a patriotic official who had suffered from the corruption of the ancien régime as had so many other Egyptians. Aziza Hussein also fit the image 'Abd al-Nasir wanted to project of Egyptian women. Like Hussein, she was well educated and had been active in social reform projects. She was attractive, pleasant, talkative, and at ease speaking to foreigners. For 'Abd al-Nasir, the image Hussein and his wife could project in Washington was of great importance. A young, energetic, modern, reform-minded couple was the ideal choice for the young, energetic, reform-minded Free Officers to make. Hussein's lack of diplomatic experience was largely irrelevant.

None of this is to suggest that Hussein was somehow a poor choice for the post. It is significant, however, that 'Abd al-Nasir was more concerned with image than experience. In the early days of the revolution, it was important for the Free Officers to project a positive, reformist, modern picture of themselves and their government, and Hussein fit the bill exactly. It is also significant that Hussein was recalled in 1958 at a time when the image 'Abd al-Nasir wanted to project had changed. No longer did he want a liberal, pro-American ambassador in the United States. Relations between the two countries had soured, and 'Abd al-Nasir wanted his ambassador in Washington to reflect the change. A young, energetic, reform-minded ambassador no longer was wanted. Instead a tougher, more aloof, less pro-American image was the new ideal. As Egypt turned away from the United States toward the nonaligned movement and as the government became increasingly socialistic, Hussein was a liability for 'Abd al-Nasir and would have been so regardless of how experienced he was as a diplomat. It is worthwhile to note that the man who replaced Hussein in Washington in 1958 had previously been ambassador to India, another nonaligned nation. For 'Abd al-Nasir, both the appointment and the recall had much to do with image and little to do with qualifications.

Hussein reluctantly accepted 'Abd al-Nasir's nomination because he viewed it as a duty and believed that he would be helping his country. Aziza Hussein recalls that Hussein was always poking fun at diplomats and at what he saw as the absurdities of protocol, warning, "I'm not a diplomat—I speak my mind."[45] In the end, however, 'Abd al-Nasir convinced Hussein to accept and persuaded him that he was the best person for the job. 'Abd al-Nasir told him that the main issue for the new ambassador would be to present Egypt's point of view on the continued British occupation of the Suez Canal Zone to American officials and to the American public.[46] Hussein agreed to accept the ambassadorship because the evacuation of the British was a cause he believed in and because he thought the post would be temporary—that as soon as he succeeded in getting American help to pressure Britain to remove its troops from the canal zone, he would be allowed to return to Egypt. He had no notions of becoming a career diplomat and was well aware that he was not suited to the post by either training or inclination.[47]

Hussein attached a few conditions to his acceptance, however. He insisted that ʻAbd al-Nasir allow him to take with him to Washington several colleagues of his own choosing as part of the new embassy staff.[48] Hussein's long-standing preference to work with staff he himself had groomed, in whose competence and loyalty he could be secure and who he believed were qualified for the job, continued in his new diplomatic career. Hussein's personal goals as ambassador were to get the British out of the Suez Canal Zone, to present the Palestinian case to the American government and the American public, and to make contacts with American governmental and nongovernmental institutions that would be beneficial for Egypt. He chose his staff members with these goals in mind.

Hussein selected Hassan Dawood, who had worked with him in the Ministry of Social Affairs for many years, to be his closest associate in the embassy and to occupy the post of counselor of the embassy.[49] Hussein also chose Galal al-Hammamsy and Mahmoud al-Riyad to accompany him to Washington.[50] Unlike Dawood, al-Hammamsy was not a close associate of Hussein, but he did have a reputation as a good journalist, and Hussein believed that he would be useful in improving Egypt's image in the United States. Al-Hammamsy was

Hussein and Gamal ʻAbd al-Nasir. Courtesy of Aziza Hussein.

appointed to the post of deputy minister for propaganda in the embassy.[51] Al-Riyad was not an associate of Hussein, either, but he was an expert on the Palestinian problem. Al-Riyad was an army officer, but because of his expertise he was chosen by Hussein to accompany him to Washington and to present the Palestinian point of view on the conflict with Israel, a point of view Hussein believed that the American public was not hearing.[52] Although 'Abd al-Nasir initially agreed to send all three to work with Hussein in Washington, he later changed his mind and did not allow army officer al-Riyad to go. Hussein also set the condition that he would not report to the Ministry of Foreign Affairs. He insisted on reporting directly to 'Abd al-Nasir.[53] Aziza Hussein recalled that Hussein and 'Abd al-Nasir were on very good terms, speaking once or twice weekly until the controversy over the Aswan High Dam.[54]

Hussein's confirmation as Egyptian ambassador to the United States was announced on March 5, 1953. The new ambassador was sent to Washington to replace Kamal 'Abd al-Rahim, who had been shifted to the post of Egyptian ambassador to West Germany. Hussein initially expected to stay for six months in Washington, thinking that the British withdrawal could be completed within this time period. In reality, however, although the agreement for withdrawal was signed in 1954, the evacuation was not completed until 1956. Hussein asked every year to be recalled to Cairo, aware that diplomacy was not his strong suit. As time passed, Hussein began disagreeing with 'Abd al-Nasir's domestic and foreign policies, and he found it increasingly difficult to represent his government. When the evacuation of the British troops from the canal zone was completed, Hussein asked again to be recalled, having completed his primary mission. Events intruded on this plan, however. Crises surrounding an arms deal with Czechoslovakia, funding of the Aswan High Dam, and nationalization of the Suez Canal Company all delayed Hussein's return to Cairo.[55]

In April 1953, Hussein set out for Washington accompanied by his wife and his specially selected staff members. Prior to leaving his post, Ambassador 'Abd al-Rahim left a memorandum for Hussein outlining the situation within the embassy and its relations with other organizations in the United States. He included with this memo three lists: businessmen and employees connected to the embassy, Americans with ties to Egypt, and those who "assist the Zionists with their propaganda." 'Abd al-Rahim also informed Hussein about the work of the Egyptian-American Association, established in 1951, noting that the activities of the association were limited and membership was slight, but he expressed his hope that the organization might do more in the future. He also urged Hussein to involve the embassy in the newly established Islamic Center in the Washington area, stressing that the goals of the center were to "publicize Islamic culture and introduce America to the Islamic world."[56]

In addition, 'Abd al-Rahim informed Hussein of routine matters of embassy business such as meetings with representatives from Arab and Asian countries, the status of relations with Congress, and the state of the embassy's finances. One issue that he particularly noted for Hussein was the lack of funding for the embassy. The government in Cairo had been remiss in financing its embassy in Washington, to the point that the embassy had to cease all publication, declare a moratorium on the travel of embassy staff, substitute paper for cloth towels in order to save laundry expenses, and economize on telephone calls, electricity, and stationery use. 'Abd al-Rahim urged Hussein to take measures to correct this situation, which had damaged the reputation of the embassy.[57] Upon his arrival in Washington, Hussein found an under-

Official embassy portrait of Ahmed Hussein. Courtesy of Aziza Hussein.

funded embassy with a poor reputation among the capital's elite—an embassy that had been ineffectual, inactive, and insufficiently funded. From this embassy, Hussein was to represent his country during one of the most turbulent periods in its history.

Negotiating for British Withdrawal

Hussein's main task upon arrival in Washington in 1953 was to enlist American support for British evacuation of the Suez base, thus ending the British military occupation begun in 1882. Hussein was a staunch supporter of this position and sought to address the issue at once. Upon disembarking from the plane in Washington, he made a statement to the press concerning the necessity of resisting aggression and foreign domination. He also stated his hope that the American public would recognize Egypt's legitimate position on a variety of issues.[58]

Hussein's primary contribution to the agreement on British withdrawal came in his efforts to present Egypt's point of view to the American audience. The embassy issued press releases throughout 1953 and 1954 stressing Egypt's rights and the validity of its insistence on British withdrawal and appealing to American sympathy for countries struggling to free themselves from the yoke of European imperialism. Other press releases emphasized Egypt's desire for peace, its lack of aggressive designs, its commitment to free passage in the Suez Canal, and its commitment to use military aid solely for defensive purposes. Hussein also played a more direct role in the negotiations. On the whole, however, Hussein's primary role in the negotiations was to serve as a diplomatic bridge between Neguib and 'Abd al-Nasir in Cairo and the American administration in Washington. This section does not seek to provide a thorough history of the events leading up to the Anglo-Egyptian agreement on the Suez base. Instead, it provides a brief overview of the American role in these negotiations and the extent to which Hussein, as Egyptian ambassador to the United States, was able to influence the American position.

The Suez base was "a vast complex of more than 50 camps, air fields, supply depots, ammunition dumps, ordnance, engineer, and motor repair shops . . . spread over an area 50 miles long and half that wide, west of the canal.

Collectively, the Ismailia network . . . comprise[d] the largest military installation in the world. British Prime Minister Sir Winston Churchill . . . said that $1,500,000,000 [had] been spent to build up this base."[59] In 1946, British foreign secretary Ernest Bevin signed an agreement to evacuate this massive military installation, but by 1953, when Hussein arrived in Washington, British troops had yet to be removed. With the start of the cold war, Britain became reluctant to give up the base, having little confidence in Egypt's ability to run the base effectively should Britain abandon it. The Egyptians were equally adamant that, after more than seventy years, the British occupation of their country had to come to an end.

The British position on the Suez base was neatly summed up by General Fetling, the base commander, when he said, "[We agreed to give up the base], but that was before the cold war and before NATO. . . . Now it no longer is one against one but something involving the whole Western world. Egypt thinks it can remain neutral and that the presence of the base will invite attack. Egypt is the land bridge to Africa and if war should come we need the base. The base needs skilled technicians and we have to provide them. The point is in brief, does the presence of 5,000 technicians violate Egypt's sovereign rights? We think not."[60] Speculating on scenarios for a third world war that would necessitate a continued British presence in Suez was a favorite pastime in the American press. One such article argued:

> British Middle East Air Force under Air Marshal Sir Claude Pelly has its headquarters in the area for a command that covers everything from the Western Mediterranean to the Persian Gulf and down through Kenya. In the Canal Zone it has bases for fighters, bombers, sea planes, and transport. . . . Defense of the Suez Canal is only one of the minor functions of British forces in this area. Since the canal was closed during World War II, it is arguable that defense of the canal from this area is no longer possible. Because of this, there is some excuse for the British moving out. If, however, the Russians in a possible World War III were to do an end run around Eastern Turkey, through Iran, Lebanon, Syria, Israel, and Northern Arabia, into Egypt, across the canal and into Africa, the need for a supply base to stop such an aggression puts another light on the matter.[61]

Such hypothetical war scenarios notwithstanding, Egyptian officials obviously disagreed with the stationing of foreign troops on their soil. In speaking internationally, however, they were shrewd enough to use cold war rhetoric to enlist support for their position. Like the British, the Egyptians conjured up the specter of communism to bolster their views, but while the British used the "communist menace" as a reason to justify their continued military presence in Egypt, Egypt used it to argue that the British should abandon the base. In a 1953 interview, Neguib stressed that the continued presence of British troops on Egyptian soil was a good way to keep communist influence strong in Egypt. In his words, "Now the one strong card [the communists] still have in their hands is the continued presence of British troops. Remove this, and you have struck a strong blow against Communism. Communism will become much weaker when the evacuation of British troops from Egypt is achieved and we are left to strengthen our internal front."[62]

The British wanted their troops to stay; the Egyptians wanted the troops to leave. The emergence of the United States as a superpower after World War II and its essentially neutral position on the issue meant it would be an effective mediator in the negotiations. The British had wanted American involvement in the negotiations from the start, often stressing the central role of American economic and military aid in the negotiations. British foreign minister (later prime minister) Anthony Eden wrote in his memoirs that he originally intended a settlement of the issue to include a phased troop withdrawal, the maintenance of the base by the Egyptians, its use by Britain and its allies in event of war, an Anglo-Egyptian air defense agreement, Egypt's participation in a regional collective security arrangement, and British and American economic and military aid to Egypt.[63]

The United States agreed to become involved in the negotiations because of its interest in setting up the Middle East Defense Organization (MEDO); American policymakers were aware that Egyptian officials would not discuss this issue before an agreement between Egypt and Britain on the Suez base was reached. One scholar summed up the situation as follows:

> The Americans were pressing the British hard to settle their dispute with the new rulers, on the grounds that if that regime collapsed the next one would

> be much worse. In these circumstances [American] Ambassador [to Egypt Jefferson] Caffery did his utmost to influence the British towards a compromise. Caffery informed the State Department that "Egypt will not participate as partner with Britain in any MEDO concept unless Britain announce acceptance principle of evacuation Canal Zone." The American eagerness for Egypt's participation in an anti-Soviet collective security network pushed its policy-makers to do everything possible to save the junta's reputation as well as that of the British.

American policymakers stressed that the price of British evacuation would be Egyptian participation in MEDO, and Egyptian officials, for their part, demanded substantial American economic and military aid as the price for participating in MEDO.[64] In late 1952, following a visit to Cairo of William Foster, the U.S. undersecretary of defense, the Egyptian government sent two of its officers to Washington to discuss Egypt's military aid requirements. Although Caffery warned Washington that these officers should not go back to Cairo empty-handed, British complaints and concerns about the effect American arms shipments might have on the conflict with Israel combined to quash any offers of American military aid that might have been forthcoming.

When Eisenhower took office in 1953, American policy singled out Egypt as the key to the defense of the Middle East. The new administration wanted to appear to support the Egyptian nationalist goal of British evacuation and, and at the same time, to support its ally, Britain. Eden wrote of his meeting with Eisenhower in early 1953, "The President agreed with me that it was essential to maintain the base in Egypt and that if we were to evacuate the canal zone before making a Middle Eastern defence arrangement we would be exposing ourselves to Egyptian blackmail. In contrast to [U.S. secretary of state John Foster] Dulles, he was clear and firm on this point. I put it to him strongly that Egypt was the key to Middle East defence but that if we were to secure a satisfactory agreement, we must act together."[65]

Although Britain and the United States agreed on what they hoped the final agreement would look like, Eisenhower did not want to appear to be siding with Britain or forcing U.S. mediation on the Egyptians. As a result, Eisenhower told Eden that the United States would not involve itself in the base negotiations except at the invitation of Egypt. Yet Egypt rejected direct American participation in the negotiations, saying in early 1953 that the first issue to be dealt with was the base, which was solely an Anglo-Egyptian issue; any agreements on regional security in which the United States might be involved were secondary and should be dealt with in separate talks.[66] In addition, Egyptian officials did not want to give the impression that Egyptian political decisions were being influenced by the United States, nor, because of domestic opposition, did they want to appear to be consenting to participation in MEDO.[67] Eden was somewhat irked at American reluctance to insist on participation in the negotiations and remarked rather pettishly in his memoirs that "it was impossible to persuade the Americans to make any further effort to attend the meeting. The Egyptians were left to act as they wish and they preferred to divide both the discussions and the allies."[68]

In May 1953, Dulles visited Cairo for talks with Egyptian officials on a variety of issues, including the status of the Anglo-Egyptian dispute over the Suez base, MEDO, and the conflict with Israel. Mahmoud Fawzi, the Egyptian foreign minister, stressed to Dulles the Egyptian view that MEDO would never work because of the Anglo-Egyptian conflict over the Suez base. Fawzi and Neguib both mentioned Egypt's desire for American aid for economic and social programs. During the course of these talks, Dulles agreed that MEDO was dead in the water and that a different form of collective security needed to be arranged.[69] The secretary's willingness to exclude MEDO from the talks allowed him to make the point that the United States was not in a position to give military aid to Egypt when it might be used against the British.[70]

Following his trip to Cairo, Dulles concluded that formation of any sort of regional collective security arrangement was a long shot. He recognized that "such British troops as are left in the area are more a factor of instability rather than stability."[71] He also agreed with intelligence reports that concluded that "any British military action against Egypt would constitute a threat to pro-Western regimes in the region and thereby increase the likelihood of Soviet penetration in the Arab world. . . . Any British military interference would put an end to American attempts to conclude peace between the Arab states and Israel."[72] In addition, Dulles believed the base to be of no strategic importance.[73] Although the bilateral talks were not progressing, the American position, while officially carefully balanced, was unofficially gravitating toward Egypt.

At this point, Hussein, who had been working behind the scenes to present Egypt's case to both the American public and American officials, entered the picture in a more direct way. After Dulles returned to Washington, Hussein solicited proposals from the U.S. State Department on how best to resume negotiations with the British. Hussein told American officials that Egypt would consent to British civilian technicians remaining at the base if Britain would withdraw its military personnel.[74] The compromise suggested by Hussein was publicly announced as the Egyptian government's position a few days later.[75] Hussein's compromise also resulted in renewed American attempts to jump-start the negotiations. Eisenhower informed Churchill that American policy now regarded settlement of the base issue as separate from and prerequisite to any talks on MEDO.[76] At the same time, however, American officials told Hussein that the United States wanted the Suez base made available to the West in the event of "general war anywhere in the world," a shift from the previous position that the base should be made available in the event of war in the Middle East.[77] During the summer of 1953, American officials continued to try to facilitate negotiations while maintaining their balanced position, but very little real progress was made.

American ambassador Caffery also played a prominent role in negotiations, echoing the Egyptian position on events in his dispatches to Washington. He continually urged the Eisenhower administration to push for an agreement, citing the growing power of opposition groups in Egypt.[78] Caffery was also worried about the American "balancing act" in the negotiations and argued in his dispatches that this balancing act appeared to many Egyptians to be American support for imperialism in the region and abandonment of its "traditional role of supporting national movements."[79]

Britain did not appreciate Washington's balancing act, either. Eden was particularly harsh in his assessment of the American position on the negotiations. He condemned the lack of American support for the British position in his memoirs, writing:

> Our Ambassador in Cairo commented that American policy in general seemed to be conditioned by a belief that Egypt was still the victim of British

> "colonialism," and as such deserving of American sympathy. It also appeared to be influenced by a desire to reach a quick solution almost at any cost and by a pathetic belief that, once agreement was reached, all would be well. These considerations, combined with a horror of unpopularity and fear of losing their influence with the new regime, particularly on the part of the United States Embassy in Cairo, and also an apparent disinclination by the United States Government to take second place even in an area where primary responsibility was not theirs, resulted in Americans, at least locally, withholding their support which their partner in N.A.T.O. had the right to expect and which would have been of great, if not decisive, influence on our negotiations. Inevitably the Egyptians exploited the equivocal American attitude.[80]

Certainly anticolonialism influenced the American position in negotiations, but Hussein's efforts to present Egypt's side of the story to policymakers in Washington and to the American press also played a role. The stress placed by Hussein on the unjust nature of the British occupation as well as comments made by Hussein and numerous other Egyptian officials that the base was bolstering anti-Western sentiment within Egypt also influenced American thinking on the issue.

Disappointed at the lack of agreement on the issue following the Anglo-American summit conference in Bermuda in December 1953, Hussein remarked rather prophetically to a North Carolina newspaper, "Quite frankly, I am afraid the Egyptian people now will say they will be friends neither to the East nor to the West, but will work out their own destiny."[81] The threat of Egyptian neutralism (read: anti-Westernism) absent a settlement of the Suez base issue was a motivating factor in American attempts to push for a quick solution.[82] Indeed, immediately following the Bermuda conference and the resulting lack of progress, Hussein and the Egyptian ambassadors to Britain, the USSR, India, and Pakistan were summoned to Cairo for a wholesale review of Egyptian foreign policy, lending credence to the view that 'Abd al-Nasir was prepared to gravitate away from the West if a settlement of the base issue was not forthcoming.

After the Bermuda conference, negotiations made no further progress until the spring of 1954. By this time, Egypt had agreed to allow British use of the base in the event of an attack on Turkey. 'Abd al-Nasir was anxious for an agreement to consolidate his own power base vis-à-vis Neguib and was aware that "Naguib's affiliations [with the Muslim Brotherhood and the old political parties] would conflict with American strategy in Egypt which was based upon supporting the military dictatorship against the parliamentary system." Anticipating that an agreement would strengthen his own position within Egypt, 'Abd al-Nasir was willing to concede on the issue of Turkey.[83] In response to Hussein's suggested compromise, the British abandoned the idea of clothing their technicians in military uniform, and the United States, to facilitate an agreement, committed itself to expanding economic aid to Egypt following the conclusion of an agreement on the base question.

The British were also increasingly anxious to conclude an agreement before their base rights expired in 1956. According to the terms of the 1936 Anglo-Egyptian treaty, after expiration of their base rights "Great Britain would have had to seek permission from the United Nations to keep its troops in Egypt, and it was doubtful whether such permission would have been forthcoming. From the British point of view, therefore, there were cogent reasons for negotiating a reasonable settlement and thus saving face prior to the expiration of the arrangement in 1956."[84] Eden stressed that an indefinite British stay in the canal zone without concluding some sort of agreement with Egypt would be absurd and self-defeating. He wrote, "If Egypt invoked international authority, the verdict was likely to be against us. The attacks on our base would be intensified; we would be unable to find any Egyptian labour; our water supply, by the Sweet Water Canal, might be cut off, or the filter plants sabotaged. So many troops would be tied down in the canal zone that we should be unable to meet any crisis elsewhere."[85]

Eden argued that by 1954, British leaders had decided that the base was not as important as they had thought it would be immediately following World War II. He wrote, "Time and modern needs were bringing changes. The Suez Canal remained of supreme importance, the base was yearly less so. . . . It did not seem likely that in this nuclear age we should ever need a base on the past scale. Smaller bases, redeployment and dispersal would serve our purpose better. . . . A treaty seemed to [the minister of defense and the secretary of state for war] a method of resolving an outdated commitment." Following this decision, the main points of the agreement, signed later that year, were resolved in a few days' time. As Eden recalls, "This agreement was a declaration of convenience for Britain and Egypt. Neither country wanted the existing state of affairs to continue."[86]

The announcement of an agreement on British withdrawal from the Suez base, signaling an end to the more than seventy-year British occupation of Egypt, came on the second anniversary of the Egyptian revolution. 'Abd al-Nasir announced the agreement in principle to British withdrawal during anniversary festivities in Cairo. The agreement was initialed on July 27, and final signing of the accord came on October 19, 1954. The main points of the agreement were as follows: termination of the 1936 Anglo-Egyptian treaty; withdrawal of all British troops within twenty months; maintenance of parts of the base by British civilian technicians; British right to reactivate the base on a war footing in the event of an armed attack against Turkey or any of the eight members of the Arab League by any country except Israel; British-Egyptian consultation about actions to be taken in the event of such an attack; immediate British troop withdrawal following the end of any such war; recognition of British rights for overflight, servicing, and landing of announced RAF flights; recognition of the international importance of the Suez Canal and mutual agreement to uphold the 1888 Constantinople Convention; Egyptian assumption of responsibility for the base after British withdrawal; and Egyptian-British consultation on arrangements for terminating the agreement after seven years had passed. The actual number of troops stationed at the base was some 83,000, and according to the agreement, Britain was required to withdraw all of them. The agreement did permit Britain to maintain certain installations with two or three thousand of its own civilian personnel (Hussein's compromise), but in evacuating the troops it ended the British military occupation of Egypt.

Hussein received numerous telegrams of congratulations following the signing of the agreement. One said, "Hearty congratulations and admiration. Thank God. At last your mighty effort in an epic struggle was crowned by historic and glorious achievement. Undoubtedly a proud record. Personal triumph for you and madam. God bless you."[87] The Washington society pages noted that at a reception for the president of Pakistan at that nation's embassy in October, "the Egyptian Ambassador and Mme. Hussein and the British Ambassador, Sir Roger Makins and Lady Makins were overheard congratulating each other on the signing yesterday of the Suez Canal agreement."[88] Mutual congratulations and Egyptian jubilation notwithstanding, however, many saw the end of British occupation in a dimmer light and argued that with the removal of Britain as the enemy, the new regime would be forced to address seriously its many internal problems. An article in an American newspaper summed up the situation as follows:

> To all outward appearances the Government of Premier Gamal Abd El Nasser is riding high. It is difficult, in fact, to exaggerate the prestige it achieved by capping the second anniversary of its revolution with the Suez pact—the brightest star in the Egyptian political firmament for the past 70 years. . . . However, all the fruits of victory are not sweet. If the presence of British forces in Suez presented each administration with a hot issue, it also furnished a means of obscuring purely indigenous shortcomings. If the British have been an irritation, they have also served as extremely valuable scapegoats for all sorts of economic ills.[89]

Yet this pessimistic view was not shared by most Egyptians, who saw the end to occupation as a major victory for the new government and a harbinger of a glorious future. American economic aid in the amount of $20 million was granted to Egypt in August 1954, and it was hoped that this aid would help the new regime achieve some of its development goals.[90]

The evacuation of British troops was completed on June 18, 1956 (a date still celebrated as Evacuation Day), and the Egyptian flag was hoisted over the Suez base, ending almost seventy-four years of British military occupation of the country. Evacuation was celebrated by military parades, complete with the display of the Czechoslovakian-bought tanks and Russian aircraft that by then made up part of Egypt's arsenal. Because Hussein was in Egypt when the evacuation was completed, Chargé d'Affaires Anwar Niazi hosted the official embassy reception in Washington to commemorate the joyous occasion and the fulfillment of Hussein's primary mission as ambassador.[91]

Arguing ʿAbd al-Nasir's Case

From 1954 until 1958, Hussein's primary task was to present ʿAbd al-Nasir's case to American officials and to the American public on various matters.

Hussein himself disagreed with many of 'Abd al-Nasir's policies during his last four years as ambassador, but in that post he was required to present those policies in the best possible light. The three main challenges Hussein had to deal with during this period were the purchase of arms from the Soviet bloc, the funding of the Aswan High Dam, and the nationalization of the Suez Canal Company. The purpose of this section is not to give a complete account of events surrounding these issues, which have been studied in great detail in secondary literature, but rather to present a general picture of events and locate Hussein within that picture.

Hussein's primary role during this period was in a public relations capacity. Although 'Abd al-Nasir occasionally asked his opinion on matters of substance, Hussein had very little effect on Egyptian policy during this period. By presenting Hussein's role in events, the importance of image in Egyptian foreign policy during this period will become clear. Hussein was not in the United States because 'Abd al-Nasir believed he could substantially influence American policy toward Egypt, nor did 'Abd al-Nasir recall Hussein to Cairo for periodic meetings in order to listen to Hussein's policy recommendations. Hussein was kept in Washington despite his own desire to return to Cairo because 'Abd al-Nasir still preferred a pro-Western orientation in foreign policy and Hussein was still the right man to project this image to the American audience.

It was particularly important for 'Abd al-Nasir to have a man like Hussein in Washington in 1954 to explain why Egypt had turned to the Soviet bloc for military aid. Although American economic and military aid had been promised to Egypt as early as 1952 as a means of prodding the government to negotiate with the British on the Suez base question, the United States was reluctant to fulfill its promise to provide military aid. British complaints about the incongruity of its NATO ally arming a country with which Britain had a dispute resulted in the United States declining to provide any aid before the conclusion of the Suez base agreement. Concerns about possible Egyptian use of American military aid against Israel also played a role in the delay of the promised aid.

In 1954, while talks on the base were still ongoing, Egypt was able to acquire an amount of small arms (guns, mortars, etc.) from Spain. On the whole, however, Egyptian officials were content to wait for an arms deal until the base issue was resolved. Part of the reason for this attitude was practical—

the regime was primarily concerned with social and economic reform, and until 1955, there were relatively few problems on the Egyptian-Israeli border (most hostilities in the Arab-Israeli conflict were then occurring on Israel's border with Jordan).[92] In addition, hopes for peace with Israel were raised with the 1952 revolution, and American, Egyptian, and Israeli sources saw some sort of peace agreement as a distinct possibility.[93] In such an atmosphere, military aid was not an immediate concern. Egyptian officials also did not press the issue because most of them believed American promises of future aid and preferred waiting for Western military aid as opposed to acquiring aid immediately from other sources. Although some officials may have doubted whether the American government would carry through with its promised aid, Hussein honestly believed that military aid would be forthcoming after the conclusion of the base agreement.[94]

For various reasons, events did not unfold as Hussein had expected. The evacuation of British troops from the Suez base resulted in increased Israeli fears of Egyptian attacks on Israel. The Eisenhower administration attempted to formulate a more balanced approach to Middle Eastern policy, part of which included a program of military aid to Iraq and Egypt. Military aid to Iraq began in April 1954, but congressional opposition to further assistance meant that Egypt did not receive its promised aid. Israeli policy became more hard line, in part due to fear of attacks from Egypt and in part due to the perception that U.S. policy was shifting to favor the Arab nations.[95]

In February 1955, Israel led an attack on the Egyptian-controlled Gaza Strip in response to border incursions, ending hopes of a peace agreement between the two countries and beginning a period of increased border clashes that eventually culminated in war in 1956. 'Abd al-Nasir felt that the attack on Gaza undermined his position both within Egypt and among other Arab leaders. The conclusion of the Baghdad Pact (a defense agreement between the United States, Turkey, and Iraq) two days before the Gaza incident made 'Abd al-Nasir even more wary of American intentions. The effect of the attack on Gaza and the signing of the pact (which gave Iraq greater prominence in the Arab world) was to harden the Egyptian stance. In order to bolster his own position, 'Abd al-Nasir viewed the acquisition of new arms as crucial, and "the Egyptian leadership promptly intensified its campaign to get arms from the United States." The new American ambassador to Egypt, Henry Byroade, "was bombarded with such demands. ʻAbd al-Nasir said that only new arms supplies for Egypt could forestall army and popular support for retaliation [against Israel]. ʻAbd al-Nasir's CIA contacts took up his cause, but despite the sympathy of Alan Dulles, the CIA chief, no help was obtained."[96]

By April of 1955, the USSR had already offered "to help any Middle East country not already aligned with the West,"[97] and ʻAbd al-Nasir, exasperated with the failure of American officials to respond to his repeated requests for arms, warned both the American and British ambassadors to Egypt that "if they refused to supply him with arms he would try to get them from the Russians."[98] Soon thereafter, ʻAbd al-Nasir attended the Bandung Conference of nonaligned nations (a move Hussein advised against), where he discussed the arms situation with Chinese leader Zhou Enlai and asked about the possibility of acquiring arms from the Soviet bloc. Zhou conferred with Soviet authorities, and "according to [RCC member] Salah Salem, the Soviet ambassador in Cairo conveyed a positive response to them on 6 May 1955."[99]

Yet ʻAbd al-Nasir waited until the end of July before contacting the Soviets to arrange a deal. Continued optimism that the United States would come through on its previous promises, a lack of interest in further weakening relations between the United States and Egypt, and the fact that the Egyptian military was unfamiliar with Soviet-made arms all combined to make the regime reluctant to close the deal.[100] Yet when ʻAbd al-Nasir failed to get any assurances of American aid in late May, he told Byroade of the Soviet offer. This offer was not taken seriously in Washington, where Dulles thought that the USSR would not actually arm Egypt and that Egypt would not really buy arms from the Soviet bloc. When the deal was concluded, however, U.S. officials sought to block the delivery of arms. Dulles warned Soviet foreign minister V. M. Molotov about the dangers of selling arms to the Arab states, and Kermit Roosevelt, the head of the CIA's Middle East section, warned ʻAbd al-Nasir of the consequences of allying Egypt against the West.

Hussein was in Cairo when he got word of the arms deal. He had not been consulted about or warned of the upcoming agreement with the Soviet bloc; it came as a total surprise. Upon hearing of the deal, he went to see ʻAbd al-Nasir, expressed his disapproval of the agreement, and reminded him that just a short time previously, the United States had orchestrated the overthrow of Guatemala's left-wing government and that he needed to be careful.[101] Before returning to Washington, Hussein tried to smooth things over between 'Abd al-Nasir and American officials. He arranged a dinner party at his father-in-law's house for Kermit Roosevelt (CIA), Eric Johnston (Eisenhower's special representative), Ambassador Byroade, 'Abd al-Nasir, and Field Marshal Abdel Latif Amer and Wing Commander Abdel Latif Baghdadi (both of whom were RCC members). Unfortunately, the party was not a success, and Byroade and 'Abd al-Nasir exchanged harsh words, which resulted in the abrupt departure of 'Abd al-Nasir and the two RCC members before the meal.[102]

While personally disagreeing with the arms deal, Hussein's task was to present Egypt's point of view to the American audience upon his return to Washington. He needed to simultaneously allay fears within the American administration that Egypt would be "lost to the commies" and respond to allegations that the arms deal signaled Egypt's preparation for war with Israel. Through embassy press releases, speeches, conversations with American officials, and statements to the press, Hussein tried to address these issues.

An embassy press release issued on September 29, 1955, chronicled Egypt's attempts to acquire arms from the Western powers, stressing Egypt's patience with Western delays in providing military aid and its preference for Western supplies:

> Egypt's need to establish an army adequately equipped for her defense was long since recognized by the great powers, including the U.S. Proof of this recognition is that in 1952, the U.S. signed an agreement with the Egyptian government for reimbursement purchase of American arms. Year after year Egypt repeated her requests for arms, and waited, watching meanwhile a constant flow of aid, military and otherwise, going to Israel. . . . Britain and France agreed to furnish Egypt with small arms. These agreements were not kept. Even though Egypt paid for arms from Britain, all of them were not received. France, angry at Egypt's liberal attitude toward the natural and legal aspirations of the people of North Africa . . . not only tossed aside her agreement to sell arms to Egypt, but she even announced that she had begun shipment of tanks and jet planes to Israel. No word of protest went to France, despite the avowed policy of the West for maintaining the balance of power in the Middle East. The inevitable effect of these disappointments, coupled with Israeli boasts of superiority, and the general recognition in public opinion of that superiority, brought humiliation to the proud hearts of the

> Egyptian people. Day after day they have been reminded that they are weak, and that they can perish at the hands of their enemy. No people can be expected to maintain a policy of merely waiting in the sort of atmosphere which has existed for too long in the Middle East.[103]

In an extemporaneous speech to the Overseas Writers' Club in November 1955, Hussein again presented Egypt's point of view on the issue, remarking that Egypt had been patient but that the Israeli raid on Gaza signaled to the Egyptian government that the acquisition of arms was necessary:

> The West has always been in the past our only source of arms supplies, and for three years Egypt looked in vain for arms from the West to meet her legitimate defense requirements, while at the same time arms were pouring into Israel. During the comparatively calm period following the Anglo-Egyptian agreement on Suez, however, we were given to understand by the Western powers that Israel had no intention of attacking us. We could only hope that they were not wrong in their appraisals of Israel's intentions, but this hope was soon dashed when Israel launched its unprovoked assault on the Gaza Strip on February 28 [1955]. Although we used restraint, the incident spurred us to new efforts in our quest for arms. Now we looked everywhere for them.[104]

Responding to American concerns that the purchase of Soviet-made arms from Czechoslovakia meant increased communist penetration into Egypt, Hussein remarked, "This is a strange contention, because Israel has purchased arms from Czechoslovakia without evoking such fears. Besides, the deal is purely commercial, without any strings attached. It signifies no change in our position vis-a-vis the West. We are opposed to communism, which has never been under such rigid control in Egypt as it is today. We bought arms, not ideology. We have 600 communists in jail and, unlike Israel, Egypt has outlawed communism."[105] Hussein also repeatedly argued that Egypt, as a Muslim country, could never embrace communism and its attendant doctrine of atheism.[106]

Hussein also emphasized the commercial nature of the deal in talks with American officials, saying that "the arms deal was no more than a commercial transaction with no political strings attached to it," informing Dulles that Egypt was determined to resist and prevent the spread of communist influence in the region" and stating Egypt's preference for the Western alliance.[107] In a 1955 speech to the American Legion, Hussein expanded upon this theme, saying:

> We searched for arms wherever we could find them to meet our legitimate defense needs. We have no intention of opening the door to any ideology, and we are anxious to maintain our friendship with the US. We would like the US to understand our conditions and problems in the honest and open way, not in the twisted way presented by our opponents. Unfortunately, we have not the vast means at our opponents' disposal for making our case better known here, but we appeal to the Americans' sense of justice, which we fully trust.

Hussein also ridiculed the argument that the acquisition of Czech arms threatened the balance of power in the Middle East, noting that "this balance is strongly in favor of Israel, which has a marked superiority over the combined Arab states."[108] In embassy press releases as well as in numerous of Hussein's speeches and remarks to the press, Egypt's desire for peace, its adherence to UN resolutions, and its lack of aggressive or expansionist aims were stressed.

Since Hussein was neither consulted about nor warned in advance of the arms deal, it came as rather a shock to him. Although he warned ʿAbd al-Nasir of the possible consequences, he was not in a position to influence the president's decision making on the issue. Hussein's role in the acquisition of arms from the Soviet bloc came after the deal was concluded; his responsibility was to make the deal understood in the American press, among the American public, and, most importantly, by American officials. Egypt needed to retain American goodwill, particularly since it was seeking American support and funding for the centerpiece of its development efforts, the Aswan High Dam.

Even prior to Hussein's arrival in Washington in April 1953, the Aswan High Dam was recognized as an important issue for the new ambassador. Before leaving Cairo, Hussein met to discuss the issue with various Egyptian officials, including the minister of commerce and production, Hilmi Baghet Bedawi, and the minister of finance, ʿAbd al-Galil al-Amari.[109] The dam was envisioned as an essential component of Egyptian development. It was to provide massive amounts of hydroelectric power and at the same time allow irrigation of vast tracts of previously nonarable land.

American cooperation in the project had always been assumed by the Egyptian government because "Americans, after all, led the world in dam engineering and irrigation projects. The American government had also indicated a keen interest in Egyptian economic development as part of its larger strategy of fighting Communism by fighting poverty."[110] Neguib had initially requested American aid for the project in November 1952, before the completion of feasibility studies.[111] In 1953, the Egyptian government officially requested American aid in completing these preliminary studies and the same year also requested financial support from the World Bank. Yet by December 1953, the Egyptian government had gotten no firm funding commitments from either the United States or the World Bank. Nonetheless, the regime decided that construction of the dam was necessary and that it would proceed with or without outside aid.[112] At this point, the American embassy in Cairo became a champion of the dam project, arguing that the dam was crucial to the economic development of Egypt.[113] In November 1954, "an international panel of consulting engineers met for several weeks in Cairo and finally gave the go-ahead for construction on the dam." Early the next year, the World Bank stated its approval of the project but also made clear its reservations about funding issues. One scholar sums up the issue as follows:

> Dire as the need for the dam was, however, the Bank was unwilling to shoulder the entire burden itself. In particular, estimates for the total foreign currency requirements of the project ran at approximately $300 million, and Bank economists assayed that Egypt did not represent a "good bankable risk" for a loan of that size. Consequently, funding for construction would have to come from a number of sources, with a US grant in aid representing a significant component of total financing.[114]

'Abd al-Nasir's underhanded dealings with Hussein during the funding controversy colored relations between the two men and, in Hussein's view, also undermined the negotiations. Hussein returned to Cairo annually to meet with 'Abd al-Nasir and other officials and to discuss issues. After preliminary agreements had already been concluded with the World Bank to finance the dam, Hussein received a note from the British ambassador via the U.S. Department of State. The note included minutes of a meeting between the American ambassador to Egypt and RCC member Gamal Salem, during which Salem objected to many portions of the preliminary agreement. Hussein, who had not been informed about the conference, immediately traveled to Cairo to confront 'Abd al-Nasir about this secret meeting. 'Abd al-Nasir professed to know nothing about it. Hussein told him to fix the situation, warning him that this interference with the preliminary agreement would likely sour the deal. Alhough 'Abd al-Nasir said he would send an aide to the American embassy to discuss the issue, he never did so.[115]

By late 1955, there was still no firm American commitment to help fund the project, and rumors of Soviet offers of aid for the dam were commonplace. Egyptian newspapers began reporting in October that the USSR had offered to build the dam, and references to the Soviet offer were frequent in American embassy dispatches. By this time the arms agreement between Egypt and the Soviet bloc had been completed. In November, an Egyptian delegation traveled to Washington to secure some sort of firm American commitment to the project. They returned to Cairo with documents attesting to the World Bank's willingness to grant an initial loan of $200 million, an American commitment to provide $54.6 million, and a British contribution of £5.5 million.[116]

When an American mission to Egypt to investigate peace talk potentials between Egypt and Israel returned empty-handed in early 1956, American and British officials began suggesting that the time had come to change the focus of Western policy in the region and to begin working with other governments in the area.[117] Niazi reported that the American press had begun to take an anti-Egyptian turn as well and suggested that Egyptian officials in the Middle East take a more conciliatory stance vis-à-vis the West.[118] In late March, Hussein met with an American official who warned him that Egyptian policy needed to take a more pro-American turn.[119] By this time, U.S. policy had already changed and was officially oriented toward isolating Egypt, although there were vague discussions of allowing 'Abd al-Nasir back into the Western fold should Egyptian policy become more pro-American.[120]

The deterioration of Egyptian-American relations continued. In May, 'Abd al-Nasir gave official recognition to the People's Republic of China, which may or may not have negatively influenced American thinking on the dam project; in any event, it was not a move designed to win American approval.[121] By this time, "it was apparent to most involved—on both the Egyptian and American sides—that there was little chance that the United States would in any way participate in funding the High Dam. All that remained was the end game." In order to delay final refusal of funding, the U.S. Department of State issued a document asserting that the Egyptian economy was not strong enough to support the construction of the dam. In mid-May, Hussein returned to Cairo to consult with ʿAbd al-Nasir. ʿAbd al-Nasir, who apparently had given up on the possibility of American aid, told Hussein to accept all conditions on American financing for the project.[122]

Hussein returned to Washington in early July 1956 and met with Dulles on July 19 to discuss the financing of the dam project. But the American decision had already been made. In a now legendary show of tactlessness, Dulles (who had already distributed information on the U.S. refusal to the press outside) met with Hussein, allowed him to state Egypt's willingness to accept U.S. conditions on funding, and only then informed the ambassador that the United States had declined to fund the project. Though Dulles may have relished the episode as a chance to put Egypt in its place (seizing the opportunity to refer to ʿAbd al-Nasir as a "tin-horn Hitler"), he did cite two specific reasons for the U.S. refusal: "First, the austerity such a large project would demand from the Egyptian populace would arouse resentment toward the United States, and second, . . .the American public would oppose aid to a country which seemed to be working against the interests of the United States."[123] The American decision was made without consulting the other financing sources—Britain and the World Bank—though Britain quickly followed suit. Bank president Eugene Black was taken aback by the American announcement and stated that in his view, Dulles "made a mistake in turning down this project."[124]

Despite public opinion that the dam project had not been funded by the American government because the Egyptian ambassador had not negotiated hard enough, Hussein did not feel that the failure to secure American funding was a personal one. Instead, he believed that once ʿAbd al-Nasir concluded the arms deal with a Soviet bloc country, the United States would not support the High Dam no matter how hard he tried to convince Dulles.[125] The primacy of

American political concerns also ensured that whatever efforts Hussein made would be of no avail:

> Throughout the 1950s, the High Dam project never really ceased to be an economic project for the Egyptians. However, in high-level discussions in the US Department of State and among the National Security Council, it was never anything but political. While Egypt's leaders continued to view the High Dam as a key to the economic future of Egypt, Secretary of State Dulles and his subordinates in the Department of State regarded it as a mere bargaining chip in a bid for regional peace. Although the Egyptian government record is significantly less clear than the American one, Egyptian officials appear not to have grasped entirely the disinterest which high levels of the American government directed toward internal conditions in Egypt.[126]

The High Dam at Aswan was eventually completed, with Soviet funding, in 1970—the same year 'Abd al-Nasir died of a heart attack.[127] Two years later, Egyptian president Anwar Sadat asked Soviet advisers to leave Egypt, ushering in a new era of Egyptian-American aid cooperation.

Soviet aid for the dam was not immediately forthcoming, oft-repeated American fears and Egyptian expectations notwithstanding. 'Abd al-Nasir was prepared for this and had already decided upon a way to generate funds for the construction of the High Dam. When Hussein was in Cairo early in the summer of 1956 to consult about the dam, 'Abd al-Nasir spoke to him of his plans to nationalize the Suez Canal Company, asking Hussein his opinion about nationalization. Hussein, still somewhat optimistic about American funding for the High Dam, responded by asking what the reason for nationalizing the company would be since, according to the treaty, the canal would revert to Egyptian control in only twelve years. Hussein opposed nationalization as a pointless measure and called 'Abd al-Nasir's attention to the international opposition that would result from such an action. Although 'Abd al-Nasir listened to Hussein's opinion, he told Hussein to prepare for nationalization—to prepare to make 'Abd al-Nasir's case in America.[128]

Upon returning to Washington, Hussein asked several trusted staffers, including Dawood, to work on a secret project, preparing a booklet about the history of the canal and Egypt's reasons for nationalizing the Suez Canal Company. The booklet was to be prepared and available for distribution when ʿAbd al-Nasir nationalized the canal. When ʿAbd al-Nasir made his famous speech in Alexandria on July 26, 1956, nationalizing the Suez Canal Company, the booklet, called *The Suez Canal: Facts and Figures,* was quickly printed and distributed in the United States, Canada, and Mexico, and copies were sent to Egypt.[129] This is most likely the document that ʿAbd al-Nasir subsequently sent to Egyptian embassies around to world in order to enlist support for the Egyptian position.

This booklet, issued in the form of an embassy press release in the United States, began by reviewing the history of the canal itself and the terms of the original concession granted to French engineer Ferdinand deLessups in 1856. It argued that the grants made by the khedive to the company (including granting uncultivated lands to the company for rent-free use, tax-free rights to exploit mines and quarries in the vicinity of the canal, and complete exemption from all duties and customs for anything connected to the construction of the canal) were unjust because they were not ratified by the Ottoman sultan, as was required legally. According to this booklet, the sultan opposed these grants and demanded both the cessation of the use of forced labor to build the canal and the return of all lands to Egypt. The booklet argued that the French commission of inquiry into the Ottoman dispute with Egypt and deLessups that sided against the sultan was a further injustice and had no legal basis. The commission's requirement that the Egyptian government pay an indemnity of 38 million francs in return for halting forced labor on the canal (forced, unpaid labor having been used for eight years prior to this ruling) and a further 46-million-franc indemnity for the return of lands adjoining the canal was presented as further evidence of this injustice.

The booklet then turned to a discussion of the cost of the construction of the canal. It argued that Egypt had contributed to the building of the canal the sum of some 338 million francs in the form of shouldering the expenses of scientific missions, purchasing shares, paying the indemnities discussed above, paying further indemnities in return for the later renunciation of customs exemptions, undertaking restoration projects, and providing unpaid labor during the construction of the canal. This total was, according to the booklet, some 60 percent of the money used to build the canal, which "explodes the myth that the canal was built almost entirely with French and other foreign capital. Actually it was Egyptian hands which dug the canal and Egyptian capital which helped most in implementing the project."[130]

It also argued that the British were the first to violate the principle of the neutrality of the canal when, in 1882, the invading British forces used the area as a base for attacks against 'Urabi's forces. It presented the signing of the 1888 Constantinople Convention as a response to British violations of the canal's neutral character.[131] The convention, the booklet noted, stipulated in Article 1 that "the Suez Canal shall always be free and open in time of war as in time of peace, to every vessel of commerce or war, without distinction of flag."[132] Yet, the booklet continued, previous British use of the canal as a military base and British restrictions on shipping through the canal during both World War I and World War II were further precedents for the area not being a neutral zone.

The booklet then defended nationalization of the Suez Canal Company:

> It was an Egyptian company, operating under an Egyptian act of concession and subject to Egyptian laws and sovereignty. In nationalizing the company on July 26, 1956, the Egyptian government was exercising a sovereign and legal right, a right upheld by the International Court of Justice. The same right has been exercised by many other nations, including Britain and France. The Egyptian Government, instead of following the example of other nations, by confiscating the assets of the company, has decided to compensate the stockholders by paying them the full value of their shares according to the closing prices of the Paris Bourse for the date preceding that on which the law of nationalization came into force.[133]

Having thus established the right of Egypt to nationalize the company, the booklet then provided the rationale behind nationalization. It stressed the need to use revenues from the canal for improvements of the canal itself, which the company refused to do, criticized this refusal to make necessary improvements, and argued that the company preferred to spend canal revenue on projects unrelated to the canal because its operating concession would soon expire. The company, it argued, did not care about the best interests of Egypt or the maintenance of the canal. It simply wanted to make as much money as possible from the canal before its concession expired.

The booklet refuted claims that nationalization would have a deleterious effect on the operation of the canal, pointing out that 85 percent of company employees were Egyptian, maintenance of the canal was not a complicated matter, all current staff would be retained, and tolls would not increase. It contended that nationalization of the company and the neutrality of the canal were unrelated issues since the company had nothing to do with decisions on passage but instead was responsible solely for operation and maintenance. The document then proceeded to reaffirm Egypt's commitment to the 1888 convention, refuting arguments that Egyptian refusals to allow Israeli passage of strategic goods through the canal was in violation of the convention, and stating that according to Article 10 of the convention Egypt was within its rights to restrict passage when such restrictions were necessary to the defense of the country. Finally, it addressed itself (albeit obliquely) to the crux of the issue—the future of the Aswan High Dam project—noting, "If the Government decides to use a portion of this surplus [of revenue] in continuing the development and improvement of the canal and the balance in carrying out its much needed economic objectives, this should be a source of gratification to all who are interested in the peace and prosperity of Egypt and the whole Middle East."[134]

Hussein, in statements to the press and in official embassy press releases, often referred to the fact that American policy had long recognized the right of nations to nationalize assets within their own borders. British nationalization of the coal, steel, and transportation industries had been recognized by the American government, and even Mexico's retroactive actions against American oil companies in the 1930s had been acknowledged to be legitimate. By referring to these historical precedents, Hussein attempted to present Egypt's nationalization of the Suez Canal Company as merely another such action, in consonance with actions of other governments and in accordance with international law. Hussein recorded in his ambassadorial diary that his main focus was presenting the legality of nationalization to American officials and persuading them that war would not be profitable for any party involved.[135] Thus, Hussein presented the nationalization in a language he thought the American audience would hear and understand. Nationalization was presented as a normal act of free countries; American recognition of the right of nationalization was stressed; and the entire drama was presented as another chapter in Egypt's resistance to imperialist domination. In other words, the image 'Abd al-Nasir needed Hussein to present was the image of a small nation resisting foreign domination and struggling to fund its own development through an action internationally recognized as legal and legitimate. Although Hussein personally disagreed with the nationalization, he was, in 'Abd al-Nasir's view, still the right man for the job.

A substantial amount of secondary and primary source literature exists on virtually every aspect of the resulting Suez Canal War. These events will not be examined further here, except to note Hussein's own role in them. Hussein recorded in his diary after the Israeli attack in 1956 that he constantly emphasized that Egypt had done nothing to provoke the attack, and he stressed to American officials the Arab perception that Israel would act in accordance with American wishes. Hence, argued Hussein to American officials, if the United States did not do something to oppose the Israeli action, Arab nations would perceive this as American support for the aggression.[136]

During the war (known in Egypt as the tripartite aggression), Hussein coordinated the response of other Arab countries to events. He wrote in his diary that he encouraged the Arab ambassadors to respond positively to American efforts to support a UN solution and that these positive responses should be backed up by whatever the Arab countries could do to show their support for the American position.[137] He talked almost daily with representatives from the U.S. Department of State as well, drawing their attention to the devastation and loss of life in the canal zone as a result of British, French, and Israeli attacks.

In addition to Hussein's attempts in his conversations with American officials to publicize the human and material damage done to Egypt during the war, the Egyptian Embassy published and distributed a booklet entitled *Anglo-French-Israeli Aggression Against Egypt.* The booklet presented Egypt's point of view on the war, stressing the atrocities and human rights violations committed by British, French, and Israeli troops. It chronicled the events in the United Nations related to the war, reproduced 'Abd al-Nasir's statement on Egypt's independence and neutrality, and included numerous pictures of the aftermath of the bombings in the canal zone towns of Port Said, Isma'iliyah, and Suez. It also contained the account of a Swedish journalist who, according to the booklet, was the only journalist able to avoid British censorship of news stories in the occupied areas. The booklet repeated Egypt's demand for a full-scale UN probe into all actions taken during the war and invited UN investigations of British and French accusations of a Russo-Egyptian plot to destroy area oil pipelines.

One American journalist praised Hussein's efforts to explain the Egyptian point of view of the crisis and attributed American opposition to the aggression in part to Hussein's efforts:

> The composed and moderating tone exercised by the American administration may well have been influenced by the Egyptian ambassador to Washington, Achmed Hussein. Mr. Hussein deservedly enjoys the esteem of the State Department and the whole diplomatic corps in Washington, as he would in any other capital. . . . Mr. Hussein, without the slightest obsequiousness to power, has ardently striven to strengthen Egypt's relations with the United States. . . . The sudden, brusque, badly rationalized, rude and highly undiplomatic withdrawal of the offer [of American aid to finance the Aswan High Dam] certainly could not enhance Mr. Hussein's prestige in Cairo, nor in any way aid in pacifying Western relations with Egypt.[138]

On the whole, however, and despite American opposition to the aggression, most journalists saw the nationalization of the canal company as another anti-Western move by 'Abd al-Nasir's increasingly Soviet-friendly government. Even the gossip columns and society pages harped on this theme, and in November 1956, Washington society pages printed large photos of Hussein shaking hands with Soviet ambassador Georgi Zaroubin at a party at the Soviet embassy held to commemorate the October Revolution. The papers also made sure to note that American and European officials boycotted the party (with the exception of Supreme Court justice William O. Douglas and his wife, who apparently had not gotten word that the American contingent had decided to decline the invitation).[139] Columnists remarked that because of these absences there was plenty of "elbow-room" at the party, except around Hussein, who "stood explaining the Suez Canal situation to some students from the University of Pennsylvania."[140]

On the whole, Hussein's personal role in the Suez crisis was similar to his role in the other events of that time. Hussein's primary responsibility was to present 'Abd al-Nasir's case to American officials and to the American public, and he did so with much success. Hussein's speeches, comments to the press, and embassy press releases all testify to the efforts made by the ambassador to make the rationale for Egyptian policy accessible to the American audience. That there was a growing rift in Egyptian-American relations during this time is clear, as is the fact that Hussein had very little influence on 'Abd al-Nasir's foreign policy. However, Hussein effectively presented 'Abd al-Nasir's case in the United States, and in the end, the ability of a diplomat to put the best face on his or her country's actions is one of the primary criteria for judging diplomatic success.

Hussein was also involved in several other projects as Egypt's ambassador to the United States. One issue was the purchase of American wheat under U.S. Public Law 480 (PL 480). Hussein successfully negotiated for Egypt to purchase wheat in Egyptian currency and to transport the wheat on Egyptian vessels. He succeeded in getting technical aid for agricultural projects from the U.S. Department of Agriculture. He was also able to make arrangements for more Egyptian students to study in American institutions. Dawood recalled that Hussein's biggest successes while ambassador were the agreements regarding the transport of wheat to Egypt, an agreement with the American govern-

Ahmed and Aziza Hussein aboard the *Queen Elizabeth*.
Courtesy of Aziza Hussein.

ment not to decrease the amount of food aid sent to Egypt, and removal of conditions on the food aid (American officials had wanted to condition the food aid on Egyptian purchase of only American-made goods, but Hussein convinced them to drop all conditions except that Egypt not trade with communist-bloc nations, a condition that was subsequently dropped as well).[141] These successes combined with his public relations efforts were some of Hussein's contributions to strengthening Egyptian-American relations and improving his country's image abroad. His efforts are all the more important when seen in light of the increasing political tension between the American and Egyptian governments.

Improving Egypt's Image

Egypt's image in the United States was not good when Ahmed Hussein took up his post as ambassador. Hussein and his wife were a welcome change, able to relate to Americans in a positive way and to project the image of a modern, progressive, new Egypt. Favorable comments such as the following became common in American newspapers beginning in 1953.

> Gone from the Embassy is Farouk's picture and also the quiet air of apology that one used to sense among Egyptian diplomats. In its place is a proud new enthusiasm for the new republic and a free democratic atmosphere. Contributing much to this change are the new Ambassador and Mme. Hussein. . . . A smiling bon vivant, Ambassador Hussein is a man of serious accomplishments. He set up Egypt's first social security system. As a cabinet minister under the Farouk regime, he tried to set up other reforms but resigned when he was unable to do so. His slender, black-haired wife did much to help rural Egyptians by setting up welfare centers in the villages. Both are as democratic as America and as friendly as we like to think we always are.[142]

Arriving at Washington National Airport on April 19, 1953, Hussein declared that his "chief duty will involve untiring efforts to increase Egyptian-American understanding and to express the Egyptian point of view to the American people,"[143] and despite the deterioration of official relations between the two countries, Hussein achieved this goal.

One of the first obstacles faced by the Husseins in Washington was the confusion in the American press about Hussein's identity. In both New York and Washington, major newspapers carried stories about the new ambassador's "political past," confusing him with the other Ahmad Husayn, leader of the Young Egypt Party. Newspapers carried stories of Hussein's supposed arrests, his fascist affiliations, and his sympathy for the Axis during World War II, and they blamed him for the January 1952 riots in Cairo.[144] This confusion was soon put straight, and subsequent articles carried correct accounts of his career.

In accordance with his goal of increasing American understanding of Egypt, Hussein undertook to expose the American public to the culture of his country. One of the first things the new ambassador did was to arrange for over three hundred works of art by Egyptian artists to be shipped to Washington. While some remained on display at the embassy, most were exhibited in various American cities.[145] The art of ancient Egypt also served to expose Washingtonians to Egyptian culture. Although a substantial array of Egyptian antiquities and Islamic art had been housed at the embassy since 1950, they had not been widely displayed. Hussein arranged for a permanent display of the objects in the embassy and opened the exhibit to the public for a limited period of time.[146]

The doors of the embassy were also opened to various social clubs and associations, such as the YWCA, whose members were invited to the embassy to see films and listen to talks on Egyptian topics. Other activities, such as donating a chandelier to the new Islamic Center, donating Egyptian fare to an Washington charity bazaar, putting the Egyptian embassy on the annual Washington House and Embassy Tour list, and hosting charity events at the embassy were also common. The press department of the embassy made an effort to present an alternative, more positive view of Egypt, publishing pamphlets on Egyptian culture, society, and politics from ancient times to the present. Positive reports on Egypt by American writers were also reproduced by the embassy, accompanied by photos showing the progress of the new regime and photos showing military officials embracing religious officials of all faiths.[147]

The Husseins also worked hard to establish personal and professional links with various people both within and outside the government. Hussein established personal contacts with Walter Lippmann and other famous journalists in Washington, and soon Egyptian embassy functions were attended regularly by most well-known Washington-based journalists. Hussein cultivated personal relationships with members of the American government, including Henry Byroade, Kermit Roosevelt, and members of the CIA (whose names Dawood was reluctant to mention). Before the deterioration of relations between their two nations, Hussein helped persuade John Foster Dulles and his wife to visit Egypt for the first time, and Dawood personally escorted Mrs. Dulles on her tour of the country. The Husseins also forged links with various American universities and women's organizations, often through the efforts of Aziza Hussein.[148]

In addition to formal projects, Hussein also tried to establish personal friendships as a means of improving his nation's image in the United States. Often these personal relationships and the energy with which Hussein and his wife pursued the social side of Hussein's ambassadorship brought even more positive results. It is surely no exaggeration to say that Aziza Hussein played a key role in improving Egypt's image in the United States. In her role as a diplomat's wife, Aziza Hussein played hostess to numerous parties and social events, joined various women's organizations in Washington, was quick to assent to interviews with the press, and spoke to a wide array of audiences on social, political, and economic topics.

Aziza Hussein remembers that the previous ambassador and his wife had not been popular in America. They were not a sociable couple, they rarely spoke to the media, and their aristocratic demeanor made them somewhat unpopular with Washington insiders as well as with embassy staff; one embassy staffer described 'Abd al-Rahim as "a bit of a tyrant" whose "cold formality" made him rather difficult to work for. When the Husseins came to Washington, things changed. Hussein became something of a father figure to many younger embassy staffers, teasing and joking with them as he passed their desks in the morning, leaving a faint scent of cigar smoke and aftershave lotion in his wake.[149]

Dawood recalls speaking to a member of the press corps shortly after Dawood's arrival in the capital. This journalist said he had instructed his secretary to decline immediately any invitation to any event held at or sponsored by the Egyptian embassy.[150] This situation changed when the Husseins arrived. In sharp contrast to the rather retiring former ambassador, the Husseins

Ahmed Hussein, ca. 1955. Courtesy of Aziza Hussein.

burst onto the Washington social scene. They attended and hosted tea parties, receptions, dinners, lawn parties, and every other form of proper diplomatic entertainment current in the American capital. Newspapers described Hussein as affable, hearty, and a bon vivant and described his wife in flattering terms as well. After remarking on the sudden and unexpected departure of the former ambassador, a 1954 article went on to comment, "Since the Husseins came they have done-over the Embassy and have entertained at numerous afternoon, early evening, and dinner parties. They are young and the hostess is pretty and vivacious."[151] Heeding the Washington wisdom that more deals are made over the dinner table than in a government office, the Husseins entertained at every possible occasion. Receptions for Egyptian writers and archaeologists, dinners in honor of American, Egyptian and Arab League officials, celebrations of Egyptian holidays, teas for American charities, and a party for visiting (though not performing) Egyptian singing sensation Umm Kulthum were just a few examples of events on the Husseins' busy social calendar.

Aziza Hussein was frequently photographed and became something of a darling of the writers of the Washington society pages. Her photograph appeared with considerably more frequency than did Hussein's, and her youth and beauty were often subjects of comment. She was described as chic, charming, attractive, handsome, slender, fashionable, graceful, popular, pretty, lively, beauteous, glamorous, elegant, friendly, gracious, vigorous, courageous, adventurous, with an infectious laugh, "one of the youngest and best looking of diplomatic wives,"[152] well educated, widely traveled, a leading intellectual, and a prominent feminist. Numerous articles about Aziza Hussein's activities appeared in the press, and her own positive image helped build a more positive image for her country as well.[153]

But perhaps the most important way in which Aziza Hussein helped improve Egypt's image in the United States was simply by being an example of a modern, educated, liberal-minded Egyptian woman. Her education and intellect were referred to almost as frequently as her beauty and charm, and she was often used to emphasize the fact that the status of women in Egypt was improving. "No one could better typify the progress of the modern Egyptian woman than Mme. Ahmed Hussein, wife of the Egyptian Ambassador to the United States. A tall, striking brunette with a dynamic personality, Mme. Hussein combines the charm and femininity of her veiled predecessors in the

Ahmed and Aziza Hussein cutting a cake decorated like the UAR flag, just before leaving Washington in 1958. Courtesy of Aziza Hussein.

harem with the new freedom and education which is becoming the rule rather than the exception in today's Egypt," wrote one Washington journalist.[154] Another column cited her "social service zeal,"[155] while still another referred to Aziza Hussein as "a remarkable woman," saying, "She is a most attractive woman, both in appearance and in intellectual approach. Observing her chic self-possession, one would hardly guess she came from a world that, until a few years ago, insisted all women shield their faces with veils and abstain from any attempt to influence men in political, economic, or social activity."[156] While one might well take issue with the ways in which these writers characterized Egyptian women prior to the 1952 revolution, Aziza Hussein was a prominent, visible example that American stereotypes of Egyptian women were erroneous. This young, active, modern, educated woman was the perfect diplomatic wife to represent Egypt in Washington society immediately after the revolution, and ʿAbd al-Nasir knew it.

One article remarked, "Few Ambassador's [*sic*] wives have ever been so deluged with requests to make speeches as Mme. Ahmed Hussein, wife of the Egyptian Ambassador. Not only is she pleasing to look at, but her delivery and command of the English language as well as her vast experience and knowledge of the social problems in Egypt makes her very much in demand."[157] As already mentioned, Aziza Hussein had been on an American lecture tour in 1952, where she spoke in twelve cities in five days. When she returned to the United States as the wife of the new ambassador, she was inundated with requests to continue giving public speeches.[158]

Aziza Hussein accepted virtually every invitation to speak, most often discussing either social reform in Egypt, referring frequently to her own and her husband's experiences with the Rural Social Centers project, or choosing to talk about the broader theme of the role of women in the Muslim world. She worked hard to combat American stereotypes of Egyptian and Muslim women, arguing that the veil was not required by Islam and that Islam was not hostile to Judaism and Christianity but was instead "based on the Judeo-Christian principles of one god and the brotherhood of man."[159] She stressed the progress made by women in Egypt since the 1920s, citing increased enrollment of girls in all levels of the educational system and the existence of female doctors, lawyers, scholars, journalists, social reformers, and educators. She argued that "the gradual freeing of women does not represent the influence of the West, but is rather a return to the original ideals and practices of Islam. 'The coming of Islam,' Madame Hussein explained, 'raised women from mere possessions to be bought, sold, and inherited, to legal individuals with property rights. In the Moslem religion, it is a duty to seek knowledge and acquire education.' "[160]

Aziza Hussein spoke at the University of Chicago, the American Foreign Policy Conference, Princeton University, the Women's National Democratic Club, the Congressional Club, the United Nations, and the Library of Congress, among other venues, and often referred to the natural friendship between Egypt and the United States. In 1956, she spoke at the conference of the General Federation of Women's Clubs in Washington. That year, the Cairo Women's Club won the federation's first prize for community service for establishing the first rural day care center in Egypt in the village of Sindiyun. Accepting the award on behalf of the CWC, Aziza Hussein used the occasion to stress the importance of such links between the United States and Egypt. As one newspaper remarked, "At a time when strained relations between Egypt and other nations was reaching its peak, an attractive Egyptian woman leader was extolling the 'basic goodwill' existing between the women of this country and her own."[161]

Aziza Hussein also spoke on political topics, sometimes replacing her husband when embassy business called him away from speaking engagements. In 1953, she spoke forcefully on the continued British occupation of the Suez Canal Zone, dubbing it "the 'one last ally' of communism in Egypt."[162] While Hussein was ambassador, Aziza Hussein represented Egypt on several UN committees, sponsoring a resolution urging governments to abolish what she viewed as antiquated marriage customs such as polygamy and arranged marriages.

While remarking on Aziza Hussein's beauty, intellect, and public speaking ability, the society pages, in keeping with 1950s American values, were also quick to produce evidence of the domestic skills of the new ambassador's wife. References to her excellent cooking were frequent in Washington newspapers of the 1950s, and some of her recipes appeared in a 1955 issue of the national women's magazine *Good Housekeeping*.[163] One of the most often-repeated stories was how she taught U.S. secretary of state John Foster Dulles's wife, Janet Dulles, to make proper Turkish coffee.[164] Stories about her sewing skills were popular as well, and several society page articles praised Aziza Hussein's home-sewn gowns when describing the fashions worn at embassy parties.

All in all, American newspapers portrayed Aziza Hussein as something of a renaissance woman—educated, intelligent, self-possessed, a competent speaker and social reformer, yet also beautiful, charming, fashionable, a gracious hostess, a good cook, a skilled seamstress, and a dutiful wife. The frequency of press coverage of her activities and the favorable tone of the articles written about her helped improve Egypt's image, and particularly the image of Egyptian women, in the United States. When Aziza Hussein was awarded the Medal of Perfection by 'Abd al-Nasir for her efforts as a diplomatic wife, the American media were delighted.[165] Such press coverage of Aziza Hussein was particularly important at a time when Egyptian-American relations were deteriorating and Egyptian government policy was increasingly being criticized in the United States.

Yet despite their social successes, the Washington years were not always easy for the couple. Hussein's young niece, daughter of his sister Namizar, came to the United States for cancer treatment during Hussein's embassy years. Doctors in Washington concluded she had little chance of survival. Hussein asked Dawood to make plane reservations for himself and his niece on the next flight to Cairo; when Dawood returned to Hussein's office, he found the ambassador alone and in tears, the only time Dawood ever saw Hussein cry. Hussein took his niece back to Cairo, where she passed away a few days later.[166]

By 1958, after five years in a post he had not wanted to accept, Hussein had accomplished quite a lot. He succeeded in his primary ambassadorial mission, completing British evacuation of the Suez Canal Zone. He represented 'Abd al-Nasir's government to the best of his ability even when personally disagreeing with the government's policies. He succeeded in improving Egypt's image in the United States while ambassador. In short, he did what he was sent to Washington to do. Although Hussein accepted the post and remained as ambassador because he felt he had a duty to serve his country, 'Abd al-Nasir wanted him there at least in part because of the image he and his wife projected. The young, energetic, modern, educated Husseins were well received in Washington, and the ties they established there served 'Abd al-Nasir's purpose. By 1958, however, the president's policies began to take a new direction, and suddenly a popular, pro-American ambassador became a liability rather than an asset.

6

Hussein's Legacy

In 1958, Ahmed Hussein resigned from government service. Although he lived some twenty-five years in retirement, Hussein never again accepted a public post. However, Hussein's influence on development thinking in Egypt did not end with his retirement in 1958 or with his death in 1984. His colleagues and the students he trained continue to be involved in development projects both in Egypt and internationally, and current projects owe much to Hussein's philosophy of social reform. Though the prospect for new projects to achieve substantive progress is debatable, efforts are underway on the part of Hussein's colleagues and students to influence national leaders. By reentering the debate on development, Hussein's associates hope to reclaim Hussein's contributions to the history of Egyptian development and help guide current development projects in a manner consistent with Hussein's successful projects.

Resigning and Retiring

The immediate catalyst for Hussein's resignation was the formation of the United Arab Republic, but other issues played a role as well. Hussein was increasingly frustrated with 'Abd al-Nasir's domestic policies and did not like his anti-Western stance. Hussein was also ready to leave the post he had never particularly wanted and that he had thought would last less than a year. For his part, 'Abd al-Nasir began to realize that although Hussein had been the perfect man for the job in 1953, by 1958, someone different was needed. Image was still important to 'Abd al-Nasir, but the type of image he wanted his man in Washington to project had changed.

Hussein had accepted his ambassadorial appointment reluctantly and had frequently requested to be recalled to Cairo. As the 'Abd al-Nasir regime began dismantling Hussein's successful rural programs and increasingly oriented itself toward the Soviet Union, Hussein could not refrain from telling 'Abd al-Nasir that he was making a mistake. He also had an increasingly difficult time defending Egyptian policy in the United States. Aziza Hussein recalled that "an ambassador is one who has to deal in a lot of tricks and diplomacy and to be very calm, not to be involved emotionally with the things that he is doing. He should be like a lawyer who can stand up for something even if he doesn't believe that his country is doing the right thing. He has to pretend and to go along. [Hussein] couldn't do that."[1]

The problems also had a personal dimension. Hussein was unable to deal with the harsh criticism of Egyptian policy in the United States, and in a sense, he took the criticism personally. Aziza Hussein recalls that "every half hour you heard news about Egypt. We were the enemy, . . .although we had so many [personal] friends who loved us immensely. He couldn't reconcile these two things. To have so many personal friends and yet to represent a country that is being damned every day."[2] Hussein's own desire to get out of the diplomatic game coupled with the growing tension between the country he represented and the country in which he lived were reasons for his repeated requests for reassignment to Cairo.

In 1958, 'Abd al-Nasir decided to follow up on his pan-Arabist ideas and unite Egypt with Syria, forming the short-lived United Arab Republic. Hussein advised 'Abd al-Nasir against the merger, arguing that Syria and Egypt were very different countries, 'Abd al-Nasir's pan-Arabist ideas notwithstanding. Hussein was also very concerned about the communist movement in Syria, a political ideology he had always abhorred. During a three-month stay in Cairo in 1958, Hussein made his position clear. He told 'Abd al-Nasir that if he went ahead with the merger he would have to appoint a new ambassador; Hussein would not be able to defend this action to the American government or the American public, nor would he be able to represent Syria.[3] According to Dawood, Hussein considered the union with Syria to be one of his biggest disappointments as ambassador, second only to the American refusal to support the High Dam project.[4] 'Abd al-Nasir responded to Hussein's request to be replaced by telling Hussein that he still needed him in Washington. Hussein re-

Official embassy portrait of Mme. Aziza Hussein. Courtesy of Aziza Hussein.

luctantly returned to the American capital, and two days later, in a move that can only be described as a planned insult, ʿAbd al-Nasir recalled him, implying that Hussein was not able to represent Egypt because he was too easily influenced by American officials.[5] The recall was so abrupt and unexpected that a welcome-back party planned for the Husseins in Washington quickly became a preliminary farewell party, and the Husseins returned to Cairo permanently shortly thereafter.[6]

As Aziza Hussein recalls, "ʿAbd al-Nasir wanted to make a show of it. That is what peeved my husband. Because [Hussein] had dealt with [ʿAbd al-Nasir] openly and decently and [Hussein] thought that [ʿAbd al-Nasir's actions] were not decent. We understood this to be a political gimmick. [ʿAbd al-Nasir] wanted to show people that [Hussein] is a stooge of the Americans, and that that was the reason he was being recalled. This is the thing that [Hussein] would never forgive [ʿAbd al-Nasir] for." She also recalls that ʿAbd al-Nasir "knew very well that Ahmed Hussein was not an American stooge, and yet he decided to play that card because he had so many communists around him, trying to influence him, and they were always putting a wedge between him and my husband."[7] It is ironic that Hussein, whose programs had been considered by some as dangerously leftist in the 1940s, was in 1958 being presented by 'Abd al-Nasir as not nearly leftist enough.

After Hussein's return to Cairo, the president sent several officials to persuade Hussein to accept another government post, including a post as 'Abd al-Nasir's own roving ambassador.[8] In addition to courting him with offers of government positions, 'Abd al-Nasir awarded Hussein the Order of Merit in June 1958 for his many contributions to Egypt.[9] Hussein, who had never cared for titles or awards, was not impressed with these overtures. He had had his fill of government service under the 'Abd el-Nasir regime. Hussein declined all offers of new posts, having become thoroughly disgusted with politics and with 'Abd al-Nasir himself. 'Abd al-Nasir's treatment of Hussein and his response to Hussein's request to be recalled to Cairo confirmed in Hussein's mind that the president could not be trusted. According to Aziza Hussein, Hussein was so incensed at the poor treatment he had received that he responded by saying, "I would rather go to jail than to put my hands in the hands of 'Abd al-Nasir [cooperate with 'Abd al-Nasir]." Aziza Hussein commented that the reason Hussein was so upset by the president's underhanded dealings with him was that Hussein himself was not a politician. She added that "most politicians are doing this all the time. It's not that 'Abd al-Nasir did something strange. He was not unusually bad to my husband. He had to play those tricks . . . But my husband was a different type. He went with a full heart, put his heart into his job and got the support of everyone. . . . He was not a politician at all."[10]

Even more significant than his disappointment with his treatment on a personal level was his overwhelming sense that 'Abd al-Nasir's policies had destroyed everything he had worked to accomplish.[11] Aziza Hussein offered this evaluation of the 'Abd al-Nasir years, one that her husband shared: "It was a lot of show, a lot of demagogy. People are still considering his contribution to be tremendous, and maybe it was in a way. But to us, we consider that he lost many opportunities. He really could have done much more for the country, including the Aswan Dam, including everything. He lost many opportunities. And he realized it at the end."[12] Dawood concurred, saying, "Now we are under the impression that Gamal 'Abd al-Nasir has freed the country of the British and so on and so forth and has done lots for the people and built the

High Dam and all these things, without stopping to think what happened at the grassroots [level]." [13] Yet this was the level of evaluation most important to Hussein, and in Hussein's view 'Abd al-Nasir's government was headed toward failure. The continuing anti-American direction of the government made Hussein feel that all his efforts to present a positive image of Egypt in the United States had been in vain,[14] and the dismantling of his RSC program affected him deeply. According to Dawood, Hussein "was not one of those people who are ambitious to have a high political position in the community. All he wanted was to serve his country by improving the life conditions of the poor people. And at that time he thought that there was no chance to do this, so there was no reason for him to continue [in government service]." [15] More significantly, according to Aziza Hussein, her husband in fact lost all hope. "He said, 'This is no use. Whatever we do, it all gets destroyed.' " [16]

This sense of hopelessness pervaded Hussein's years in retirement. When he retired in 1958 at age fifty-six, Hussein was still a relatively young man. Yet he lived the next twenty-five years of his life in virtual seclusion, leaving home rarely. His withdrawal from participation in public life was almost total. He refused most invitations out and did not enjoy holding dinner parties or social gatherings in his home. After accepting two invitations to parties in Cairo, Hussein refused to go to any other such functions. Aziza Hussein says that Hussein had had enough of that sort of thing while ambassador and did not enjoy it anymore.[17] More significantly, the defeats he had suffered while ambassador coupled with the demise of his successful social reform programs affected Hussein deeply—to the point that he became generally pessimistic and withdrawn. Aziza Hussein recalled that her husband "retreated from everything because he was so shocked and disappointed" by events.[18]

In the late 1970s, the Food and Agriculture Organization (FAO) of the United Nations organized a conference on rural development. The aim of the conference was to present the different development experiences of rural nations in order to determine an appropriate model for developing countries. Mohamed Riad el-Ghonemy, a former colleague of Hussein's from the Ministry of Social Affairs, was at that time working for the FAO, as were several other prominent Egyptians, including Sayed Marei and Adel Bishai. El-Ghonemy suggested Hussein as chairman of the meeting, and the FAO agreed. After much persuasion, Hussein acceded to el-Ghonemy's request to come to Rome to chair the conference. A few days before the conference was to open, however, Hussein changed his mind and refused to go. Aziza Hussein and el-Ghonemy both say that this was typical of Hussein in retirement. Hussein had lost his enthusiasm for public work, and although he might be persuaded temporarily to agree to reenter public life, he would change his mind beforehand, as in the case of the FAO meeting.[19]

In retirement, Hussein refused all requests for interviews from the press and even from private individuals.[20] British official Anthony Nutting requested an interview with Hussein to discuss Hussein's experience in rural reform and government service, and Hussein warned him that although he would be welcome in Cairo and welcome in his home, Hussein would not discuss the issues with him. Nutting came to Cairo, apparently hoping Hussein would change his mind once he was there, but Hussein categorically refused to discuss matters of substance with him. Aziza Hussein attributes this to her husband's reluctance to discuss the past, a time he simply wished to forget.[21]

Although unwilling to discuss issues or become involved in national affairs, Hussein did continue to see old friends, many of whom, like Dawood, had been colleagues and students. In retirement, Hussein did occasionally go to the Gezira Sporting Club, where he practiced golf or simply sat and drank coffee with friends. However, the refusal to give interviews, the lack of public involvement, and the reluctance to socialize on the part of a man who had been known for his social commitment, his cadre of followers, and his jokes gave rise to much speculation. Although rumors of his house arrest were greatly exaggerated, Hussein was not unaware of the domestic political climate. According to Dawood, when meeting with friends at the club, Hussein was careful to avoid giving "the impression that we were talking politics, because at that time, you didn't know what would happen to you if [you criticized the government]."[22]

Despite his personal withdrawal, Hussein continued to read voraciously on a wide variety of subjects in German, English, and Arabic and to follow national and world events through the newspapers, radio, and television. His relationship with his wife also kept him somewhat connected to national events. Hussein encouraged Aziza Hussein to remain active in political affairs and, in a sense, participated vicariously in public life through her, encouraging her to travel and giving her advice on her continuing studies, the articles she wrote,

Playing golf at the Gezira Club. Courtesy of Aziza Hussein.

and her activities in the UN, International Planned Parenthood Foundation (IPPF), and numerous national organizations. Hussein's career advice to his wife, though, was colored by his personal background and experience in government service. He vigorously opposed the idea of Aziza Hussein taking any paying jobs, as he believed it would put her in a vulnerable situation; in his view, women put themselves at risk by subjecting themselves to the authority of male bosses. Hussein also came to believe that volunteer work was more rewarding than government service and encouraged his wife to pursue her career goals through participation in voluntary organizations. In the 1970s, Aziza Hussein was contacted by officials of the Sadat government and asked to become minister of social affairs; she responded by saying she would consider the offer and consult with her husband. Her own inclination was to decline the offer, and Hussein, based on his own experience, encouraged her to refuse the post.[23]

When Egypt went to war with Israel in 1967, Hussein saw his judgment of 'Abd al-Nasir vindicated. In his view, the war was a colossal mistake—a result of a failed government that refused to face political and military realities.

Hussein with his father-in-law at the Gezira Club. Courtesy of Aziza Hussein.

Hussein saw the 1967 war as tangible proof of the mess that 'Abd al-Nasir had gotten the country into. Aziza Hussein recalls that both she and her husband believed the 1967 war to be a sort of wake-up call for the government and that 'Abd al-Nasir began, at long last, to see what had gone wrong in Egypt and to blame himself for his nation's woes in his final years.[24]

When 'Abd al-Nasir died in 1970 and Anwar Sadat became president, Hussein was sixty-eight years old. Sadat's gradual reversal of 'Abd al-Nasir's "Arab socialism" and Sadat's *infitah* program must have been a welcome change for Hussein, who had always believed in the free-market system. The initial expansion of political freedoms must also have been welcomed by Hussein. Dawood recalled that Hussein valued freedom very highly and believed that "there is nothing in the world worth anything more than freedom and the free choice of what [one] wants to do and what [one] wants to believe in." He also viewed Sadat as a good politician, believed his decisions in the 1973 war with Israel were sound, and though not overly optimistic about the Camp David Accords, did not oppose the peace. Yet despite cautious approval of some of Sadat's actions, Hussein was not impressed with Sadat himself.[25] He was aware of Sadat's political past, including his sympathies for the Axis during World War II. He believed Sadat to be morally weak and considered that a

Hussein in retirement. Courtesy of Aziza Hussein.

politician's morals and principles were more important than his or her policies. Hussein saw his judgment of Sadat vindicated with Sadat's later mass imprisonments of his political opponents. Hussein argued to his friends and family that Sadat's actions reflected his weak moral fiber and showed what sort of a man Sadat really was.[26]

The change of leadership did not bring about any change in Hussein's views. Perhaps because of his experience with 'Abd al-Nasir as well as because of his own standards of behavior for public officials, Hussein did not see the changes Sadat brought to Egypt as indicators of an improved government. He also did not see any reason to resume his former public life. Although Egypt had a new president, Hussein did not think it had a new government. He remained in retirement and, after a long and productive life as one of Egypt's most dedicated and most successful social reformers, Hussein passed away in 1984 at the age of 83.[27]

Al-Ruwaad: Continuing Hussein's Reform Ideas

Perhaps one of the most important indicators of Hussein's historical importance is that his ideas and his influence on those he taught and those with whom he worked did not die with him. Hussein was a role model for his students and for the generation of young people entering government service in the 1930s and 1940s. Hussein's devotion to reform, a devotion born out of sincere belief, his standards of conduct and behavior, and his overall idealism were infectious. Dawood said that even though Hussein was often depressed and pessimistic after he retired, he "never lost hope that this country sometime would find the road to prosperity. He thought that people can do wonders if they are properly guided and honestly dealt with. [Because of his teachings] we always listened to him and we went and lived in the villages [where there] was no electricity, no running water, no entertainment, nothing at all, but we worked and stayed in our small rooms . . . because of the fellahin, 24 hours a day without much reward."[28]

Hussein was able to convey his own beliefs and his own passion for reform to his colleagues and his students in a way that made them share his views. Dawood remembered Hussein as "the ideal man," saying, "I think you cannot meet anyone whom you prefer to work with better than Ahmed Hussein. . . . We always considered him as our godfather." To his colleagues, Hussein was the sort of man "who could oblige you to work as hard as you can without waiting for a reward." Calling Hussein a true intellectual and a "first-class team leader," Dawood also remarked that leading a group of independent, educated intellectuals was not easy, but Hussein was "admired by each one of us to the extent that if he told us to go and throw ourselves in the lake, we would do that." Dawood recalled that one of Hussein's greatest sources of satisfaction was his relationship with his students and colleagues. He always took great joy in their successes and was pleased that he was able to create "a school of thought which believes in what he believes in."[29]

Hussein's influence was not limited to ideas of social reform. El-Ghonemy, one of Hussein's many former students, summed up Hussein's influence on his students by saying, "All the students of Ahmed Hussein followed his principles throughout their lives in every area of life and work."[30] Dawood said of Hussein's former students and colleagues, "The youngest of us is over 70 now, but we still have Ahmed Hussein in our hearts and our minds all the time."[31] In the words of one of Hussein's associates, "To us, [Ahmed Hussein] was like Gandhi."[32]

Few of the original members of al-Ruwaad, the group Hussein founded during his teaching days and whose members worked with Hussein in his early programs, are still living, including Dawood, who passed away in 2001. But another group, "second-generation" Pioneers comprising Hussein's former students (who also call their group al-Ruwaad), has taken up Hussein's torch. Today, the second-generation Pioneers continue to meet periodically to discuss the reform ideas of Hussein, his impact on their personal and professional lives, and the prospects for rural reform in Egypt. This group began meeting in the late 1970s and at that time decided to compile a record of Hussein's ideas, projects, and accomplishments in the arena of rural social reform. While the goal of recording Hussein's achievements did not come to fruition, nevertheless, as Aziza Hussein remarked after a 1997 meeting of the group, "Through

Some of the "second generation" Pioneers: *top row, left to right:* Abdul Latif el-Heneidy, Ahmad Saber Yousef, Mohamed Riad el-Ghonemy, Kamal al-Din al-Wardany; *bottom row, left to right:* Aziza Hussein, Salah el-Nimaky, Anwar Abdul Razzak al-Abd, Ahmad Fathi al-Diffrawy, Omar Rashed al-Mikawy. Photograph taken by author.

these disciples, a school of thought continued to exist and to articulate [Hussein's] concepts and principles, [and these disciples] spread [Hussein's ideals] not only in [Egypt] but throughout the world" in their capacity as government experts and UN officials.[33]

Despite periodic lapses, the group has continued to meet, and, spurred on by the author's biography project, has become even more active in national affairs, despite the members' advanced ages. In coordination with the National NGO Council on Population and Development (NCPD), the group has sponsored conferences on rural development in 1997, 1999, and 2000, published several collections of articles on the same topic, and met with government officials (including Ibrahim Muharram, director of the Shuruq program) to discuss ways to include Hussein's reform ideas in national policy. Indeed, the enthusiasm that these men, all of whom are advanced in age, still have for Hussein and his ideas is overwhelming. Their discussions of Hussein's programs and ideas are impassioned. The fact that they still meet to discuss Hussein's reforms testifies to the impact he had on those who worked with him. The eagerness, emotion, and intensity with which these former colleagues of Hussein speak about him and about events that occurred over forty years ago is perhaps the best indication of how important Hussein and his ideas have been in Egypt. A prominent NGO official remarked that Hussein was the genesis of many current projects of development in Egypt, saying, "Before the New Valley, before Toschka, before Nasser, before land reform, there was Ahmed Hussein."[34] In the words of one of the Pioneers, "The story of Ahmed Hussein is the story of development thinking in Egypt."[35]

But it is a story still waiting for a happy ending. Were Hussein alive today, he would be disappointed with the conditions of life in most of rural Egypt. Continued population pressures have exacerbated many of the problems existing when Hussein began his work, and continued high illiteracy rates (especially for women) would sadden him, according to his wife.[36] Despite the continuation of social security, the implementation of land reform, and further efforts toward land reclamation, rural development projects since Hussein's resignation have been few and relatively unsuccessful. After the failures of the 'Abd al-Nasir regime, the Sadat government generally avoided the issue of rural development, in keeping with Sadat's view of rural areas as hotbeds of communism. While various NGOs have been active in social service provision in rural areas, only in recent years has the government of President Hosni Mubarak begun addressing the issue of rural reform.

In 1994, the Egyptian government began the Shuruq ("sunrise") project, a new program administered by the Ministry of Local Administration (MLA) and the Organization for the Reconstruction and Development of the Egyptian Village (ORDEV), which has as its primary goal "achieving integrated and sustainable development."[37] The similarities between the RSC program and the rhetoric of the Shuruq literature are striking. The program is framed as an aided self-help project that aims to involve actively the rural population in all aspects of decision making and project implementation. Project literature stresses RSC-type methodology—drawing up a community resource map, using focus group discussions to determine people's needs and priorities, using community contributions as partial financing, forming committees, and having one female and one male specialist per rural area.[38] The rhetorical similarities are perhaps less striking, though, when one notes project director Muharram's connections to 'Abd al-Nasir-era propagandists, including those who drew from the RSC literature to publicize the failed CU program.

There are several indications that the similarities between the RSC and Shuruq projects are limited to language. Two years after Shuruq was inaugurated, it began receiving funding from USAID as part of its program to promote democratization and popular participation in local government in Egypt. USAID agreed to provide $30 million to Shuruq in three tranches. After releasing the first tranche of $10 million, USAID determined that Shuruq was not meeting its participatory goals and withdrew its funding from the project. Concerns about Shuruq have not been limited to USAID staff or American officials, however. Although the project has been widely praised in the Egyptian media, many independent observers fault the project for its failure to truly involve local populations. Aziza Hussein, who has been asked to serve on several Shuruq committees, is not overly optimistic about its prospects, saying that the program "refers to past methods of development, but there are signs of nonparticipation." She also argues that despite the participatory rhetoric of the program, it is, in reality, another centrally designed and centrally run government development program. Noting the high level of bureaucracy and central organization of the program, Aziza Hussein contends that the essential component the new program lacks is spontaneity—the participation of the people in every phase of the project, where ideas for reforms arise spontaneously from the interactions of the populace. In her words, Shuruq "is a top-down program pretending to be a bottom-up program."[39] An incident in the province of Bani Suef illustrates this point. In 1997, a local businessman brought suit against government officials for what amounted to coercing financial contributions to Shuruq from local businesses. Controversy has also engulfed project director Muharram, whose methods and management strategies have been frequently criticized. What is more serious, Muharram was recently accused by the Central Audit Agency for various acts of malfeasance, including misappropriation of funds. Though the accusations were later withdrawn and prosecution was terminated, some continue to question Muharram's leadership ability and commitment. Nevertheless, Muharram remains in charge of the Shuruq program and continues to champion it as a beneficial means of rural development.

Despite these problems, there may yet be some hope for the Shuruq project. The consensus of observers seems to be that the Shuruq project is problematic because it relies too heavily on centralized decision making; were it to be administered differently and were it to live up to the participatory rhetoric contained in its literature, it might well bring substantial benefits to the rural population. The reentry of the second-generation Pioneers into the debate on rural development is calculated to bring about such results, and the inclusion of Muharram and various local and national government leaders (as well as academics and NGO staff) in their conferences and meetings is no accident; their goal is to encourage Shuruq leaders to direct the project away from the mistakes of the centrally run and unpopular CU program and toward the successful model of the RSCs. Perhaps with the advice and guidance of this cadre of specialists, all of whom were part of one of the most successful rural reform programs in Egyptian history, Hussein's Rural Social Centers project, the Shuruq program will steer Egyptian social reform efforts away from centrally planned projects and will herald a return to the successful models of aided self-help developed by Ahmed Hussein. With current development thinking emphasizing a macroeconomic approach, Shuruq may well be the last chance for implementing a successful integrated rural development program in Egypt.

. . .

Ahmed Hussein was a social reformer by training and inclination, a diplomat when his country needed him, and an idealist in every facet of his life. His own career and the projects he created and implemented are alone worthy of study. Yet Hussein's importance is not limited to the impact his ideas of reform have had on those with whom he worked, nor is he significant solely for providing a successful model of development. Hussein was also, in a sense, a mirror of the age in which he lived. His own experiences in prerevolutionary government, in postrevolutionary service, and in subsequent retirement and dissatisfaction with the new regime are in many ways typical of an entire generation of Egyptian intellectuals and public servants.

Prior to the revolution, Hussein, like many others of his class and position, tried to generate change within Egyptian society. Hussein and his coterie, as well as other reformers of his time, believed that Egyptian society needed to be reconstructed. The recommended reforms took varied shapes, as did the reasons for reform. Some saw reform as the only alternative to revolution, others saw it as a way for the government to control society, and people like Hussein saw it as a moral duty.

Hussein's career began in the late 1920s, at the very beginning of real interest in social reform in Egypt. He lived at a time when proposals for change were commonplace and the elite's refusal to make comprehensive reforms was even more so. Like many of those who proposed reforms, Hussein was a member of the wealthy elite. Perhaps it was because he was keenly aware of the reluctance of those of his class to embrace reforms that might serve to undermine their own social and economic position that Hussein's reforms took a more gradual approach. The programs he implemented reflected his desire for rapid reform coupled with a degree of realism. His programs were designed not to achieve quick, wholesale reform but to work slowly and to gradually convince the elite that change was positive and not to be feared.

Although Hussein was an insider in the sense that he was a member of the upper class—the same elite whose support he was trying to get for his programs—in his work he was a political outsider. He did not believe in the dogma of any political party; he had his own belief system, his own system of ideals that guided his work. He was certainly not the only unaffiliated politician or public official of his day, just as he was not the only reform-minded intellectual. But for Hussein, not joining a party was not just a choice he made;

it was, for him, almost a prerequisite for his work. Operating outside of the traditional party framework, Hussein was able to continue his programs despite the vagaries of politics in prerevolutionary Egypt. Hussein's lack of interest in politics was not a choice made for the sake of expediency or a way to ensure his programs would not be targeted for elimination by rival political groupings. It came from his sincere belief that the political parties were not operating for the good of the people; perhaps he even doubted whether they ever could.

Hussein's reform programs were part of the intellectual legacy inherited by the leaders of the 1952 revolution. His ideas, like those of many of his contemporaries, provided the Free Officers with much of their subsequent plans of social and economic change. Proposals made for land and other rural reform in the 1930s and 1940s, the expansion of voluntary social service programs, and Hussein's own emphasis in his projects on governmentally aided self-help all testify to the currency of social reform in the two decades preceding the revolution. To some extent these ideas may have provided the peasantry with a vague idea of what real change might mean. In a way, moderate, gradual reform programs like Hussein's may also have presented the ancien régime with its last hope. By refusing to endorse such change, the political parties not only betrayed the hopes of the majority of the people, they may also have ensured the downfall of the entire political system. In a climate where professing social reform had become the epitome of political correctness and where many actually believed that reform was possible, the refusal of the parties, and particularly of the Wafd, to make reform a real priority rather than another empty campaign promise was devastating.

Hussein was among those who believed that reform was still possible when he joined the Wafdist cabinet in 1950, but it took a little more than a year for him to realize that those in control of the political system were using reform as a pawn in a game of political power. His resignation garnered so much press attention not just because he was a faithful public servant who had been treated badly but because it was emblematic of the wider failure of the government to make use of the currency of reform ideas, of the rich debate on the various means of social reform that was everywhere in Egyptian society. Reform was not tied to any particular party, but the failure of the most popular and populist party to endorse the idea with concrete measures made many intellectuals and reformers like Hussein simply retreat and wait for events to take their course. With the failure of the parties to champion gradual reform, a more drastic solution became an eventuality rather than a mere possibility.

The revolution owed much to Hussein and his contemporaries because of the proposals and ideas of reform they bequeathed to the new leaders. The prerevolutionary reformers may also have paved the way for revolution by succeeding in making social change a powerful buzzword in Egyptian society. Certainly real commitment to change was evident, but by making it a political necessity for all leaders to espouse reform symbolically, they unknowingly may have helped prepare the country for revolution. Reform may have been just a politically correct catchphrase for the politicians, but for most people it was something else. The frequency of the calls for reform had been intensifying throughout the 1940s, people had begun to expect a government response, and at some point, the regime would have to either "put up or shut up." As it happened, the last Wafdist government failed to take any real action on reform. The opportunity for reform presented by the debates and by the intellectual climate in Egypt was not taken. In setting the stage for reform that did not happen, Hussein and his colleagues may have unwittingly opened the back door of the Egyptian political theater to revolution.

Whether or not Hussein and those like him unwittingly contributed to the revolution, almost all reformers greeted the change in regime with a degree of optimism. After the failure of the political parties to embrace the reformist agenda, the revolution brought the first hopes of real, wholesale change in years. In Hussein's case, the optimism was tinged with caution. At the same time that he wanted to believe in the social reformist zeal of the Free Officers, he was skeptical of their methods. He would not accept a position in the cabinet because he knew that a military government would not allow him the freedom to effect reform on his own terms. Still, he wished the new government well and tried to influence the new leaders' ideas of social, and particularly rural, reform.

In accepting the post of ambassador, Hussein showed his willingness to work with the new government. He believed in his main mission—freeing Egypt from British military occupation. He believed initially that the revolution was a positive step, and he tried to convey that point of view to the American public. But he also expected 'Abd al-Nasir to deal honestly and fairly with him, and in this he was disappointed. 'Abd al-Nasir knew Hussein was intelligent and accomplished, and these qualities helped make him the ideal ambassador to the United States immediately after the revolution. But 'Abd al-Nasir was much more interested in the image Hussein could project and the public relations efforts he could put forth than he was in Hussein's policy recommendations. As the president began to work around Hussein, rather than through him, in his dealings with American officials, Hussein's disappointment grew—disappointment not only with 'Abd al-Nasir himself, but with the regime as a whole.

Egyptian policy toward the United States began to take a less favorable turn beginning in 1954. In the context of the cold war, the U.S. perception was that a country that was not pro-American was pro-Soviet. Hussein was a liberal, a believer in freedom and in free enterprise. He was opposed to communism, and he was pro-American in his orientation. He wanted to believe in the revolution, but his enthusiasm began to wane with the new direction in Egyptian policy. Like many of the reformers, liberals, and intellectuals in Egypt, Hussein's initial optimism was dulled by events. He personally disagreed with many of 'Abd al-Nasir's policies, both at home and abroad, and by the late 1950s had become thoroughly disillusioned with the revolution.

The political spin put on his recall by 'Abd al-Nasir was the last straw for Hussein. His subsequent resignation from the diplomatic corps, his refusal to work with 'Abd al-Nasir, and his withdrawal from public life are symbolic of the fate of an entire class. Many upper-class reformers, liberals, and intellectuals who originally welcomed the revolution had by this time realized that the revolution was not bringing the kind of change and reform they had hoped for. Worse still, for many of them, their own contributions to social change prior to the revolution were being dismissed, devalued, and denounced. Hussein's successful rural reform program was changed to meet the ideology of the new government. The changes made to the program not only destroyed the program but more broadly implied that the program that had garnered so much international acclaim and support and had brought so many benefits to the peasants was essentially worthless.

Hussein's recommendations to 'Abd al-Nasir on issues of social policy fell on deaf ears. 'Abd al-Nasir's government was not interested in the recommendations of the Fellah Association, which was viewed as an upper-class relic of prerevolutionary days. Hussein's opinions on foreign policy were similarly dismissed. The group of reformers of which Hussein was an important part prior to the revolution had contributed enormously to the framing of the debate on poverty and social reform. When the revolution came, they expected their contributions to be acknowledged, their advice to be listened to and perhaps followed. When this did not happen, many of them, Hussein included, simply gave up. Hussein's retirement is thus symbolic of a larger dissatisfaction with the revolutionary regime on the part of many of those who had prepared the political ground for the new government. When it became clear that the new government did not particularly want their help or advice, these experts quietly withdrew their support and expressed their dissent through nonparticipation.

There is not much detail available on Hussein's life after retirement. His disappointment with 'Abd al-Nasir ran deep, and his withdrawal from public life was total. Hussein lived for twenty-five years in retirement and from all the available evidence lived the quiet life of an ordinary retiree, socializing with family members and close friends, traveling occasionally, playing golf, reading,

Hussein as a senior citizen. Courtesy of Aziza Hussein.

and supporting his wife in her career. Hussein had served Egypt for thirty years, and the documentation on his public life, his programs, and his career is vast. Yet there is virtually no information available on Hussein outside of his professional life. He was an intensely private man, and his private life was just that. Part of the reason for this separation of public and private lives may lie in his class origins; the separation between work and personal life was a natural one for many upper-class Egyptians of his time. Part of the reason also lies in his dedication to his career. For Hussein, his work was essentially his life. The destruction of his programs hit him hard because he saw it not only as the ruin of his important work, which was devastating enough, but, in a broader sense, as the destruction of his entire life by the 'Abd al-Nasir regime. His unwillingness to grant interviews or speak to anyone about the past after retiring illustrates the depth of his disappointment, and his disappointment is the disappointment not just of an individual but of an entire class.

The tragedy of Hussein's story is that his successful social reform programs were eliminated by the new government, his ideas of reform were dismissed for decades, and his own career was cut short. The hope and the lesson of Hussein's story is that one person can make a difference—one individual can have an impact. The motto of al-Ruwaad was, "The strength of the nation is in the strength of the individual, so with ourselves we must start," and no one was a better example of that than Hussein. He had significant influence on the development of reform thinking in Egypt. His programs brought substantial relief and benefits to those who participated in them. His vision of a reconstructed rural Egypt only partially came true, but elements of his work survived the revolution. The resurrection of the notion of aided self-help and community development that took place on an international level in the early 1970s shows the historical importance of reformers like Hussein. The introduction of the Shuruq development program could mean a return to his ideals in the context of government-sponsored development in Egypt. Hussein was a dedicated reformer and an idealist, and his programs were uniquely successful. Yet Hussein's story is not only his; it is also the story of a whole generation of reformers and intellectuals. In looking at the career of Ahmed Hussein, we are looking not only at one man and his reforms, but in a larger sense we are looking at the whole idea of change within Egyptian society and at the history of Egypt itself.

Notes

Glossary

Bibliography

Index

Notes

1. Origins of Hussein's Reform Ideas

1. Aziza Hussein, interview with the author, Cairo, Oct. 24, 1996.

2. Hussein, the eldest child, died in 1935 shortly after completing his medical degree. Namizar died in 1958, Abdul Aziz in 1984, Muhammad in 1992, and Aisha in 1993. Muhammad married the daughter of Abboud Pasha, a successful industrialist in the prerevolutionary period who was widely vilified and whose property was expropriated after the revolution. Muhammad and his wife were forced to leave Egypt as a result of the controversy surrounding Abboud Pasha; they lived in London until Muhammad's death. Aziza Hussein, letter to author, June 8, 1997. Amr Shalakany, Ahmed Hussein's great-nephew, relates the following story about how Hussein's sister Namizar got her name: "Ahmad Hussein's mother, Khadiga Nagdalih, was the cousin of Egypt's great poet Ahmad Shawky, 'amir al-sho'raa' or the prince of poets. Their connection is Shawky's grandmother Namizar, who was a Greek concubine in the Khedive's harem, captured during the 'morah' war, and then married off to Shawky's grandfather. There is a famous episode of her bringing Shawky before Khedive Ismail and the latter throwing gold at Shawky's feet to distract his attention . . . My grandmother was called Namizar after her." Amr Shalakany, interview with author via e-mail, May 12, 1999.

3. Donald M. Reid, *Cairo University and the Making of Modern Egypt* (Cambridge: Cambridge Univ. Press, 1990), 18.

4. Ibid.

5. Ibid. The number of students rose as well. Robert L. Tignor states that "the number of students in the primary schools rose from 5,761 in 1890 to 8,644 in 1910; those in the secondary schools increased from 734 to 2,197 over the same twenty-year period." Tignor, *Modernization and British Colonial Rule in Egypt, 1882–1914* (Princeton, N.J.: Princeton Univ. Press, 1966), 323.

6. Abu al-Futouh Ahmad Radwan, *Old and New Forces in Egyptian Education* (New York: Bureau of Publications, Teacher's College, Columbia Univ., 1951), 94.

7. Reid, 18.

8. Ibid., 18–19.

9. Radwan, 101. For a thorough summary of British educational policy in Egypt, see David Chapman Kinsey, "Egyptian Education under Cromer: A Study of East-West Encounter in Educational Administration and Policy, 1883–1907" (Ph.D. thesis, Harvard Univ., 1965).

10. Radwan, 100.

11. Ibid., 102.

12. Tignor, 323. Tignor notes that under Isma'il, English and French were taught as foreign languages, but Arabic was the language of instruction in most other subjects, and French was used where suitable. As British influence increased, so did the emphasis placed on English-language instruction: "An increasing number of non-linguistic courses were offered in either English or French, rather than Arabic. The culmination of this program to establish English as the first language in the government schools occurred about 1900, when a large number of courses in the primary schools were given in English; in the secondary schools all subjects except Arabic and sometimes mathematics were either in English or French" (325–26). After 1900, the nationalist movement in Egypt (whose cause was supported by some in the British parliament) sought to reinstate Arabic as the primary language of instruction, and "Arabic instruction was gradually reintroduced into the curriculum of primary and secondary schools. In the primary schools all courses were taught in Arabic. An increasing number of subjects in secondary schools were taught in Arabic, as trained Egyptian teachers became available" (327).

13. Ibid., 323.

14. In A. B. DeGuerville, *New Egypt* (London, 1905), 161, cited in Radwan, 101–2.

15. DeGuerville, 160, cited in Radwan, 104.

16. This was in addition to the study of the religious sciences at al-Azhar University.

17. Reid, 45.

18. Gordon A. Craig, *Germany: 1866–1945* (New York: Oxford Univ. Press, 1978), 424.

19. David Phillips, "Transitions and Traditions: Educational Developments in the New Germany and in their Historical Context," in David Phillips, ed., *Education in Germany: Tradition and Reform in Historical Context* (London: Routledge, 1995), 254.

20. Ibid., 255.

21. Fritz Kellerman, *The Effect of the World War on European Education* (Cambridge, Mass.: Harvard Univ. Press, 1928), 52.

22. Frederic Lilge, *The Abuse of Learning: The Failure of the German University* (New York: Macmillan, 1948), 145.

23. Kellerman, 52.

24. Lilge, 146.

25. Ibid.

26. Ibid.

27. Kellerman, 5.

28. "Friedrich Aereboe," in *Deutschlands, Österreich-Ungarns und der Schweiz. Gelehrte,*

Künstler und Schriftsteller in Wort und Bild (1908; reprint, Hannover:Bio-Bibliographischer Verlag Albert Steinhage, 1911).

29. 'Ali Hussein Pasha to Ahmed Hussein, letters, Amr Shalakany Family Archives.

30. Ahmed Hussein, "Der genossenschaftliche Bezug landwirtschaftlicher Bedarfsartikel. Sein Aufbau, seine Durchführung, sowie seine Bedeutung f.d. Einzelbetrieb u.f.d. Volkswirtschaft" (Ph.D. thesis, Landwirtschaftliche Hochschule, Berlin, 1927), 58.

31. Aziza Hussein, interview, Oct. 24, 1996.

32. Ibid.

33. Hassan Dawood, interview with the author, Cairo, Oct. 31, 1996.

34. Aziza Hussein, interview, Nov. 13, 1996.

2. The Professor and the Inspector

1. By 1950 the Cooperative Department within the Ministry of Social Affairs was composed of the following sections: the Agricultural Cooperatives Section, responsible for supervising agricultural cooperatives; the Agricultural Economic Section, responsible for supervising the economic affairs of agricultural and industrial cooperatives; the Consumers Cooperative Section, responsible for supervising the consumer cooperatives, the wholesale societies, and the petroleum, drug, thrift, lending, and building societies; the Auditing and Statistical Section, responsible for supervising audits of accounts, keeping statistics, and arranging financing by the Agricultural Credit and Cooperative Bank; the Social Welfare Section, responsible for supervising the welfare activities of the societies, disseminating propaganda about the societies, and supervising and sponsoring the formation of cooperative unions and advisory cooperative councils in the provinces; the Supplies Section, responsible for arranging with the Ministry of Supply and various firms and factories to supply the cooperatives; the Legal Research Section, responsible for registering and modifying the statutes and rules of the societies, publishing official notices and registrations, dissolving and liquidating the societies, engaging in necessary court cases, giving legal advice, studying cooperative problems, and generally dealing with any issues related to the implementation of Cooperative Society Law no. 58 of 1944; and the Administrative Section, responsible for supervising the clerical and administrative work of the Cooperative Department and its inspectorates, preparing the budget, and supervising expenditures. Ministry of Social Affairs, *Social Welfare in Egypt* (Cairo: Ministry of Social Affairs, 1950), 45.

2. Ahmed Hussein, "Brief Summary of Ahmed Hussein's Qualifications, Positions Held, and Some Facets of his Activities," unpublished, undated document, Hussein Family Archives.

3. When World War I began, the nominal head of Egypt was the khedive, 'Abbas II. During the war, however, he fled to Switzerland and was deposed by the British when they declared their protectorate over Egypt. The British installed Husayn Kamil as ruler in 1914 and gave him the title of sultan. In 1917, Fu'ad succeeded his brother, Husayn Kamil, and his official title was

Sultan Ahmed Fu'ad. The monarchy was not declared until 1922, when Fu'ad's title became King Fu'ad I.

4. Don Peretz, *The Middle East Today,* 5th ed. (New York: Praeger, 1988), 217.

5. Ibid. See also Afaf Lutfi al-Sayyid Marsot, *Egypt's Liberal Experiment, 1922–1936* (Berkeley: Univ. of California Press, 1977), chap. 2. The Wafd won 151 seats, the Liberal Constitutionalists won 7, the Hizb al-Watani (Nationalist Party) won 2, and independent candidates won 15 seats.

6. Marsot, 218–19. See his chap. 2 for full details.

7. Ahmed Hussein, "Social Reform in Egypt with Special Reference to Rural Areas" (paper presented at the Colloquium on Islamic Culture sponsored by the Library of Congress and Princeton University, 1953), 3. Hussein gives the date 1908 in Ministry of Social Affairs, *Social Welfare in Egypt,* 41. "Agricultural cooperative" is used to describe a system in which the farmers jointly own agricultural and irrigation machinery and in which farmers' credit and other agricultural and economic needs are met by the cooperative, rather than by the individual farmer.

8. Ministry of Social Affairs, *Social Welfare in Egypt,* 41.

9. Other cooperatives also eventually emerged for the production and supply of petrol and drugs. Ibid.

10. Ibid.

11. Ahmed Hussein, "Social Reform in Egypt," 3.

12. Hussein attributes this in part to Saad Zaghlul's interest and intervention. Ministry of Social Affairs, *Social Welfare in Egypt,* 41.

13. Egypt officially became independent in 1922, although the agreement with Britain listed several reservations on independence, including British rights to station troops in Egypt.

14. The Ministry of Social Affairs listed 135 agricultural cooperative societies in *Social Welfare in Egypt,* 42, but the table accompanying the text lists 139. Roger Owen states that "the Egyptian Government was also active at this time in trying to improve the conditions in which peasant agriculture was practised. Laws of 1923 and 1927 paved the way for an expansion of the co-operative movement so that by 1931 there were 538 societies with 53,000 members." Owen in P. J. Vatikiotis, ed., *Egypt since the Revolution* (London: George Allen and Unwin, 1968), 61.

15. Ahmed Hussein, "Social Reform in Egypt," 4.

16. Statement by 'Abdel Latif Amer, in Ministry of Social Affairs, *Second Social Welfare Seminar for Arab States of the Middle East: Lectures—Discussions—Reports* (Cairo: Ministry of Social Affairs, 1950), 375.

17. Ministry of Social Affairs, *Social Welfare in Egypt,* 42.

18. Ibid.

19. Ibid. The text of this source says 297, but the table says 514.

20. Ahmed Hussein, "Social Reform in Egypt," 4.

21. Ibid., 5.

22. Jacques Berque, *Egypt: Imperialism and Revolution,* trans. Jean Stewart (New York: Praeger, 1972), 407.

23. Ibid., 408–9.

24. For details, see ibid., 410–15.

25. Leila Ahmed, *Women and Gender in Islam* (New Haven, Conn.: Yale Univ. Press, 1992), 191.

26. Berque, 438.

27. Ibid., 442–43.

28. Ibid., 449–50.

29. Ibid., 451.

30. Ibid., 461.

31. For more information on the EASS, see al-Jam'iya al-Misriyya lil-Dirasat al-Ijtima'iya, *Al-Jam'iya al-Misriyya lil-Dirasat al-Ijtima'iya: Mahdiha—hadaruha—mustaqbaluha, 1938–1994* (Cairo: al-Jam'iya al-Misriya lil-Dirasat al-Ijtima'iya, 1994). This source says that the project started in 1937. Mohamed M. Shalaby says the General Assembly of the EASS decided to begin the project in spring 1939, the same year the Ministry of Social Affairs was established. Shalaby, *Rural Reconstruction in Egypt* (Cairo: Egyptian Association for Social Studies, 1950), unnumb. appendix. Assuming Shalaby's date is not a typographical error, the probable reason for this discrepancy is different dating techniques; for instance, the EASS publication may list the date the first step toward the project was taken, while Shalaby may be dating the actual beginning of the project differently. Shalaby listed the other projects of the organization as a survey of the causes of rural and urban poverty (begun in 1938), the al-Manayil and Shatanuf projects of village reconstruction (begun, he says, in 1939), the inauguration of the Social Service Bureau of the Cairo Juvenile Court in 1940, whose services, Shalaby says, "in making psychological, medical, and social studies of delinquent children, followed by sympathetic advice and supervision while readjusting to their home environments, have proved of such worth that the Ministry of Justice on March 22, 1941, officially recognized the Bureau and designated detention homes at some institutions. In consequence the Bureau is now a definite part of the Juvenile Court system." The fifth project of the EASS was the foundation of a boys' club in 1941 "in which children and young men found suitable means for their development so that they might become good citizens, capable of cooperating with other members of their community for the improvement of their conditions. The services of the Club are now extended to girls in the district. This club served another purpose as well, namely, as a training center for leaders who wished to help administering similar clubs."

32. Cited in Karl de Schweinitz, *Social Security for Egypt,* vol. 2 (Washington, D.C.: Federal Security Agency, 1952), 71.

33. M. Fouad el-Bidewy, "The Development of Social Security in Egypt" (M.S. thesis, Columbia Univ., 1951), 40. El-Bidewy cites a pamphlet, *El Rowwad Settlement* (Cairo: Press el Eetmad, n.d.).

34. Aziza Hussein and M. Riad el-Ghonemy, interview with the author, Cairo, Jan. 17, 1998.

35. Galal, in Ministry of Social Affairs, *Second Social Welfare Seminar,* 105.

36. De Schweinitz, *Social Security for Egypt,* 71. He says the group began in 1929. There seems to be some confusion about the date the group began. El-Bidewy cites a document in support of his date (see note 33 above). Jacques Berque says that the association began in the late 1930s and early 1940s and "included certain personalities who were later to play an important role: Muhammad 'Awad, 'Abbas 'Ammar, Sulaiman Huzzayin, Ahmad Husain, etc. It was supported by Ali Mahir." Berque, 641, n. 5.

37. Shalaby, appendix. Founding members (aside from Hussein) included 'Ali Maher Pasha, Dr. 'Abd al-Moneim Riad Bey, 'Abd al-Salaam al-Shazli Pasha, Muhammad 'Abd al-Khaliq Hassouna Bey, and Ahmed Negib al-Hilali Pasha, who later figured prominently in Nahas's selection of Hussein as minister of social affairs in 1951 (see chap. 3). See *Al-Jam'iya al-Misriya,* 24, 28.

38. Ibid., 29.

39. Edwin Muller, "New Ideas in Old Egypt," *Rotarian,* July 1946, 44.

40. Shalaby, 2.

41. Ibid., 17, citing "Dr. W. W. Cleland, original plan accepted by the Committee, the Association files." However, officials at the EASS told me repeatedly that they no longer keep old files such as these.

42. Ahmed Hussein, "Egypt's War on Poverty," *United Nations World* 5 (March 1951): 69.

43. Shalaby, *Rural Reconstruction,* says work began in 1939, but al-Jam'iya al-Misriya lil-Dirasat al-Ijtima'iya reported that work began in 1938.

44. See Shalaby, 29–38, for details.

45. Ibid., 28–39.

46. There has not been much written about the Shatanuf project. Although anecdotal reports on the reform projects in al-Manayil exist, no such reports exist from Shatanuf. Since Shatanuf was a larger village, the survey undertaken by the staff there took a longer time to complete (ibid., 29), and one might likewise expect that projects were slower in developing as well.

47. Ibid., 28–39.

48. Muller, "New Ideas," and other sources say Shalaby was a graduate of the Faculty of Agriculture, but Shalaby himself says he was a graduate of the Faculty of Commerce. See Shalaby, 18. It is likely that many writers took for granted that Shalaby was from the Faculty of Agriculture because all subsequent social-agricultural specialists came from that faculty. Ibrahim el-Menoufi was the social-agricultural specialist in Shatanuf.

49. Shalaby received his diploma in social work from the Cairo School of Social Work in June 1940.

50. Shalaby says this research was done thoroughly but never published. See Shalaby, 17.

51. Ibid., 22.

52. Ibid., 23.

53. Muller, "New Ideas," 44.

54. Ibid., 45.

55. Shalaby, 23.

56. Muller, "New Ideas," 44–46. This article gives an account of the al-Manayil project based on Muller's two visits to the village, one prior to the project's implementation and one six years after the project began. It and Shalaby's work are two of the few surviving anecdotal accounts of the program.

57. Shalaby, 23.

58. Muller, "New Ideas," 44–46.

59. Shalaby, 24.

60. Muller, "New Ideas," 44–46. Muller notes that "strings were pulled" to get the government to establish the school in al-Manayil, but he does not elaborate on this. It is possible that Hussein and some of the other influential board members in the EASS prevailed upon their governmental acquaintances to urge acceptance of the petition.

61. Shalaby, 24.

62. Muller, "New Ideas," 45; and Shalaby, 25.

63. Shalaby, 26–28.

64. Ibid.

65. *Al-Jam'iya al-Misriya,* 36.

66. Muller, "New Ideas," 44–46. There are no statistics available on the decrease in infant mortality. When I was in al-Manayil in the summer of 2000, many of the older residents of the village remembered Kabil. Both they and younger residents who had heard of the Rural Social Centers program from their older relatives often remarked on Kabil's popularity and nursing skills, always adding "and she was very pretty!"

67. *Al-Jam'iya al-Misriya,* 34–35.

68. The villagers had expressed an interest in the societies and had promised to join but had not paid any dues before that time. Shalaby reports that the shares were sold for 50 piasters each. Shalaby, 27.

69. According to the Cooperative Law of 1926, the minimum amount was LE 100. Shalaby, 27–28.

70. Ibid., 28.

71. Ibid., 29.

72. Ibid., 30.

73. Ibid.

74. Muller, "New Ideas," 46. Later on, centers also offered the construction of home lavatories for contest winners. Ministry of Social Affairs, *Second Social Welfare Seminar,* 265.

75. Shalaby, 33.

76. Muller, "New Ideas," 44–46.

77. Ibid., 45–46.

78. Ibid., 46; and Shalaby, 32.

79. *Al-Jam'iya al-Misriya,* 35.

80. Muller, "New Ideas," 46.

81. Shalaby, 36.

82. *Al-Jam'iya al-Misriya,* 34.

83. Ibid., 36; and Shalaby, 35.

84. *Al-Jam'iya al-Misriya,* 36.

85. Muller, "New Ideas," 46. El-Bidewy cites *Conference Report on Extension Experiences Around the World* (Washington, D.C.: U.S. Department of Agriculture Extension Service and Office of Foreign Agricultural Relations, May 16–20, 1949), 35, which gives a similarly positive opinion of the al-Manayil project and says: "Al-Manayel is well on its way of progressive development. It is serving Egypt as a model for similar improvements in other rural communities. In its story we find clearly demonstrated the superiority of the extension educational technique over the prevailing practice of effecting improvements in rural life by orders and regulations from above. We also observe the important role played by the pattern of local culture in a program involving social and technical change" (99).

3. The Ministry of Social Affairs and the Rural Social Centers

1. Peretz, 221–22.

2. Ibid., 222. For a comprehensive history of the Brotherhood, see Richard P. Mitchell, *The Society of the Muslim Brothers* (London: Oxford Univ. Press, 1969).

3. Ibid., 225.

4. See Misako Ikeda, "Sociopolitical Debates in Late Parliamentary Egypt" (Ph.D. thesis, Harvard Univ., 1998). Ikeda lists the following books as indications of increased interest in rural life: Mirrit Ghali, *Siyasat al-ghad* (The policy of tomorrow), 1938; Taha Hussein, *Mustaqbal al-thaqafa fi Misr* (The future of culture in Egypt), 1938; Hafiz 'Afifi, *'Ala hamish al-siyasa* (On the margin of politics), 1938; and Ibnat al-Shati (the pen name of 'Aisha 'Abd al-Rahman), *Al-Rif al-misri* (The Egyptian countryside), 1936, and *Qidayat al-falla* (The issue of the peasant), 1938.

5. See Berque, "Emergent Groups and Latent Classes," in *Egypt,* for more details.

6. Ikeda cites el-Ghonemy's article, which appeared in the February 1948 issue of *al-Mujtama' al-Jadid.* Ikeda, 37–40.

7. 'Abbas 'Ammar, *The People of Sharqiya: Their Racial History, Serology, Physical Characters, Demography, and Conditions of Life,* 2 vols. (Cairo: 1944). Cited and summarized in Ikeda, "Sociopolitical Debates." A portion of the work appears as an article: 'Abbas 'Ammar, "Conditions of Life in Rural Sharqiya," *Sociological Review* 32 (July 1940), 171–215.

8. Ikeda.

9. Berque, 485, 489–90.

10. Ali Fu'ad Ahmed, *'Ilm al-ijtima' al-rifi* (Cairo: Dar al-Thaqafa wa-al-'Ulum lil-Tiba'a wa-al-Nashr, 1960). This is a good account of the history of rural social service.

11. Ibid., 212.

12. Nancy Elizabeth Gallagher, *Egypt's Other Wars: Epidemics and the Politics of Public Health* (Syracuse, N.Y.: Syracuse Univ. Press, 1990), 13.

13. Foreword to Ministry of Social Affairs, *Social Welfare in Egypt.*

14. See Jeremy Bentham, *An Introduction to the Principles of Morals and Legislation* (Oxford: Oxford Univ. Press, 1996).

15. Adam Smith, *The Theory of Moral Sentiments* (Indianapolis, Ind.: Liberty Classics, 1976).

16. Roger Girod, Patrick de Laubier, and Alan Gladstone, eds., *Social Policy in Western Europe and the USA, 1950–1980* (New York: St. Martin's Press, 1985). For more detail on the theoretical aspects of the development of social welfare policies, see, for example, Edward Craven, ed., *Regional Devolution and Social Policy* (London: Macmillan), 1975; Neil Gilbert and Harry Specht, *Dimensions of Social Welfare Policy* (Englewood Cliffs, N.J.: Prentice Hall), 1986; Leon H. Ginsburg, *Understanding Social Problems, Policies, and Programs* (Columbia: Univ. of South Carolina Press), 1994; Raymond Plant, Harry Lesser, and Peter Taylor-Goodby, *Political Philosophy and Social Welfare* (London: Routledge and Kegan Paul), 1980; and S. P. Sen, ed., *Social and Religious Reform Movements in the Nineteenth and Twentieth Centuries* (Calcutta: Institute of Historical Studies), 1979.

17. See Joseph G. Jabbra, *Bureaucracy and Development in the Arab World* (New York: E. J. Brill, 1989).

18. Some efforts by Coptic and women's groups went beyond simple reactive service provision, most notably the Oeuvre des Ecoles Gratuites des Villages de Haute-Egypte, founded by Henry Habib Ayrut. According to Margot Badran, this organization included groups of women who "visited villages to learn about local needs and . . . [gave] basic instruction in health and hygiene, and [distributed] gallabiyahs (tunics), soap, medicine, and food parcels. The volunteers also gave peasant women literacy lessons. Before leaving an area the volunteers and local townswomen set up permanent centers under the society's auspices." Margot Badran, *Feminists, Islam, and Nation: Gender and the Making of Modern Egypt* (Princeton, N.J.: Princeton Univ. Press, 1995), 120–21.

19. Robert Bianchi, *Unruly Corporatism* (Oxford: Oxford Univ. Press, 1989), 64.

20. Ibid., 65.

21. Ibid., 72.

22. Peretz, 220.

23. Ibid.

24. Ibid., 221.

25. Ibid.

26. Ikeda, citing speech on May 14, 1945. See also Roel Meijer, "The Quest for Modernity: Secular Liberal and Left-Wing Political Thought in Egypt, 1945–1958" (Ph.D. thesis, Univ. of Amsterdam, 1995).

27. Ikeda, citing article in *Majallat al-Shu'un al-Ijtima'iya,* June 1944, 27–34.

28. Ibid.

29. Gallagher, 124.

30. Ibid., 125. Many women's associations had been active in social service provision since the 1920s. For a good account of the activities of these associations, see Badran.

31. Gallagher, 126.

32. See Ikeda for details of the debate on poverty from 1945 to 1952.

33. Ikeda, 37–39, citing Shishini's speech, recorded in *Madabit* (parliamentary records) of the Chamber of Deputies, Dec. 25, 1945, 362–63.

34. Ikeda.

35. Ibid.

36. Ibid., citing Sadiq Sa'd.

37. Ikeda notes that this plan was later included in a book al-Barrawi coauthored with Dalawir 'Ali called *Our Social Problems.*

38. Ibid., citing speech in *Madabit* of the Chamber of Deputies, March 1, 1948, 1066–67.

39. Ikeda, citing *Legal Fatwa,* June 8, 1948 (Cairo, Confidential U.S. State Department Central Files, 883.2/6–848, 3, translation). Ikeda says that although the preface of the fatwa does not identify the source of the document, Heyworth-Dunne attributed it to the Brotherhood. Ikeda, 51.

40. Ikeda, citing Muhammad al-Ghazali, "The Reflection on Religion and Life," *al-Ikhwan al-Muslimun,* June 5, 1948, 6–9.

41. Ikeda.

42. Aziza Hussein, interview, Oct. 24, 1996.

43. Aziza Hussein, interview, Jan. 28, 1998.

44. Aziza Hussein, interview, Oct. 24, 1996. Although in Egypt it is not customary for a wife to take her husband's last name, Aziza came to use Hussein as her last name. Foreign press reports referred to her as Mrs. Hussein and as Mme. Ahmed Hussein, and she became accustomed to this. Her father, however, was unhappy with this development, although Aziza told him that since his own father's first name was Hussein, she could (even sticking to custom) legitimately use Hussein as her third name. Aziza's father, interestingly, had also changed his name. The family name had been Dahroug, and while in school, her father was called Sa'id Dahroug. However, his teachers told him that Dahroug sounded too "peasant-like" and suggested he change his name to Sa'id Shukri (a name that sounded more Turkish and hence more upper class). He agreed; a brother also changed his second name to Hilmi for the same reason.

45. Ibid.

46. Ibid.

47. Ibid.

48. Muhammad was born in June 1923 and became a gynecologist. Hussein, who was born in 1922, was born deaf and mute and did not pursue a career. Leila was born in January 1925 and became a professor of anthropology. Esmat was born in 1920 and married and raised a family. Aziza herself was born in May 1919. Aziza Hussein, letter to author, June 8, 1997.

49. Aziza Hussein, interview, Oct. 24, 1996.

50. Aziza Hussein's mother, Hekmat Aref, died in March 1967, and her father, Said Shukri, died in August 1969. Aziza Hussein, interview, Oct. 24, 1996.

51. Ibid. Aziza Hussein also recalled one instance of this. Hussein loved to dance, and while a student in Germany he was quite an accomplished dancer. However, after marriage Hussein would not dance in public any longer because he did not want people to see his wife dancing.

52. Aziza Hussein, interview, Jan. 28, 1998.

53. Aziza Hussein, interview, Oct. 24, 1996.

54. Aziza Hussein, interview, Jan. 1, 1999.

55. Ibid.

56. Austin Moore, a Fulbright scholar at Farouk I University in 1951 and 1952, is one who falls into this category. He wrote that "during the late 1930s and through the 1940s the condition of the masses became so deplorable that the government was forced to put through a kind of new deal program. This included such reforms as increased public education, social security, and the establishment of social centres for recreation and health in the *fellaheen* villages. These reforms were enacted by a generally unwilling government which had the intention of using them as little other than sops to public opinion. Education was made compulsory for certain categories, but only on paper. A pitifully inadequate social security program went into partial effect. Roughly 120 of Egypt's 4000 villages received social centres. The reform program was, in the main, mere window dressing. It could not be financed without taxing the few great families who own most of the land." Austin L. Moore, *Farewell Farouk* (Chicago: Scholars' Press, 1954), 20–21. Comments such as these, however, are unnecessarily harsh. While it is true that the social centers program and the social security program were slow to develop, these programs were earnest attempts by competent government authorities to improve living conditions in rural areas. Nor are Moore's remarks about funding accurate, at least as regards the social centers project. It is strange that Moore selected two of the most successful (social centers and social security) prerevolutionary projects to bolster his criticisms of the pre-1952 government.

57. By 1966, the percentage of the population living in rural areas, while still a majority, had changed. The 1966 census showed a total population of 30,075,858, of which 17,691,356, or 59 percent, lived in rural areas and 12,384,502, or 41 percent, lived in urban areas. Central Agency for Public Mobilization and Statistics, *Statistical Handbook: 1952–1968* (Cairo: CAPMAS, June 1969), 9.

58. Ministry of Social Affairs, *Social Welfare in Egypt,* 11.

59. Beatrice McCown Mattison, "Rural Social Centers in Egypt," *Middle East Journal* 5, no. 4 (1951): 463–64. She based this on figures given by Issawi, Ayrout, Hussein, and the Ministry of Social Affairs. For a good summary of the conditions of rural life in prerevolutionary Egypt, see el-Bidewy, chap. 6. See also H. Sirgany in Ministry of Social Affairs, *Second Social Welfare Seminar,* 125–28, for a good summary of the conditions of life in an average Egyptian village.

60. Ministry of Social Affairs, Fellah Department, *Annual Report on the Rural Welfare Centers, 1942* (Cairo: C. H. Pallemans, 1942), 10.

61. Shalaby, 38.

62. Ministry of Social Affairs, *Social Welfare in Egypt,* 11.

63. Ibid., 12.

64. Dawood, interview, Oct. 31, 1996. Note that 1942 and 1941 are both given in various sources as dates for the establishment of the first six centers. Also see Fellah Department, *Annual Report.*

65. Isma'il Sidqi was asked to form a new government in 1946 in the aftermath of violent anti-British riots. When Sidqi became prime minister in 1946, he promised that he would renegotiate the 1936 Anglo-Egyptian treaty, thereby making Egypt fully independent and retaining Egyptian control over the Sudan. Gallagher reported that "although he [Sidqi] was unaffiliated with any political party, he was closely associated with the palace and with business and industrial interests and was considered a 'strong man' who could restore order." She also reported that Sidqi was largely unsuccessful in suppressing the anti-British riots and demonstrations and the increasing number of labor strikes and that the formation of the Committee to Combat Poverty, Ignorance, and Disease was perhaps "an effort to direct national attention to a less politically sensitive arena." Gallagher, 106–7. However, there were many proposals for reform in the 1940s, and in January 1946, the Egyptian press began calling for further social reform. In mid-January, prior to the state visit of King Ibn Saud of Saudi Arabia, articles began appearing in the Egyptian press criticizing the lack of government action on social issues, government corruption, and inertia and waste. The Senate also began pushing for more reform measures, including Makram Ebeid's call for individual income taxes and his criticism of the high rates of illiteracy and disease. The *New York Times* carried an article summarizing the criticisms of the Egyptian press. See Clifton Daniel, "Move for Reform Renewed in Egypt," *New York Times,* Jan. 21, 1946, 6.

66. 'Ali Fu'ad Ahmed, 214.

67. The committee was the subject of a Memorandum of Conversation between Radi Bey, undersecretary of the Ministry of Social Affairs, and William J. Handley of the American Legation in Cairo on Apr. 3, 1946. Enclosure to Dispatch no. 1452 of April 3, 1946, from the American Legation at Cairo, in *Confidential U.S. Department of State Central Files: Egypt, 1945–1949.* This memorandum reports the Egyptian view that the committee would be a positive step. American and British sources were more skeptical, noting the problems caused by population growth and lack of land reform and the failure of the committee to deal with them. Even so, the British felt they should contribute medical assistance to the committee, as Gallagher reports. Gallagher, 107. Gallagher reports that the Ministry of Agriculture submitted proposals for reform to this committee and says that the Ministry of Agriculture proposed expanding the existing Rural Social Centers program (107). Its proposal, though, was not for an increase in the number of RSCs. Rather, the Ministry of Agriculture proposed the creation of "agriculture units" that would operate in conjunction with the RSCs. The agricultural units

would help the fellahin choose the best seeds and get rid of pests and would provide stud animals, maintain a demonstration plot, create a nursery for fruit trees, distribute vegetable seeds, and create a veterinary unit and a slaughterhouse. Other plans proposed to the committee by the Ministry of Agriculture included improving drainage and improving seed stocks, increasing technical research, increasing pest control, increasing mechanization of agriculture, increasing cattle breeding, providing buffalo and cattle to certain small farmers, improving the land itself, expanding vegetable cultivation, providing decent housing for farm laborers, expanding agricultural and domestic cooperative societies, expanding cottage industries, and regulating "relations between landowners and tenants." Memorandum of Conversation.

68. Ibid. In this document Handley cites the *Egyptian Gazette* of Apr. 1, 1946, as reporting that Faruq's visit to the committee meeting was "only the second occasion in the King's reign that he had taken part in a meeting at the Presidency of the Council of Ministers." The *New York Times* also remarked upon this fact as evidence of royal concern for the fellahin. See "Egypt's King Pushes for War on Poverty," *New York Times,* Apr. 1, 1946, 13.

69. Gallagher, 67–68; and Memorandum of Conversation. In this memorandum, Handley reports that the Egyptian press in the week prior to the memo "carried glowing accounts of the improved working conditions that the King had introduced at the Royal Estate at Inchass." Handley also notes the following: "The recent visit of the King to one of the committee's meetings was, according to Radi Bey, very significant and indicated the concern which the Palace is feeling over the lack of social reform in Egypt. Radi Bey said that the King was very harsh in his comments on the attitude of many wealthy Egyptian landowners towards their workers. When one of the committee members suggested that visits by these landowners to the King's estate at Inchass might bring about a change in their attitude, the King said that he did not think receptions at Inchass would be of much avail, and, emphasizing his point by gestures, he declared that these landowners should be made to change their ways. He thoroughly approved of the law now under study [and which Hussein succeeded in having passed while minister] which will force landowners to improve the social conditions of their workers."

70. Memorandum of Conversation.

71. El-Ghonemy and Aziza Hussein, interview, Jan. 17, 1998. The booklet on the exhibit stresses the need for peasants to make more money on their own and stresses cottage industries as potentially "the most effective way of raising their standard [of living] generally." Ministry of Social Affairs, Fellah Department, *Souvenir Booklet: Exhibition of Rural Cottage Industries* (Cairo: Ministry of Social Affairs, 1946), 3, English section. Note the emphasis in the booklet on "safe" projects, the use of nonthreatening rhetoric to garner the support of conservatives, and the emphasis on peasants learning how to help themselves (the implication being that the government did not need to help them by, for instance, changing the land tenure system). The booklet is full of pictures of peasants engaged in uncontroversial activities such as playing volleyball, listening to the radio, planting improved seeds, making rugs, and so on. Another souvenir booklet on the RSCs themselves was prepared in 1950.

72. "Egypt's King Pushes for War on Poverty."

73. There is some discrepancy here. Some sources say five centers were begun, others say six. Hussein himself sometimes said five and sometimes said six. In a speech delivered at the Second Social Welfare Seminar for Arab States of the Middle East in 1950 (and originally prepared for the first such seminar, held in Beirut in 1949), Hussein says that the first five centers were begun in May 1941, and six more were established in 1943. However, the only source that lists the first centers by name is a 1942 Ministry of Social Affairs publication, written by Hussein himself while director of the Fellah Department, that lists six original centers. This list is the one reproduced here. Fellah Department, *Annual Report.* Also, Ali Fu'ad Ahmed says five centers were begun in 1941 and six in 1942. Ali Fu'ad Ahmed, 212.

74. The Pioneers, interview with the author, Cairo, Jan. 22, 1998. In de Schweinitz, *Social Security for Egypt,* 62–63, de Schweinitz, the chief of the United States Point Four Social Security Mission to the Ministry of Social Affairs in Egypt, related the story of how one man came to the Fellah Department to ask for a social center in his village. The official in the Fellah Department said that a social center would not work in his village since he was the only villager interested in founding one there. The villager then asked for a social worker to come to his village and explain the social center scheme to the people there. After spending two weeks in the village and giving nightly talks on the social centers, the people of the village were all ready to request a center. As de Schweinitz wrote, "The people were convinced because they were ready to be convinced. They had found the social worker to be a good neighbor and they therefore believed that the Social Center of the Fellah Department of the Ministry of Social Affairs would also be a good neighbor to them." This example is cited by de Schweinitz as evidence of the importance of the social security workers getting involved in their communities and determining the resources in their communities so as to be better able to serve the people. (The booklet was prepared by the Point Four team as a training manual for those persons working on the social security program in Egypt). It is also a good example of how talks such as those given by Hussein to explain the social centers project worked.

75. Ministry of Social Affairs, *Social Welfare in Egypt,* 12; on page 31 Hussein describes the procedure for financing the centers: "At the end of every year each committee prepares its budget proposals and programme for the following year. This is sent to the [Fellah] Department for approval and provision of Government grant-in-aid which depends on the enthusiasm and activity of the Committee which will have to provide an equivalent sum from public donations."

76. Hussein did use foreign aid for educational purposes, sending students abroad to be trained. His idea was for his students to go abroad for education and return to reconstruct rural Egypt. Examples of those who did master's or doctoral work abroad and returned to work in Hussein's programs: Hassan Dawood, M. Riad el-Ghonemy, Ali Fouad, and Salah al-Abd, among others. See also Ministry of Social Affairs, *The Fellah Department,* 31–32, for an account of overseas training missions.

77. Ministry of Social Affairs, *Social Welfare in Egypt,* 12.

78. Ahmed Hussein in Ministry of Social Affairs, *Second Social Welfare Seminar,* 263; and

the Pioneers, interview, Jan. 22, 1998. The Pioneers tell a story about one such incident. The *nazir* (overseer) of 'Ali Maher's estate came to see one of the staff in the Fellah Department in order to request that a rural social center be built on 'Ali Maher's estate. The staff member refused the application on the basis that the center would be dominated by Maher and not be able to function effectively. When Maher learned that the application had been refused, he was incensed and went personally to Ahmed Hussein to get Hussein to reverse the decision. Hussein not only refused to change the verdict of his staffer, he also explained the reasons for the refusal in such compelling terms that Maher was forced to agree with him and left, placated and in full agreement that his estate should not have a rural social center. Also see Mattison, 466. Mattison says that two other factors were also taken into consideration: whether or not the village had an agricultural cooperative society and whether or not there were "any serious conflicts between families which might obstruct the smooth running of the center."

79. Ministry of Social Affairs, *Social Welfare in Egypt,* 12.

80. Ahmed Hussein, "Some Aspects of Agricultural and Rural Life Developments in Egypt" (Washington, D.C.: U.S. Department of Agriculture, 1955), 7, emphasis in original.

81. Ibid., 8; the masculine pronoun for doctor is used here with precision—all doctors at the social centers were male. In Ministry of Social Affairs, *Social Welfare in Egypt,* 27, Hussein wrote: "The Supreme Council for the Fellah agreed when it was decided to extend these Centres that the Ministry of Health should supply them with doctors, but on account of their scarcity the Ministry has not been able to carry out its undertaking. The Fellah Department however did not remain idle; it came to an arrangement with various doctors living in towns close to these Centres to extend their medical services to the *fellahin* served by the Centre against payment from funds collected by the *fellahin* and subsidised by the Ministry of Social Affairs from funds for health services in the area covered by the Centre. The number of doctors with whom these arrangements were made reached 54 between October 1947 and the end of 1948." Also see Ahmed Hussein, *Rural Social Welfare Centres in Egypt* (Cairo: Ministry of Social Affairs, 1951), 22; and Hussein's statement in Ministry of Social Affairs, *Second Social Welfare Seminar,* 265.

82. Ministry of Social Affairs, *Social Welfare in Egypt,* 15; Mattison, 470.

83. The Pioneers, interview, Jan. 22, 1998.

84. Various sources gave different periods of time for the training course: Mattison (470) said four months; the Pioneers (interview, Jan. 22, 1998) said it was six months in Cairo plus 6 weeks in the field; other sources said eight months in total; and Hussein said four months in Cairo, two months in the field (Ministry of Social Affairs, *Second Social Welfare Seminar,* 262).

85. Mattison noted that since it was hard to attract educated young men to rural areas, "special incentives are offered him. . . . For instance, in addition to his regular salary as an Egyptian civil servant of his particular rank, the social-agricultural worker receives a free house in the Center and a special village allowance. Recently particular provision was made to pay him for overtime, since his duties are so heavy and of such a varied nature that it is virtually a 24-hour a day job. The provisions applying to the advancement of other civil servants are applica-

ble to him also and at present advancement is fairly rapid due to expansion of the work of the Fellah Department. To keep his interest stimulated and to prevent his becoming stale on the job, he receives frequent visits from experts from the Ministry and attends regional and national conferences where he may compare notes with his fellow-workers. Every two years he is sent to the Cairo School of Social Work for additional study." Mattison, 468. El-Ghonemy recalled that advancement in the Fellah Department was largely dependent on fieldwork experience—those working in the field were given priority. El-Ghonemy, interview, Jan. 17, 1998.

86. The Pioneers, interview, Jan. 22, 1998.

87. Mattison noted, "It is a big step for a young woman of only twenty or twenty-one to leave her family and move to a village to take up a job which will involve a great deal more than nursing. Consequently, special inducements similar to those offered the social-agricultural worker are also offered to the nurse—living quarters in the main Center building, a special (though smaller) village allowance, and overtime pay. As a government servant, of course, she is eligible for advancement under civil service regulations." Mattison, 469.

88. The Pioneers, interview, Jan. 22, 1998.

89. Mattison said that only males were allowed ("Rural Social Centers," 470), but Aziza Hussein and members of the Pioneers said both men and women were members. It is likely the women were members but did not participate in meetings to the same degree as men.

90. Ministry of Social Affairs, *Social Welfare in Egypt,* 31.

91. Hussein in Ministry of Social Affairs, *Second Social Welfare Seminar,* 263.

92. Ministry of Social Affairs, *Social Welfare in Egypt,* 32.

93. The Pioneers, interview, Jan. 22, 1998.

94. Ministry of Social Affairs, Fellah Department, *Souvenir Booklet,* 3.

95. El-Bidewy, 50, citing letter to him from the director general of the Fellah Department of the Ministry of Social Affairs, dated Feb. 18, 1950.

96. The Pioneers, interview, Jan. 22, 1998.

97. Ahmed Hussein, "Some Aspects," 9.

98. Ministry of Social Affairs, *Social Welfare in Egypt,* 16.

99. Ibid.

100. Ibid., 17.

101. Ibid.

102. Ibid.

103. Ibid., 18.

104. Ibid., 18–19.

105. Ibid., 19.

106. Ministry of Social Affairs, *Social Welfare in Egypt,* 52. Also see Gallagher, 124–26.

107. Ministry of Social Affairs, *Social Welfare in Egypt,* 52.

108. Ibid.

109. Ibid., 53.

110. Shalaby, 11, citing Census Department Pocket Annual Report, 1946. The total population was 19 million, based on the 1947 population census.

111. Ministry of Social Affairs, *Social Welfare in Egypt,* 27.

112. Mattison, 473.

113. Mahmoud Abdel Azim Bey, "Health Aspects of Social Welfare," in Ministry of Social Affairs, *Second Social Welfare Seminar,* 298. He also said that public health programs begun after 1945 resulted in significant drops in mortality rates but the drops were limited to the urban population, and he noted that "the mortality among infants and children between 1 and 5 years is alarming. It amounts to 50 percent of the total mortality rate of the whole population."

114. Mattison, 474; Ahmed Hussein, *Rural Social Welfare Centres,* 26. It is possible that the government's desire for more young men to be accepted into military service played a role in health initiatives, but it is more likely that Mattison and Hussein cite this statistic simply because it was one of the few ways of assessing health care at the time. Death rates and statistics on military service were regularly kept by the government, but more comprehensive health statistics were not.

115. Ministry of Social Affairs, *Social Welfare in Egypt,* 29. See also Mattison; Ahmed Hussein, *Rural Social Welfare Centres*; and Ahmed Hussein in Ministry of Social Affairs, *Second Social Welfare Seminar,* 265.

116. Ministry of Social Affairs, *Social Welfare in Egypt,* 22.

117. Ibid. Also, Hussein noted in the same source, "The Fellah Department made arrangements with Pont Limoun Sports Club in Cairo to train annually 40 young men selected from the different Centres on account of their exceptional qualities and ability to read and write. These men are trained in various games and club activities, music, and other means of entertainment. The first group completed their course of training in July 1949 and are working as Sports coaches in Village Centres under the supervision of the Specialists. Other groups are being trained annually until every Centre will have its own club leader."

118. The Pioneers, interview, Jan. 4, 1999. The trust the villagers put in the RSCs and their staff is also illustrated by a story told by Ahmad Fathi al-Diffrawy, another social-agricultural specialist and one of the Pioneers, who reported that the women of one village were to take a bus tour of Cairo arranged by the village's RSC. However, a problem arose when trying to find a suitable driver. The men of the village refused to allow a strange man to drive the women's bus. However, they agreed to allow the social-agricultural specialist to drive the bus because they knew him and trusted him with the women. Ibid.

119. Ministry of Social Affairs, *Social Welfare in Egypt,* 25.

120. Ministry of Social Affairs, *Fellah Department,* 18.

121. Ministry of Social Affairs, *Social Welfare in Egypt,* 25.

122. El-Bidewy noted in 1951 that "at present education is compulsory for boys and girls up to the age of twelve. Education up to secondary schools and including schools covering the compulsory ages is free as is also technical education." El-Bidewy, 140.

123. Ahmed Hussein, "Social Reform in Egypt," 2.

124. Also see Ministry of Social Affairs, *Fellah Department,* 18, and Ministry of Social Affairs, *Second Social Welfare Seminar,* 27–30, for a report on Rural Basic Education. This committee recommended rural schools be administered similarly to the al-Manayil model, although the al-Manayil project was not cited specifically.

125. Shalaby, 27. Also, a training program for rural teachers was begun in Egypt in 1946. The project was summarized by Mohamed Fouad Galal in Ministry of Social Affairs, *Second Social Welfare Seminar,* 105: "The establishment of rural schools in Egypt started in 1943, but the problem of training teachers who are specifically fit to teach in these schools was not considered before 1946 when the establishment of a rural training college near the Barrage was decided. It was, however, in 1947, that the initial steps were taken to carry out the decision. A farm fifty *feddans* wide, was attached to the school. The school was considered as a centre for research in the problems of rural education as well as a centre for training rural teachers. The Underlying Philosophy: the objectives of the school were formulated on a simple and clear basis, namely training those teachers who could carry out teaching in rural schools in such a manner as to train the rural pupil to be a good citizen possessing a deep understanding of the problems of rural life, ability to participate in the life of rural society, and an attitude of willingness to serve the community in a way which leads to continuous progress in the countryside."

126. Ahmed Hussein, "Social Reform in Egypt," 3.

127. Ministry of Social Affairs, *Fellah Department,* 16–17. The reason that classes were available for males up to age 25 and females only up to age 15 was not stated, but it is probable that several factors influenced this decision: early female marriage in rural areas, sheltering of girls after puberty, and the belief that males needed and would benefit more from an education than would females.

128. Ministry of Social Affairs, *Social Welfare in Egypt,* 20.

129. The Pioneers, interview, Jan. 22, 1998.

130. El-Ghonemy, interview, January 17, 1998.

131. The RSCs were criticized by ʿAbbas ʿAmmar in 1954 for not doing enough for village women. As part of his plan to reorganize the Egyptian village, ʿAmmar advocated that each village have a village center and that there be a female and a male social worker in each village. ʿAmmar, remarking on the activities for women in the RSCs, said that they were largely confined to health matters and that "social-work aspects are relegated to the background, and performed with amateurism and intermittent improvisation." See ʿAbbas M. ʿAmmar, *Reorganization of the Egyptian Village on the Basis of Regional Decentralization* (Sirs al-Layyan: Arab States Fundamental Education Center, 1954), 20. He cited the experiment at Sindiyun as one of two successful models for future social work with village women, the other example being a Fellah Department-WHO joint project in Gharbiyah in 1951, where students from the Women's High Institute for Social Services in Cairo worked with the village women to help them respond to their needs. After the revolution women were targeted for participation and leadership in reform initiatives to a much greater extent than before the revolution. For details

on some of the training programs begun to train female leaders in rural areas, see UAR Ministry of Social Affairs, *Training for Social Welfare* (Cairo, 1967), a booklet published for the Conference of the Ministers of Social Affairs in Africa, held in Cairo Apr. 10–13, 1967.

132. Aziza Hussein, *Women in the Moslem World* (Washington, D.C.: Egyptian Embassy Press Department, n.d.), 23.

133. Ibid., 24–25. An article in the Christian Science Monitor in 1956 summed up the project as well in part of its coverage on the activities of various women's clubs around the world. See Jessie Ash Arndt, "Women Around the World Build Better Communities," *Christian Science Monitor,* May 16, 1956.

134. Aziza Hussein, interview, Nov. 13, 1996.

135. Aziza Hussein, *Women in the Moslem World,* 25–26.

136. Ibid.

137. Aziza Hussein, interview, Oct. 24, 1996, and *Women in the Moslem World,* 26–27. Day care centers in urban areas did not develop at the same time, however. In a 1974 speech, Aziza Hussein criticized the lack of day care facilities in urban areas, saying that it was a major obstacle to employment for women. See Barbro Blomberg, "I Egypten Finns Kvinnans Rättigheter Bara på Papperet," *Arbetet* Aug. 14, 1974.

138. Aziza Hussein, *Women in the Moslem World.* By 1970, the number of nursery schools run by the Ministry of Social Affairs had skyrocketed. There were 601 nursery schools in rural areas, 351 in urban areas, and 26 in desert areas. The total number of children attending these schools was 46,998. The Ministry of Education also began a nursery school program, and by the same year, the total number of children attending those nursery schools was 12,469. Aziza Hussein and Nagiba Abdel Hamid, "Report on Egypt" (prepared for the regional conference on "Education, Vocational Training and Work Opportunities for Girls and Women in African Countries," May 17, 1971), 15–16.

139. Aziza Hussein, *Women in the Moslem World,* 27.

140. Ministry of Social Affairs, *Social Welfare in Egypt,* 14. The canvassing done by Hussein had been at the very beginning of the program, in order to introduce the program to the rural population. As centers were established and proved to be successful, the need for Hussein to travel around rural Egypt explaining the program was obviated.

141. For more details on the budget of the Ministry of Social Affairs, see ibid., 123; and el-Bidewy, 143.

142. Shalaby, 5, 11. American diplomatic officials believed that Hussein's programs in general were very long term and that Hussein was overly optimistic, given the larger structural problems in Egypt, such as the land tenure system. Speaking about Hussein's plans to decentralize the functions of the Ministry of Social Affairs, Jefferson Patterson said, "In this respect Dr. Hussein's hopes are based on the very successful experiments with the devolution of responsibility to local committees etc., in the Village Welfare Centers Program. Dr. Hussein's hopes in this area [decentralization of ministerial functions] as in other respects are very optimistic and very long term, so that in many respects they appear unrealistic by comparison with the present

state of Egypt. However, Dr. Hussein seems firmly entrenched politically, is energetic and shows good practical sense so that with patience and resolution his hopes may be realized. Whether or not in the long run the experiment is successful it is nonetheless an important and desirable one in a country where local initiative and responsibility have long been stifled by a centralized regime of only pretended effectiveness." See Document 883.002/5–349, 1949, in *Confidential U.S. Department of State Central Files: Egypt, 1945–1949.*

143. El-Ghonemy, interview, Jan. 17, 1998. El-Ghonemy stated that as early as 1946 Hussein established a research unit in the Fellah Department to collect periodically from the villages the data on wages, rental values, tenancy arrangements, and family expenditure.

144. Ahmed Hussein, "Social Reform in Egypt," 10. Hussein himself was a proponent of land redistribution even before the revolution. He was well aware, however, that tremendous opposition existed to any sort of radical reform plan. While in the Ministry of Social Affairs, Hussein formulated a ministry policy designed to gradually persuade the elite of the necessity of wholesale reform. Evidence of Hussein's own preference comes not only from his postrevolutionary praise of Nasser's land reform law but also from a conversation with American diplomatic officials where he expressed the view that lack of land reform was providing the communist movement within Egypt with effective ammunition against the monarchy. See *Confidential U.S. Department of State Central Files: Egypt, 1950–1954* (774.00/8–350, Aug. 3, 1950). Aziza Hussein, Hassan Dawood, and other former colleagues also recalled that the lack of progress on land reform was a factor contributing to Hussein's resignation as minister in 1951.

145. Shalaby, 4.

146. El-Bidewy, 68. Also, Ministry of Social Affairs, *Second Social Welfare Seminar,* 6. It should be noted that el-Bidewy also advocated national economic improvement, an increase in crop area, land reform, land reclamation, and industrialization as methods of raising the overall standard of living, although he viewed these as long-term solutions. He presented emigration and birth control as two further options, both of which he dismissed, birth control because of the cultural and religious difficulties he saw in implementing such a program. El-Bidewy, 75–76.

147. Hussein continued, saying, "The rural population reached the figure of about 15 millions living on an area of about 6 million *feddans* (acres)—an area which can by no means satisfy their needs, despite the fertility of the land and its abundant produce." Ministry of Social Affairs, *Second Social Welfare Seminar,* 261.

148. El-Ghonemy, interview, Jan. 17, 1998.

149. Memorandum of Understanding. Handley reports, "One of the problems that the committee has to solve, according to Radi Bey, is how to prevent overlapping of functions between the various ministries; for example, each of the ministries would like to establish a center in the villages, and this would obviously entail much unnecessary expense and cause poor utilization of personnel in view of the obvious overlapping that would take place."

150. Shalaby, 47. El-Bidewy agreed that this was a serious problem and called for making governmental positions in the arena of social reform and social work independent appoint-

ments, rather than political ones. For details on his recommendations, see el-Bidewy, chap. 7. Shalaby also suggests the creation of a new body to be called the National Council of the *Fellah* Affairs, which would report to parliament and "have the advice of the different ministries." The council, he argued, should be made up of technical personnel, experts with fieldwork experience, and "non-officials who have some outstanding position in their communities and some technical knowledge in the *Fellah* affairs." For more details of Shalaby's notion of a new governmental body to eliminate service duplication and competition, see Shalaby, 48–51. It should also be noted that after the revolution, the new regime did create a body called the Permanent Council for Public Welfare Services, which was similar to the one Shalaby envisioned.

151. El-Ghonemy and Aziza Hussein, interview, Jan. 17, 1998. This is also mentioned in Ministry of Social Affairs, *Fellah Department,* 11, and in el-Bidewy, 95. El-Bidewy mentioned this decision to coordinate the activities of the various ministries, although he makes no reference to whether the new body undertook any coordination projects. Later in his work, he stressed the need for further coordination efforts (146). Also, Ali Fu'ad Ahmed mentions this coordination program and the Higher Council for Workers and Peasants Affairs. Ali Fuad Ahmed, 215. Hussein mentioned this program in his 1950 speech at the Second Social Welfare Seminar for Arab States of the Middle East. Ministry of Social Affairs, "Second Social Welfare Seminar," 263–64. He also says that the reason Menoufia [Minufiyah] was chosen as the location for the coordination efforts was because it "is the most overcrowded centre in the country with a population of 300,000 persons, all of whom are of the small farmers' class."

152. Ministry of Social Affairs, *Social Welfare in Egypt,* 15.

153. El-Ghonemy and Aziza Hussein, interview, Jan. 17, 1998. Hussein mentioned this program in Menoufia [Minufiyah] in his 1951 book, *Rural Social Welfare Centres,* 12.

154. Mitchell, 218–20.

155. Ibid., 221.

156. Ibid., 36–37. The definition of the group as a political organization, among other things, came at its fifth conference in 1939. Mitchell noted, however, that the Brotherhood did receive financial contributions from the Ministries of Education and Social Affairs during the Sidqi cabinet. He says that these contributions were made with a view to supporting the Brotherhood as a bulwark against the popularity of the Wafd and the potential popularity of the communists, but that the contributions were funneled into the Brotherhood "as legitimate contributions to the education, social, and welfare services of the society." Ibid., 42. Law no. 49 also supports Bianchi's argument that the main purpose of the creation of the ministry was social control.

157. Ibid., 283–88.

158. Ibid., 289–91.

159. Ibid. See chap. 10, "The Solution: Reform and Action," for a complete account of the Brotherhood's reform programs. Mitchell cites *al-Ikhwan al-Muslimun,* June 18, 1946, 1. In this article, the author advocated that the village *'umda* should be reeducated and should fulfill these duties.

160. El-Ghonemy, interview, Jan. 28, 1998.

161. Aziza Hussein, letter to the author, May 26, 1997.

162. The Department of Health became the Ministry of Health in 1936. Gallagher, 10, 13. Ali Fu'ad Ahmed reported that Abd al-Wahid al-Wakil was one of the first employees of the Ministry of Social Affairs and was transferred to the Ministry of Health in 1942. Ali Fu'ad Ahmed, 212. His transfer may have had an impact on the competition between the two ministries.

163. Gallagher, 27. Also see Ministry of Social Affairs, *Social Welfare in Egypt,* 127 for a summary of the activities of the rural health units of the Ministry of Public Health.

164. El-Bidewy, 137. See el-Bidewy, chap. 9, for a more detailed summary of the various health services in rural areas.

165. Gallagher, 38. The increase in funds was a function of the malaria epidemic that swept through Egypt during this time.

166. Ministry of Social Affairs, *Social Welfare in Egypt,* 127; see 127–30 for more details about the Ministry of Public Health's activities in the monarchical period.

167. Aziza Hussein, letter to author, May 26, 1997. Also, see Gallagher for a good discussion of the three-way competition between the Palace, the Wafd, and the British in improving social and health conditions. Also see Memorandum of Conversation.

168. Gallagher.

169. Shalaby, 14.

170. Hussein in Ministry of Social Affairs, *Second Social Welfare Seminar,* 263.

171. For a good summary of how governmental programs, individual efforts, and the work of various NGOs fitted together in this period, see el-Bidewy.

172. Shalaby, 12.

173. Ali Fu'ad Ahmed, 212.

174. Shalaby, 14.

175. Ali Fu'ad Ahmed, 212.

176. See commentary by Fouad Abaza Pasha in Ministry of Social Affairs, *Second Social Welfare Seminar,* 159–60, for a summary of the services provided by the Royal Agricultural Society.

177. United States Department of State, *Confidential U.S. Department of State Central Files: Egypt, 1945–1949* (Document 883.40/6–2449, June 24, 1949, dispatch no. 627).

178. Ibid.

179. This resolution, Resolution 390D (XIII), "Use of Community Welfare Centers as Effective Instruments to Promote Economic and Social Progress Throughout the World," was passed by the Economic and Social Committee of the United Nations on August 9, 1951. The text of the resolution may be found in Official Records of the Economic and Social Council, Thirteenth Session, Supplement no. 12. Hussein stressed the importance of this resolution, noting that "Egypt became for the first time a country that offered technical expertise on a wide scale, whereas it had previously been only a recipient country." He also noted that the UN of-

fered positions to many staffers of the RSC project, and that various RSC personnel went on UN missions or took UN positions in countries such as Jordan, Iraq, Pakistan, Saudi Arabia, and Paraguay. Ahmed Hussein, *Summary of Qualifications.*

180. Ministry of Social Affairs, *Social Welfare in Egypt,* 31–32.

181. The Pioneers, interview, Jan. 28, 1998.

182. Hassan Dawood, letter to author, May 15, 1997.

183. The Pioneers, interview, Jan. 28, 1998.

184. Ministry of Social Affairs, *Social Welfare in Egypt,* 32. The reduction in the number of centers during that one-year interval was most likely the result of budget considerations rather than any comment on the worth of the program. Although the number of new centers approved varied from year to year, the project continued to expand throughout the prerevolutionary period.

185. The Pioneers, interview, Jan. 28, 1998.

186. Aziza Hussein, interview, Nov. 13, 1996; and Dawood, interview, Nov. 20, 1996.

4. Gaining International Recognition

1. Joel Gordon, "The False Hopes of 1950: The Wafd's Last Hurrah and the Demise of Egypt's Old Order," *International Journal of Middle East Studies* 21 (1989): 195. citing British ambassador Campbell and American ambassador Caffery. Campbell to Hector McNeil (Minister of State), Jan. 25, 1950 (FO 371/80347/JE1016/23); and Caffery, no. 18, Department of State Records, 774.00/1–650. Gordon reported that election results gave the Wafd 228 seats (54.5 percent); Sa'adists, 28 seats (16.3 percent); Liberal Constitutionalists, 27 seats (11.8 percent); Nationalists, 6 seats (1.5 percent), Socialists, 1 seat (0.7 percent); and Independents, 31 seats (14.6 percent).

2. Gordon, "False Hopes," 193.

3. Ibid., 196.

4. Ibid., 196–97.

5. Ibid., 197.

6. Ibid., 197, n. 17.

7. Ibid., 197.

8. Ibid., 196.

9. Ibid., 197.

10. El-Bidewy, 76. Hussein talked about the importance of this and other projects in a lengthy interview in "10 alif masaken sha'abi b-iskandiriyyah, tahaqiq al-'adala b-wad' jadad l-ujur al-'amal," *al-Ahram,* Aug. 2, 1951, 2. It should be noted that this project shared its name with a similar scheme put forward by Kitchener in 1913; the two projects were separate, however.

11. Ministry of Social Affairs, *Fellah Department,* 30.

12. El-Ghonemy, interview, Jan. 17, 1998; and letter to the author, Apr. 17, 1998. Also see

M. Riad el-Ghonemy, *The Political Economy of Rural Poverty* (London: Routledge, 1990), 160, 247.

13. Ministry of Social Affairs, *Fellah Department,* 30. Also see Fellah Department, *Annual Report,* 3–4.

14. El-Ghonemy, *Political Economy.*

15. Ministry of Social Affairs, Fellah Department, *Souvenir Booklet,* 17–18, English section.

16. El-Bidewy, 76, citing Ministry of Social Affairs, *Social Welfare in Egypt,* 135.

17. El-Bidewy, 80, for example, was against caps on ownership and in favor of progressive taxation, "whereby the taxes paid by the wealthy would be passed on to the needy by the state in the form of free services, social, health, and educational." He opposed wholesale land reform, saying that it would cause too much "friction and social problem[s]."

18. See Ministry of Social Affairs, *Fellah Department,* 34–35, for an outline of these proposals. The percentage to be expropriated from large landowners would be figured as follows: "The government—wherever the totality of land owned by farmers possessing five *feddans* downwards is less than a certain proportion of the "zimam" (total landed property of the village)—should expropriate against ordinary price the area in excess of this proportion from the biggest landowners. This expropriation will be effected according to a progressive scale rising in proportion to the largeness of the estate." The Fellah Department took an official position against the legal restriction of landholdings, saying that if the other recommendations were followed, "the expansion of large ownerships [would be] undesirable to big landowners. It is believed that this would make it unnecessary to issue a legislation on the restriction of large ownerships" (36).

19. Ministry of Social Affairs, *Social Welfare in Egypt,* 40.

20. Ibid., 35.

21. Aziza Hussein, interview, Dec. 3, 1996.

22. Ahmed Hussein, "Social Reform in Egypt," 6.

23. This plan is summarized in Ministry of Social Affairs, *Social Welfare in Egypt,* 113–18. For the full text of Hussein's report, see Ahmed Hussein and Mahmoud Riyad, *Mashru' l-taufir al-sakan lil-tabaqat al-mahduda al-dakhil fi Misr* (Cairo: Matabi' Madkur, 1949).

24. Ministry of Social Affairs, *Social Welfare in Egypt,* 114.

25. Ibid., 115–16.

26. Ibid., 111.

27. This law (Law no. 41) was passed in 1944. For more details on its provisions and the provisions of other labor laws prior to the revolution, see ibid., 61–71.

28. Ministry of Social Affairs, *Social Welfare in Egypt,* 111.

29. Ibid.

30. The law became effective in February 1951.

31. In the prerevolutionary period several laws were passed dealing with industrial and commercial workers. A system of workman's compensation was introduced in 1936 (and

amended in 1950) as a form of social insurance. In addition, Law no. 85 of 1942 recognized industrial and commercial unions and protected union members; Law no. 86 of 1942 institutionalized accident insurance for industrial workers; Law no. 41 of 1944 regulated individual employment contracts; Law no. 72 regulated working hours; a 1947 law regulated the proportion of foreign versus Egyptian workers; a 1948 law regulated conciliation and labor disputes; Law no. 76 of 1950 dealt with collective agreements; and a 1950 law dealt with compensation for vocational diseases. El-Bidewy, 44.

32. Ministry of Social Affairs, *Social Welfare in Egypt,* 109.

33. El-Bidewy, 42–43. He noted that in the struggle over which point of view would prevail, "it is interesting to observe the progress which one [viewpoint] made over the other group in their struggle for security through legislation. The industrial laborer had every advantage. The growing industries took him from the village to the urban area, bettered his standard of living, improved working conditions and he became a member of the masses. The movement the laborers instigated had its force and strength in their united numbers and their strikes made more effective their demands. The authorities were urged under this pressure to take steps toward a solution and to protect laborers in industries. The technical cooperation between Egypt and the International Labor Organization, which began in 1931 (Egypt became a member in 1936), contributed to the speeded progress of this movement on the part of the industrial laborer, and it left far behind the problem of public assistance for the benefit of the poor, or the majority of the population, who were scattered in rural areas. Of course the wealthy class, which owned most of the land, were less concerned with this problem because of the heavy tax burden a national public assistance program would impose on them. Consequently, the farm laborers were completely ignored and neglected and were further subjects of poverty, disease, and ignorance. Furthermore, the industrial laborer had the sympathy of the public authorities who were interested in insuring their rights in industries dominated by foreign interests. It should also be noted that the coincidence of industrial development with that of social welfare and general improvement of the state of the individual worker brought about an alliance of industry and social well-being. Laws were developed and passed for the security and social insurance of the industrial laborers and practically no law was passed to organize any adequate public assistance program and make it the right of every needy citizen" (42–43).

34. Hussein noted that three-quarters of the population live in rural areas and work in agriculture. Ministry of Social Affairs, *The Egyptian Social Security Scheme* (Cairo: Government Press, 1950), 2. The actual percentage of those in agriculture as of 1950 was 70 percent of the population. This accounts for the varying estimates of two-thirds and three-fourths. El-Bidewy, 59, citing *The Middle East, a Political and Economic Survey* (London: Royal Institute of International Affairs, 1950).

35. Ministry of Social Affairs, *Egyptian Social Security Scheme,* 2. Using the results of the social security survey and the 1950 population census, el-Ghonemy estimated the incidence of rural poverty at the level of 56.1 percent of the total rural population in 1949–50. See el-Ghonemy, *Political Economy,* 247.

36. *Social Welfare,* 109; and Ministry of Social Affairs, *Egyptian Social Security Scheme,* 3.

37. Ministry of Social Affairs, *Social Welfare in Egypt,* 109–10.

38. Ibid., 109.

39. Ministry of Social Affairs, *Egyptian Social Security Scheme,* 1.

40. Ahmed Hussein, "Social Reform in Egypt," 7. Also see Ministry of Social Affairs, *Egyptian Social Security Scheme,* 3. Other groups also were targeted for aid. As Hussein stated in "Social Reform in Egypt": "Provisions have furthermore been made for a considerable extension of the existing public assistance scheme in order that needy groups not covered by pensions may be taken care of, for instance, divorced women with children, widows under 65 years of age and partially disabled persons. It is the hope of the Government that these groups may later on be included under the Pension Scheme."

41. Ministry of Social Affairs, *Egyptian Social Security Scheme,* 28: "The legislator is aware that these rates are below the real needs of human life, neither is he content that the present standard of living should be taken as a basis for fixing rates of pensions, but he has to be modest in fixing these rates so that the state budget might not be too heavily burdened and that the balance might be kept between the income of pensioners and non-pensioners. He also has to bear in mind the standard of wages in urban and rural areas and to ensure that the rates of pensions were not higher or equal to minimum wages." El-Bidewy, however, argued that an inadequate pension is worse than none at all and recommended that the state limit the categories for coverage further in order to assure full coverage for those eligible for pensions. El-Bidewy, 111. He also made a number of other suggestions on how to amend the social security law and praised the flexibility and provision for amendment in the original law. For details on his recommendations, see el-Bidewy, chaps. 8, 10.

42. For a further explanation of the original goals of the social security scheme, including how specific amounts for pensions were set, see Ministry of Social Affairs, *Egyptian Social Security Scheme,* 19–52.

43. This is made clear by the language of part 2, which speaks of those who are entitled to pensions. Articles 26 and 34 state explicitly the conditions under which one can forfeit his or her right to a pension and the appeals and complaints process to address situations where one feels his or her rights have not been upheld by program staff.

44. Wizarat al-Shu'un al-Ijtima'iya, *Al-Daman al-ijtima'i fi 'ashura as'ila* (Cairo: Matba'at Shirka al-'alanat al-Sharqiya, n.d.). For further information about the details of the law, see Ragheb Butrus and Ibrahim Ali al-Mahlawi, *Sharah qanun al-daman al-ijtima'i* (Cairo: Dar al-Ma'arif b-Misr, 1953).

45. de Schweinitz, *Social Security for Egypt,* ii.

46. The booklet is divided into fifteen chapters. The first five chapters trace the origins of social security on the global level, one chapter sums up the new Egyptian law, and the remaining chapters address issues facing program staffers, with chapter titles such as "Representing Social Security," "Getting the Facts," "Clear Explanation and a Fair Hearing," "Organizing One's Work," "The Community and the Social Security Committee," "Learning and Using Commu-

nity Resources," "Social Security and Social Work," and "The Administration of Social Security as a Career."

47. Ministry of Social Affairs, *Egyptian Social Security Scheme,* 3–4.

48. A separate Ministry of Labor was not created until after the 1952 revolution.

49. Hussein was minister of social affairs from January 1950 until August 1951. He actually resigned in July 1951, but his resignation was not accepted by the king until August 1, 1951.

50. Ministry of Social Affairs, *Social Welfare in Egypt,* 63. The Labor Department of the Ministry of Social Affairs provided numerous social services to urban workers during the prerevolutionary period. Hussein was not directly involved with the department, but it is important to note the steps taken by the ministry in this area. According to the Ministry of Social Affairs in *Social Welfare in Egypt,* 65–66, written in 1950, "A special survey undertaken this year [1950] by the Labour Department on 150 establishments employing more than 150 workers, has shown that they provide their workers, who total 125,000 with social and medical services above the level laid down by legislation."

These services were of various types: "Nutrition: fifty-seven establishments, employing 70,450 workers, have built up dining halls, forty of which make regular meals available to 64,000 workers: the management usually sustaining either equal or greater share in the expenses. Another group, numbering 65, have canteens and supply their workers, approximately 116,000 with food stuff at wholesale prices. Medical services: employers are required according to present labour legislation to provide medical services to their workers. The above mentioned survey has also shown that 37 establishments, employing 83,430 workers, have overpassed the minimum laid down by law and established clinics with permanent staff of doctors and nurses. These services cover both the workers and their families. Cooperative Societies: cooperative societies receive equal attention in industrial establishments. Their efforts tend to raise the purchasing power of the worker by making available consumers' goods at wholesale prices. Fifty three such societies have been actually found[ed], the membership of which is 56,850. Pensions and Saving Funds: it is gratifying to notice among the workers a tendency to form provident and saving funds. Some 63 establishments, employing 90,310 workers, have established labour provident funds. Further efforts in this field are being made under the Social Welfare Section. These efforts protect workers against borrowing money with high interest in emergencies. Housing: housing questions have occupied a prominent place in the social and constructive policy of the Labour Department. Over 23 establishments have already built workers' cities and housing quarters for their staff and workers. These vary in type and accommodation according to the various categories of the occupants. Besides the vast workers' city of the Misr Spinning and Weaving Company at Mehalla el Kubra . . . the Kafr el Dawar Textile Company has followed its example and built a city comprising fifteen villas and three hundred and one flats for its staff and two thousand one hundred and fifty eight flats and dwellings for its workers. The Shell Oil Company has also established two hundred and eighty flats for its staff and one hundred and forty for its workers in its different fields. The government has built up a workers' city in a suburban area of Cairo comprising 1100 houses and is capable of accommodating 5000 people. This project when completed will count 6000 houses holding 30,000 people. Recreational Services: industrial establishments have reached outstanding results in providing recreational services for their staff and workers. Some 60 establishments, employing 27,810 workers have organised clubs, outings, summer camps, etc., for their workers."

In addition to these company services, the ministry itself began a relief section within the Social Welfare Department, which carried out activities such as housing the homeless, providing food and housing to victims of natural disasters, providing a measure of compensation to farmers whose crops or land were decimated by natural disasters such as floods and fires, providing assistance during disease epidemics, and providing assistance to Palestinian refugees (71–79). Also, the ministry provided various charitable services to poor families through its public assistance section, began a program of public kitchens providing low-cost, subsidized meals, was in charge of supervising reformatories and homes for the disabled and elderly, included a sports section that organized various athletic and scouting activities, and regulated charitable and philanthropic societies (80–108).

51. Ibid., 35. More details about future programs are included here. These plans also included land reform, but the source does not attribute the plan to any specific person.

52. Dawood, interview, Nov. 20, 1996.

53. Jon Alterman, "Egypt and American Foreign Assistance, 1952–1956" (Ph.D. thesis, Harvard Univ., 1997), 65, citing Harry S. Truman, "Inaugural Address," *Public Papers of the Presidents of the United States: Harry S. Truman, 1949* (Washington, D.C.: Government Printing Office, 1964), 114, 115. Also see Jon Alterman, *Egypt and American Foreign Assistance, 1952–1956* (New York: Palgrave Macmillan, 2002).

54. Alterman, "Egypt," 66–68; see Alterman, ibid., for discussion of the roots of interest in international aid policy.

55. Ibid., 74.

56. Ibid., 51–55, citing *Measures for the Economic Development of Underdeveloped Areas* (New York: United Nations, 1951).

57. The first United Nations Social Welfare Seminar for Arab States of the Middle East was held in Beirut in 1949. The information on his participation in these conferences was taken from Ahmed Hussein, *Summary of Qualifications.*

58. Attendance at the conference was seven hundred. Ministry of Social Affairs, *Second Social Welfare Seminar,* 6. For a complete list of participants, experts, and observers, see ibid.

59. Ahmed Hussein in ibid., 1.

60. Ibid. See committee reports, 27–81.

61. Ibid., 5, 7.

62. Ahmed Hussein in ibid., 2.

63. Gordon, "False Hopes," 197–98; also, Gordon's note 20: "A series of corruption trials initiated by the military junta in 1953, point to the areas of greatest abuse. The govern-

ment pressed charges against works minister 'Uthman Muharram [Hussein's relative] for ten separate cases, two of which involved Madam Nahhas as a codefendant. The court, which found Muharram innocent in two cases, stripped him of all political rights for five years and fined him LE 12,000, a fraction of what the prosecution sought. See *al-Ahram,* October 21, 1953. Sirag al-Din, whose trial quickly became a full-scale indictment of the Wafd and Wafdist rule, initially faced charges for conspiring to fix cotton prices, accepting bribes, allowing the King to transfer state funds abroad, and using public funds to pave private roads. The court sentenced him to fifteen years and sequestered his assets. (Ibid., 31 January 1954)."

64. Gordon, "False Hopes," 198.

65. Ibid., 199. See this article for more details on the downfall of the other "professors."

66. Ibid., 203–4.

67. Ibid., 205.

68. Gordon cited British and American diplomatic dispatches—Stevenson to Morrison, July 31, 1951 (FO 371/90115/JE10110/23), and Caffery desp. 223 (774.00/7–3151)—and neatly summed up the issue, saying "[Hussein's] sin was ignoring party interests in the assignment and promotion of officials. In June 1951, when Husayn was attending the International Labour Organization (ILO) conference in Geneva, the acting minister, 'Abd al-Latif Mahmud, minister of agriculture and a Sirag al-Din ally, nullified a series of appointments approved by Husayn. In place of Husayn's nominees, the acting minister promoted less qualified and ethically suspect party loyalists. Upon his return from abroad, Husayn sought redress from Nahas. Failing to attain a clear promise from the prime minister, he resigned." (Gordon, "False Hopes," 205). While diplomatic dispatches may mention Hussein's decision to resign as occurring after his arrival in Egypt and after no redress was forthcoming, the Egyptian press reports agree with Dawood's account of the sequence of events. As Dawood was with Hussein aboard ship, and the U.S. and British diplomats were not, credence must be given to the eyewitness account.

69. Dawood, interview, Oct. 31, 1996.

70. Ibid. Dawood also related another example of Wafdist insistence on giving only party loyalists opportunities for advancement. After Hussein had resigned, Dawood was nominated by the American government to participate in an international conference on rural reform at the University of Wisconsin, based on his work on issues of land reform while a graduate student at Michigan State University and his work in the Ministry of Social Affairs. The undersecretary of the Ministry of Social Affairs called American ambassador Jefferson Caffery and suggested another man, who just happened to be a staunch Wafd Party supporter, to take Dawood's place in the conference. Caffery categorically refused, saying that the ministry could send Dawood or could not send anyone, but he would not agree to any replacements. Dawood was allowed to go to the conference.

71. Ibid.

72. Ibid.

73. Aziza Hussein, interview, Oct. 24, 1996.

74. Aziza Hussein, interview, Nov. 13, 1996.

75. Dawood, interview, Oct. 31, 1996; and "Istiqala wazir al-shu'un, al-asbab alleti bana' alaiha al-istiqala," *al-Ahram,* July 24, 1951, 2.

76. "Ahmed Hussein yaqul lil-Nahas," *Ruz al-Yusuf,* no. 1207, 12.

77. Aziza Hussein, interview, Oct. 24, 1996.

78. "Istiqala wazir al shu'un"; and "Ahmed Hussein Pasha lan yetaraja'," *al-Ahram,* July 25, 1951, 2.

79. Aziza Hussein, interview, Nov. 13, 1996.

80. Aziza Hussein, interview, Oct. 24, 1996.

81. Gordon, "False Hopes," 207.

82. "Ahmed Hussein Pasha yurfud kol al-halul wa-al-wasatat," *al-Ahram,* July 27, 1951, 2.

83. Dawood, interview, Oct. 31, 1996.

84. Aziza Hussein, interview, Nov. 13, 1996.

85. "Kashaf al-star 'an asbab istiqala Ahmed Hussein," *al-Asas,* Aug. 18, 1951, 8.

86. Dawood, interview, Oct. 31, 1996.

87. Aziza Hussein, interview, Oct. 24, 1996.

88. "Min al-hayat: Sanf nadir!" *al-Ahram,* July 28, 1951, 3.

89. *Akher Lahza,* Aug. 1, 1951, al-rasm al-hazli (cartoon).

90. "Al-Nahas Pasha khabir 'aalami fi shu'un al-daman al-ijtima'i!" *Akher Lahza,* Aug. 1, 1951.

91. "Al-Fasad huwa al-ladhi aqasa al-duktur Ahmed Hussein 'an al-wizara," *al-Ishtiraki,* July 29, 1951.

92. "A Minister Departs," *Egyptian Gazette,* July 31, 1951.

93. See, for example, "Ahmed Hussein Pasha yurfud."

94. See, for example, "Al-Wazir al-mustaqil yunthur qabul al-istaqala," *al-Ahram,* Aug. 1, 1951, 2.

95. Gordon, "False Hopes," 205.

96. Ibid., 210, citing article in *Ruz al-Yusuf,* July 8, 1951, 3.

97. Dawood, interview, Oct. 31, 1996.

98. *Jam'iyat al-Fellah: La'ihat al-nizam al-asasi* (Cairo: Matba'at Shirka al-'Alanat al-Sharqiya, n.d.).

99. Ibid., 2.

100. Ibid., 2–3, 7.

101. Dawood, interview, Oct. 31, 1996.

102. Ibid.

103. Ahmed Hussein and Carl C. Taylor, foreword to "Report of the Mission on Rural Community Organization and Development in the Caribbean Area and Mexico" (New York: United Nations, 1953). Taylor was a leading American expert on community development. He held a doctorate in sociology and had been the head of the U.S. Department of Agriculture's

Division of Farm Population and Rural Life at the end of World War II. In 1955 he joined the Ford Foundation as a community development consultant.

104. Letter to Ahmed Hussein from H. L. Keenleyside, director-general, Technical Administration, United Nations, June 6, 1952, 1–2. The letter accompanied the United Nations Technical Assistance Administration, "Instructions Manual for Expert Mission to Survey Community Organization and Development in the Caribbean." The unpublished manual was given to Ahmed Hussein.

105. Hussein and Taylor, foreword.

106. United Nations Technical Assistance Administration, terms, 1.

107. Hussein and Taylor, foreword.

108. Ibid., 1.

109. Ibid., foreword.

110. Ibid., 2.

111. Ibid.

112. Ibid., 25, 29.

113. Ibid., 3.

114. Ibid., 3–4.

115. Ibid., 6.

116. Ibid., 23–24.

117. Ibid., 7–8.

118. Ibid., 6–7.

119. Ibid., 33.

120. Ibid., 39.

121. Ibid., 12–13.

122. Ibid., 36–37.

123. Ibid., 14.

124. Ibid., 30.

125. Ibid., 15.

126. Ibid., 22–23.

127. Ibid., 31–32.

128. Ibid., 45.

129. Peretz, 227.

130. Ibid., 228.

5. After 1952: Hussein and Gamal 'Abd al-Nasir

1. For a detailed account of how cooperatives changed after passage of the agrarian reform law, see Sayed Marei, *Agrarian Reform in Egypt* (Cairo: Imprimerie de l'Institut Français d'Archéologie Orientale, 1957). Part 4, "Agrarian Reform Cooperatives," is particularly useful.

2. Hussein el-Shafii, *Statement by Hussein el-Shafii, Central Minister of Social Affairs and Labour* (Cairo: General Organisation for Government Printing Offices, 1960), 18.

3. See Sayed Marei, *Agrarian Reform Co-operatives* (Cairo: Agrarian Reform Organization Public Relations Department, 1958); and Ministry of Information, State Information Service, *Egypt's Agricultural Policy* (Cairo: n.p., 1974).

4. El-Shafii, 23.

5. State Information Service, *Egypt's Agricultural Policy,* no page numbers in original.

6. Information Department, *The Revolution in Thirteen Years, 1952–1965* (Cairo: Information Department, 1965), 66.

7. Aziza Hussein, interview, Nov. 13, 1996; Dawood, interview, Nov. 20, 1996.

8. A 1962 publication on the progress of the revolution in ten years reported that "the social center, the benevolent societies, and the rural reformation societies under the supervision of the Ministry of Social Affairs, have reached the number of 273 institutions."—That is a total of 273 of all these bodies, not 273 social centers. *The United Arab Republic, Ten Years* (Cairo: Mahslahit al-Isti'alamat, 1962).

9. Gamal 'Abd al-Nasir, "Inaugural Address of the National Union," in Information Department, *The United Arab Republic: Achievements and Future Development Plans* (Cairo: Information Department, 1960), 138–39. See also Gamal Abdel Nasser, *The Philosophy of the Revolution* (Buffalo, N.Y.: Economica Books, 1959).

10. Information Administration, *The Permanent Council for Public Welfare Services* (Cairo: Société Orientale de Publicité, 1955), 7.

11. Ibid., 96.

12. James B. Mayfield, *Rural Politics in Nasser's Egypt* (Austin: Univ. of Texas Press, 1971), 182.

13. Information Administration, *Permanent Council,* 97.

14. This figure is in sharp contrast to the amount cited by the Fellah Department in a 1950 publication, which estimated the cost of each rural social center to be LE 10,000 plus LE 3,000 per year in annual operating costs. Ministry of Social Affairs, *Fellah Department,* 28.

15. Information Administration, *Permanent Council,* 97.

16. Ibid., 13.

17. Keith Wheelock, *Nasser's New Egypt* (New York: Praeger, 1960), 120.

18. Information Administration, *Permanent Council,* 100.

19. Ibid.

20. Ibid., 176.

21. Wheelock, *Nasser's New Egypt,* 118, quoting "Abdou Salam, a ranking official at the Permanent Council for Public Welfare Services, at a press conference on August 22, 1956."

22. Ibid., 119.

23. Ibid., citing a personal interview with the minister on August 26, 1958.

24. Ibid., 118–19.

25. Quoted in ibid., 120.

26. State Information Service, *Egypt's Agricultural Policy.*

27. The Pioneers, interview, Jan. 28, 1998. This remark was made by Ahmad Fathi al-Difrawy, who worked on both projects.

28. The Pioneers, interview, Jan. 28, 1998.

29. Ibid. This remark was made by Ahmad Fathi al-Difrawy, who worked on both projects.

30. Mayfield, 178. An example of this is Charles Issawi, *Egypt in Revolution: An Economic Analysis* (New York: Oxford Univ. Press, 1963). Issawi reports only on the intentions of the government and its stated plans for expanding the program. He praises the program as "one of the most important measures of their kind carried out in the Moslem world. . . . started as an experiment in 1939" (107). Georgiana Stevens also praised the program for its rapid expansion, saying that "to speed up the program of the Combined Rural Centers, the government has recently waived the requirement of contributions from local villagers and has furnished most of the support from state funds." Georgiana Stevens, *Egypt, Yesterday and Today* (New York: Holt, Rinehart, and Winston, 1963), 170. However, this overlooks the fact that it was the insistence on villager contributions that was one of the main factors in the success of the prerevolutionary program. After the revolution, the villagers became recipients of government charity rather than organizers of their own reform programs.

31. Mayfield, 179.

32. Ibid., 184, citing Tawfiq, "Bisindilila," *al-Taliah,* Sept. 1966, 19.

33. Mayfield, 184, citing United Arab Republic, *Research on Employment Problems in Rural Areas,* UAR, 21. A 1965 publication lists statistics on health services in combined health units, collective units, social centers, and health units. The total number of expectant mothers visiting all these units was 500,304; the total number of deliveries was 112,557; the number of visiting children was 704,287; the number of child inoculations was 371,697; and the number of house visits was 880,055. Information Department, *Revolution in Thirteen Years,* 112. The statistics given, however, do not address the points Mayfield and the UN survey bring up: the percentages of people benefiting or perceiving a benefit from government services in the villages. A government publication gives two tables of the projected percentages of population in each province who will benefit from anticipated centers, but it does not give actual numbers—all the information is speculative. Information Administration, *The Egyptian Revolution in Three Years, 1952–1955* (Cairo: Information Administration, 1955), 111–12.

34. Mayfield, 185.

35. Information Administration, *Permanent Council,* 118; and Wheelock, 121.

36. Wheelock, 121.

37. Ibid., 122.

38. By 1960, the Combined Units program received only a scant three paragraphs of attention in a sixty-page speech on the activities of the government in the realm of social reform given by Hussein el-Shafii, central minister of social affairs and labor in the UAR. El-Shafii.

39. Aziza Hussein, interview, Nov. 13, 1996.

40. Ibid.

41. See, for example, "Dur al-ahlayin fil-islah al-ijtima'i," *al-Ahram,* March 17, 1951, 4, which summarizes Hussein's remarks to the new ministers of social affairs, health, and agriculture about the direction of future social policy. See also "Jam'iya al-Fellah takaram al-duktur Ahmed Hussein," *al-Ahram,* March 20, 1951, 4, which summarizes remarks made by Hussein and others during a ceremony honoring Hussein. Both these talks were given after his confirmation as ambassador.

42. Aziza Hussein, interview, Dec. 3, 1996.

43. Aziza Hussein, interview, Oct. 24, 1996, and Dec. 3, 1996.

44. Dawood, interview, Nov. 20, 1996. See also Karim Shoukri, "Strong Press Support for Ahmed Pasha Hussein as a Determining Factor in his Acceptability to the Leaders of the Revolution," unpublished paper, American Univ. in Cairo, 1984, Hussein family archives.

45. Aziza Hussein, interview, Oct. 24, 1996.

46. Dawood, interview, Oct. 31, 1996.

47. Aziza Hussein, interview, Nov. 13, 1996.

48. Dawood, interview, Oct. 31, 1996.

49. Ibid.

50. Dawood, interview, Nov. 20, 1996.

51. "Al-duktur Ahmed Hussein yajtima' bi-wazirayn," *al-Ahram,* April 16, 1953, 7.

52. Dawood, interview, Nov. 20, 1996.

53. Ibid.; and Aziza Hussein, interview, Dec. 3, 1996.

54. Aziza Hussein, interview, Dec. 3, 1996; and Dawood, interview, Oct. 11, 1996.

55. Aziza Hussein interview, Dec. 3, 1996.

56. Wizarat al-Kharijiya, al-sifara al-malakiya al-misriya b-medinat Washington, Kamal 'Abd al-Rahim ila Ahmed Hussein (foreign ministry memo from 'Abd al-Rahim to Hussein), April 8, 1953.

57. Ibid.

58. "Safir Misr fi Washington yaqul: Wajhat al-nathr al-misriya salima wa-'amaliya," *al-Ahram,* April 23, 1953, 7.

59. Peter Edson, "More than Meets the Eye," *Washington Daily News,* Aug. 4, 1954. Reprinted in Egyptian Embassy, *Egypt in Two Years: As Seen by American Writers* (Washington, D.C.: Egyptian Embassy, 1954), 2.

60. Quoted in Leonard Lyons, "The Lyons Den," *San Francisco Chronicle,* Aug. 6, 1953. Reprinted in Egyptian Embassy, *Egypt in One Year: As Seen by American Writers* (Washington, D.C.: Egyptian Embassy, 1953. 7). Fetling here refers only to the technicians at the base, not to the more than 80,000 British troops who were still in the canal zone. The agreement when eventually reached did provide for the continued presence of British technicians, but in a civilian rather than military capacity.

61. Edson.

62. Neguib, quoted in interview, "Suez—or Else!" *Newsweek,* May 11, 1953. Reprinted in Egyptian Embassy, *Egypt in One Year,* 6.

63. Anthony Eden, *Full Circle* (Cambridge: Riverside Press, 1960), 274–75.

64. Muhammad Abd el-Wahab Sayed-Ahmed, *Nasser and American Foreign Policy, 1952–1956* (London: LAAM, 1989), 72–74.

65. Eden, 276, citing from his personal message to Eisenhower.

66. Ibid., 277–80.

67. Sayed-Ahmed, 79.

68. Eden, 281.

69. *Foreign Relations of the United States, 1952–1954,* vol. 9, *The Near and Middle East* (Washington, D.C.: Government Printing Office, 1986). Document dated May 11, 1953, "Dulles Visits Cairo." Interestingly, Dulles also stated that the United States was not in need of Middle Eastern oil because there was plenty in Venezuela.

70. Sayed-Ahmed, 82.

71. Ibid., quoting Princeton University, Dulles Papers, Box 73, Near East Trip, Important Point by Dulles, 1–2.

72. Sayed-Ahmed, 83.

73. Ibid., 84, citing NA RG 59, Top Secret File (Washington talks, July 1953) bilateral with the UK Suez Canal base (July 11, 1953), 9.

74. Ibid., citing NA RG 59 Box 4015 774–00/5–553, memo of conversation, Ahmed Husayn and Undersecretary Smith, June 5, 1953.

75. Sayed-Ahmed, 84.

76. Ibid., citing D. D. Eisenhower Library, Eisenhower Papers as President (Ann Whitman file), Dulles-Herter series, Box No. 1, Dulles folder, June 23, 1953, from Dulles to American Ambassador, London, June 17, 1953, top secret.

77. Sayed-Ahmed, 85.

78. Ibid., 86. Caffery was particularly concerned about the Muslim Brotherhood and its anti-Western orientation. It should be remembered that the Brotherhood was started in the canal town of Isma'iliyah, and its founder, Hassan al-Banna, railed against British occupation and its effects on Egyptian society.

79. Ibid., 87.

80. Eden, 284–85.

81. Sid Bost, "Envoy Says U.S. Missed Bid for Egyptian Amity," *Journal-Sentinel* (Salem, N.C.), Dec. 13, 1953.

82. See Sayed-Ahmed, 86–91.

83. Ibid., 91–92; the Turkey clause was decided earlier that year.

84. Ibid., 71.

85. Eden, 284.

86. Ibid., 288–89.

87. Aly Sorour to Ahmed Hussein, telegram, Aug. 2, 1954, Hussein Family Archives.

88. Selwa Roosevelt, "Society News: Reception Honors Pakistan Visitors," *Washington Star,* Oct. 21, 1954.

89. Stanley Ferguson, "Egypt Still Must Cure Economic Ills," *New York Journal of Commerce,* Aug. 4, 1954.

90. Sayed-Ahmed, 96: "The American scale of economic aid disappointed the Egyptian leaders, as they had expected at least $100m [million]."

91. Marie McNair, "Egypt Flies Her Flag High," *Washington Post,* June 19, 1956.

92. Sayed-Ahmed; and Fawaz A. Gerges, *The Superpowers and the Middle East: Regional and International Politics, 1955–1967* (Boulder, Colo.: Westview, 1994), 3.

93. Sayed-Ahmed, 97–102.

94. Dawood, interview, Nov. 20, 1996.

95. Sayed-Ahmed, 107. Mohamed H. Heikal noted, "There were to be no American arms for Egypt. In fact, the only guns ever to be supplied by the United States were the matched pair of silver-plated .38 Colt revolvers that Dulles had brought with him to present to Premier Naguib [during his visit to Cairo in 1953]." Even that raised eyebrows: "When Churchill heard about these pistols, he made another telephone call to President Eisenhower. This time he protested the symbolism of the guns. It was a bad sign, he said, and would encourage the Egyptians." Heikal, *The Cairo Documents* (New York: Doubleday, 1973), 42–43.

96. Sayed-Ahmed, 109.

97. Ibid., citing D. D. Eisenhower Library, legislative meeting, 9 Nov. 1956.

98. Sayed-Ahmed, 109, citing Interview with Ambassador Byroade, Washington, D.C., 1983.

99. Sayed-Ahmed, 109, citing 'Abd al-Latif al-Baghdadi, *Mudhakkirat,* vol. 2 (Cairo: al-Maktab al-Masri al-Hadith, 1977), 202.

100. Sayed-Ahmed, 110.

101. Heikal, *The Cairo Documents,* 51. Heikal was a journalist, editor, and adviser to 'Abd al-Nasir. He provides no citations for any of his sources in this book. He manages to portray Hussein as somewhat comically concerned about the effect of the arms deal. It should be noted here that Heikal repeatedly presents Hussein in a poor light, both in this book and in other works. When he published the original edition of his book *Milaffat al-Suwes* in Egypt, controversy erupted over a portion of the book in which he implied that Dulles believed Hussein was stupid. Aziza Hussein and Heikal exchanged words over this passage in the form of letters to the editor of *al-Ahram.* Heikal provided no documentation for the contention, whereas Aziza Hussein offered in rebuttal the following statement: "Henry Byroade, the American Ambassador to Egypt quoted Dulles as saying that Nasser has chosen the most intelligent man in Egypt and sent him to Washington," and she cited Hassan Dawood as a witness to the conversation. See *al-Ahram,* Nov. 12, 1986, 6. Heikal's response to the rebuttal was somewhat muddled; he merely stated that he stood by his original statement and did not intend to defame Hussein in any way. Therefore, it should emphasized that Heikal's statements about and characterizations of Hus-

sein should be taken with a grain of salt, particularly when no citations of documents or other supporting evidence is given. In addition, in his book *Cutting the Lion's Tail: Suez Through Egyptian Eyes,* Heikal states that Hussein was educated in the United States, which is untrue. He provides no documentation of any kind for this, either, nor are most references to documents written by Hussein or about Hussein footnoted, although in the preface to the book Heikal cites in a general way his own archive of documents as the source of his information. Again, these sorts of inaccuracies in his information about Hussein must be noted, as must the lack of documentation of sources.

102. Heykal, *The Cairo Documents,* 53–54.

103. "Egyptian Viewpoint on Arms Purchases; Egypt's Effort to Procure Arms" (Egyptian Embassy, Sept. 29, 1955, press release).

104. "Summary of Egyptian Ambassador's Informal Talk to Overseas Writers' Club," *Egypt News* (Press Department, Egyptian Embassy), Nov. 6, 1955.

105. Ibid.

106. Ahmed Hussein, "The New Egypt: Domestic and Foreign Policies," *Vital Speeches of the Day* 21, no. 11 (March 15, 1955), 1102–4.

107. Gerges, 36.

108. "Summary of Egyptian Ambassador's Informal Talk."

109. "Al-duktur Ahmed Hussein yajtima' bi-wazirayn."

110. Alterman, "Egypt," 211; see his chap. 5 for discussion of proposals leading up to the proposal for the High Dam.

111. Ibid., 222–23.

112. Ibid., 234, citing RG 469 DD Ops/NEA Ops/NE Central Files/Egypt Project Files, 1953–58, Box 8, Cairo to State, Dec. 21, 1953, Memorandum of Conversation between Muhammad Selim and Robert Carr.

113. See Alterman, "Egypt," chap. 5, for discussion of Embassy comments.

114. Ibid., 239–40.

115. Aziza Hussein, interview, Dec. 3, 1996. Hassan Dawood remembered that Gamal Salem would carry a revolver on his person to threaten anyone who did not agree with his opinion. Dawood, interview, Dec. 11, 1996.

116. See Alterman, "Egypt," chap. 5, and 249.

117. Ibid., chap. 5.

118. Ibid., 263–64, citing Egyptian National Archives, Foreign Ministry Archives, Box 698, Memorandum, Mar. 17, 1956.

119. Ibid., citing Egyptian National Archives, Foreign Ministry Archives, Box 397, Hussein to Cairo, Mar. 29, 1956.

120. Ibid., 266–73.

121. Sayed-Ahmed, 119. By this time, Israel had also recognized the People's Republic of China, as had other nations, and the Egyptian move came as no surprise to Dulles.

122. Alterman, "Egypt," 275–76, citing various documents. Note 156 reads as follows:

"Heikal reports the conversation in three of his books: in Arabic in *Milaffat al-suwes,* 449, in *The Cairo Documents,* 65, and *Cutting the Lion's Tail,* 110. Despite a liberal use of quotation marks, each of Heikal's accounts is different, although they all portray Hussein as something of a starry-eyed rube, which he certainly was not."

123. Alterman, "Egypt," 276–77.

124. Black, Dulles Oral History Project, 23, cited in Sayed-Ahmed, 120.

125. Dawood, interview, Nov. 20, 1996.

126. Alterman, "Egypt," 277; Alterman's study is based on British, American, and Egyptian government documents and gives a thorough account of events.

127. Hussein was not opposed to accepting aid from the Soviet bloc countries for the dam or for other projects, but he was completely opposed to accepting aid only from the communist bloc nations. Aziza Hussein, interview, Dec. 3, 1996.

128. Dawood, interview, Nov. 20, 1996. The canal concession would have expired in 1968. Heikal's contention in *Cutting the Lion's Tail,* 111, that Nasser told Hussein to buy a book on the canal is inaccurate according to both Dawood and Aziza Hussein. Heikal's condescending and rude remarks about Hussein here are consistent with his overall inaccurate portrayal of Hussein in this and other works, and like other remarks about Hussein these remarks are not documented.

129. Dawood, interview, Nov. 20, 1996.

130. Egyptian Embassy, *The Suez Canal, Facts and Figures* (Egyptian Embassy Press Department, Aug. 8, 1956), 7.

131. Signatories to this convention were Greece, Britain, France, Germany, Austria-Hungary, Italy, Russia, Spain, Turkey, and the Netherlands.

132. Egyptian Embassy, *Suez Canal,* 10.

133. Ibid., 12.

134. Ibid., 14.

135. Ahmed Hussein, diary (in Arabic), Hussein Family Archives.

136. Ibid.

137. Ibid.

138. Dorothy Thompson, "Eisenhower's Cool Composure," undated, unidentified 1956 article, Hussein Family Archives.

139. See, for instance, Marie McNair, "At Soviet Shindig: Americans Stayed Away," *Washington Post,* Nov. 8, 1956, C19.

140. Ibid.

141. Dawood, interview, Nov. 20, 1996.

142. "Egyptian Embassy Party Marks First National Day," *Evening Star,* July 25, 1953.

143. *News Review* (Beirut, Lebanon), May 14, 1953, picture caption.

144. See, for example, *New York Times,* Jan. 28, 1952, and Marie McNair, "Egypt's New Envoy Had Close Squeeze and Political Luck," *Washington Post,* Feb. 25, 1953. The problem of

the two Ahmed Husseins is a recurring one (even in newspaper indexes and references in various books in both English and Arabic), which can cause considerable frustration for the researcher.

145. "Mme. Hussein Hostess," *Evening Star,* May 5, 1953.

146. Ruth Dean, "Egyptian Embassy Opens Door to Its Art," undated, unidentified 1955 newspaper article, Hussein family archives.

147. See, for example, Egyptian Embassy, *Egypt in One Year;* Egyptian Embassy, *Egypt in Two Years;* Egyptian Embassy, *Egypt: The Youngest Republic in the World, 6000 Years Old* (Washington, D.C.: Egyptian Embassy Press Department, 1954); and Egyptian Embassy, *Egypt: As Told to an American Boy by Two Egyptian Children* (Washington, D.C.: Egyptian Embassy Press Department, 1957).

148. Dawood, interview, Nov. 20, 1996.

149. Katherine Maguire Rafferty, interview with the author via e-mail, Feb. 22, 1999. Rafferty was Hussein's secretary in the Embassy.

150. Dawood, interview, Nov. 20, 1996.

151. "Husseins Returning," *Washington Star,* Feb. 1, 1954.

152. Marie McNair, "Two Down, One to Go in Egyptian Holiday Celebration," *Washington Post,* July 24, 1953.

153. Aziza Hussein's sister Leila Shukri, who was at the time a graduate student at Cornell University, was also a popular subject of media stories when in town. Shukri's intelligence and beauty both drew favorable comment, as did her subject of study—anthropology. An oft-repeated story in the media was that when Shukri first went to live among the Navajos in New Mexico, she was so similar in facial structure to the Navajos that they mistook her for a Native American. Leila's completion of her doctorate at Cornell was also a newsworthy item.

154. "New Role of Women of Egypt Outlined," *Evening Star,* June 3, 1954.

155. *Christian Science Monitor,* article, undated, Hussein Family Archives.

156. Mary Dougherty, "Social Whirl, Mary-Go-Round," *Chicago Sun-Times,* June 1954, 34.

157. Selwa Roosevelt, "Mme. Hussein to Speak," *Evening Star,* 1955, Hussein Family Archives.

158. Hussein spoke in a number of cities, including Baton Rouge, Pittsburgh, Philadelphia, Chicago, Portland (Oregon), San Francisco, Los Angeles, New Orleans, and Washington, D.C. This tour was sponsored by the American Friends of the Middle East.

159. Selwa Roosevelt, "Mme. Ahmed Hussein Addresses Democrats," *Evening Star,* Feb. 15, 1955.

160. " 'Face Social Ills' says Egyptian Leader," *Chicago Maroon,* June 1954, Hussein Family Archives.

161. *Wausau Daily Record* (Wausau, Wis.), Sept. 26, 1956. This article is similar to a *New York Times* article by Bess Furman, "Peace Plea Made by Mme. Hussein," undated, Hussein Family Archives.

162. "Sees 'British Suez' Aid to Reds," *Utica Observer-Dispatch,* July 15, 1953.

163. "Who's Who Cooks," *Good Housekeeping,* Sept. 1955, 11.

164. See, for instance, Dorothy McCardle, "It's Not All Protocol on Embassy Row," *Washington Post,* Aug. 16, 1953.

165. The medal was given only to women, and only ten women could hold it at any one time. Incidentally, Jefferson Caffery's wife had previously been awarded the medal, making her the only foreign woman to hold the medal. Caffery was American ambassador to Egypt.

166. Dawood, interview, Jan. 2, 1999. Aziza Hussein also remembers Hussein only crying once—when his mother died. Both stories illustrate how important family was to Hussein. Aziza Hussein, interview, Jan. 3, 1999.

6. Hussein's Legacy

1. Aziza Hussein, interview, Dec. 3, 1996.

2. Ibid.

3. Dawood, interview, Nov. 20, 1996; and Aziza Hussein, interview, Dec. 3, 1996.

4. Dawood, interview, Nov. 20, 1996.

5. Aziza Hussein, interview, Dec. 3, 1996.

6. Amelia Young, "Ambassador Hussein's Recall Dismays Friends," *Evening Star,* Mar. 20, 1958, A26. Hussein was replaced in Washington by Mustafa Kamel, who had been Egyptian ambassador to India from 1955 to 1958.

7. Aziza Hussein, interview, Dec. 3, 1996.

8. Dawood, interview, Oct. 31, 1996.

9. "Wisam al-istihqaq al-duktur Ahmed Hussein," *al-Ahram,* June 5, 1958, 4. It is interesting to note that Hussein's retirement from the diplomatic corps got scant press attention. This is in sharp contrast to the journalistic uproar eight years earlier when Hussein resigned from the Wafdist cabinet.

10. Aziza Hussein, interview, Dec. 3, 1996.

11. Ibid.

12. Aziza Hussein, interview, Dec. 8, 1996.

13. Dawood, interview, Dec. 11, 1996.

14. Aziza Hussein, interview, Dec. 8, 1996.

15. Dawood, interview, Nov. 20, 1996.

16. Aziza Hussein, interview, Dec. 3, 1996.

17. Aziza Hussein, interview, Oct. 24, 1996.

18. Aziza Hussein and el-Ghonemy, interview, Jan. 28, 1998.

19. Ibid.

20. Aziza Hussein, interview, Oct. 24, 1996.

21. Aziza Hussein and el-Ghonemy, interview, Jan. 28, 1998.

22. Dawood, interview, Oct. 31, 1996.

23. Aziza Hussein, interview, Dec. 31, 1998.

24. Aziza Hussein, interview, Jan. 1, 1999.

25. Dawood, interview, Dec. 11, 1996, and Jan. 1, 1999.

26. Ibid.; and Aziza Hussein, interview, Dec. 8, 1996.

27. Hussein died of natural causes in 1984. Hussein's brother Abdul Aziz Hussein died two months before Hussein himself, and Aziza Hussein says that his brother's death had an adverse effect on Hussein's own health. Aziza Hussein, interview, Oct. 24, 1996.

28. Dawood, interview, Dec. 11, 1996.

29. Dawood, interview, Oct. 31, 1996.

30. The Pioneers, interview, Jan. 22, 1998.

31. Dawood, interview, Dec. 11, 1996.

32. The Pioneers, not attributed, told to Aziza Hussein during 1997 meeting; retold to the author by Aziza Hussein and el-Ghonemy, interview, Jan. 17, 1998.

33. The Pioneers, 1997 meeting notes, Hussein Family Archives.

34. Samir Eleish, executive director of the NCPD, interview with the author, Cairo, Dec. 31, 1998.

35. El-Ghonemy, interview, Jan. 17, 1998.

36. Aziza Hussein, interview, Dec. 31, 1998.

37. See Ministry of Local Administration, *Shrouk* (Cairo: Ministry of Local Administration and ORDEV, n.d.).

38. See ibid.; and Ibrahim Muharram, *Shuruq: Al-Tanmiyyah al-rifiyyah.* Cairo: Matabi' Dar al-Ta'aun lil-Taba' wa-al-Nashr, 1997.

39. Aziza Hussein, interview, Jan. 27, 1998.

Glossary

ardeb: a measure of dry weight.
baladi: "popular" or "native."
birsim: Egyptian clover.
bey: a title of nobility, lower than *pasha.*
eid: feast, festival, or holiday.
fatwa: formal legal opinion in Islam.
feddan: a measure of land area equivalent to 1.025 acres.
fellah: peasant or small farmer (plural: *fellahin*).
Hochschule: German technical university.
infitah: opening.
'izba: country estate.
markaz: an administrative district, subdivision of a ***mudiriya.***
millieme: a unit of Egyptian currency.
mudiriya: a province in Egypt.
mufti: title of a religious official; one who delivers formal legal opinions.
'umda: mayor or headman of a village.
pasha: a title of nobility, higher than *bey.*
piaster: a unit of Egyptian currency equivalent to 100 milliemes.
pound (LE): a unit of Egyptian currency equivalent to 100 piasters.*
qantar: a measure of varying weight comprised of 100 ***ratl;*** roughly equal to 44.93 kilograms (in Egypt).
sharia: the revealed or canonical law of Islam.
waqf: a charitable endowment (plural: *awqaf*).

*Until 1949, LE 1 = US$4.12; after 1949, LE 1 = US$2.87.

Bibliography

Archival Sources

Hussein, Ahmed, and Aziza Hussein. Papers. Letters, speeches, university lectures, diaries, photographs, press clippings, embassy dispatches, and government documents. Cairo.

Shalakany, Amr. Papers. Private archive of photographs, letters, and press clippings. Cairo.

Publications in European Languages

'Abd al-Nasir, Gamal. See Nasser, Gamal Abdel.

Adams, John Boman. "Culture and Conflict in an Egyptian Village." *American Anthropologist* 59, no. 2 (Apr. 1957): 225–35.

Adams, Sherman. *Firsthand Report, the Story of the Eisenhower Administration.* New York: Harper, 1961.

Aereboe, Friedrich. *Allgemeine Landwirtschaftliche Betriebslehre.* Berlin: Paul Parey, 1923.

"Aereboe, Friedrich." "Deutschlands, Österreich-Ungarns und der Schweiz Gelehrte, Künstler und Schriftsteller in Wort und Bild," 1908. Reprint, Hannover:Bio-Bibliographischer Verlag Albert Steinhage, 1911.

Ahmed, Leila. *Women and Gender in Islam.* New Haven, Conn.: Yale Univ. Press, 1992.

Ammar, Abbas M. "Conditions of Life in Rural Sharqiya." *The Sociological Review* 32 (July 1940): 171–215.

———. *Reorganization of the Egyptian Village on the Basis of Regional Decentralization.* Sirs al-Layyan: Arab States Fundamental Education Center, 1954.

Arndt, Jessie Ash. "Women Around the World Build Better Communities." *Christian Science Monitor,* May 16, 1956.

Aronson, Geoffrey. *From Sideshow to Center Stage: U.S. Policy Toward Egypt, 1946–1956.* Boulder, Colo.: Lynne Rienner, 1986.

Ayrout, Henry Habib. *The Fellaheen.* Cairo: n.p., 1954.

"Aziza Hussein." *Who's Who in the United Nations and Related Agencies.* 1st ed. New York: Arno Press, 1975.

Badeau, John S. "U.S.A. and U.A.R.: A Crisis in Confidence." *Foreign Affairs* 43, no. 2 (Jan. 1965): 281–96.

Badran, Margot. *Feminists, Islam, and Nation: Gender and the Making of Modern Egypt.* Princeton, N.J.: Princeton Univ. Press, 1995.

Badry, M. A., and Ahmed Hussein. *A Statistical Report on Commercial Workers and the Effect of the Minimum Wage Scheme on their Wages.* Cairo: Imprimerie Mondiale, 1953.

Baker, Raymond William. *Egypt's Uncertain Revolution under Nasser and Sadat.* Cambridge, Mass.: Harvard Univ. Press, 1979.

Baram, Phillip J. *The Department of State in the Middle East, 1919–1945.* Philadelphia: Univ. of Pennsylvania Press, 1978.

Beal, John Robinson. *John Foster Dulles: 1888–1959.* Westport, Conn.: Greenwood, 1959.

Beattie, Kirk J. *Egypt During the Nasser Years: Ideology, Politics, and Civil Society.* Boulder, Colo.: Westview, 1994.

Beinin, Joel, and Zachary Lockman. *Workers on the Nile: Nationalism, Communism, Islam, and the Egyptian Working Class, 1882–1954.* Princeton, N.J.: Princeton Univ. Press, 1987.

Bentham, Jeremy. *An Introduction to the Principles of Morals and Legislation.* Oxford: Oxford Univ. Press, 1996.

Berque, Jacques. *Egypt: Imperialism and Revolution.* Translated by Jean Stewart. New York: Praeger, 1972.

Bianchi, Robert. *Unruly Corporatism.* Oxford: Oxford Univ. Press, 1989.

Blackman, Winifred Susan. *The Fellahin of Upper Egypt.* London: G. G. Harrap, 1927.

Blomberg, Barbro. "I Egypten Finns Kvinnans Rättigheter Bara på Papperet." *Arbetet,* Aug. 14, 1974.

Bogardus, Emory S. "Social Change in Egypt." *Sociology and Social Research* 39 (May 1955): 328–33.

Brinton, Jasper Yeates. *The American Effort in Egypt.* Alexandria, Egypt: n.p., 1972.

Burns, William J. *Economic Aid and American Foreign Policy Toward Egypt, 1955–1981.* Albany: State Univ. of New York Press, 1985.

Central Agency for Public Mobilization and Statistics, *Statistical Handbook: 1952–1968.* Cairo: CAPMAS, June 1969.

Cleland, Wendell. *The Population Problem in Egypt.* Lancaster, Pa.: Science Printing Press Company, 1936.

Cooper, Chester L. *The Lion's Last Roar: Suez, 1956.* New York: Harper and Row, 1978.

Cooper, Mark N. *The Transformation of Egypt.* London: Croom Helm, 1982.

Craig, Gordon A. *Germany: 1866–1945.* New York: Oxford Univ. Press, 1978.

Crouchley, Arthur Edwin. *The Economic Development of Modern Egypt.* London: Longmans, 1938.

Dawood, Hassan Aly. "Agrarian Reform in Egypt: A Case Study." *Current History* 30, no. 178 (June 1956): 331–38.

Deeb, Marius. *Party Politics in Egypt: The Wafd and Its Rivals, 1936–1939.* London: Ithaca Press for the Middle East Centre, St. Antony's College, Oxford, 1979.

De Schweinitz, Karl. *Social Security for Egypt.* Vol. 2. Washington, D.C.: Federal Security Agency, 1952.

Dillick, Sidney. *Community Organization for Neighborhood Development Past and Present.* New York: William Morrow, 1953.

Eden, Anthony. *Full Circle.* Cambridge: Riverside, 1960.

Egyptian Embassy. *Anglo-French-Israeli Aggression Against Egypt.* Washington, D.C.: Egyptian Embassy Press Department, n.d.

———. *Egypt: As Told to an American Boy by Two Egyptian Children.* Washington, D.C.: Egyptian Embassy Press Department, 1957.

———. *Egypt in One Year: As Seen by American Writers.* Washington, D.C.: Egyptian Embassy, 1953.

———.*Egypt in Two Years: As Seen by American Writers.* Washington, D.C.: Egyptian Embassy, 1954.

———. *Egypt: The Youngest Republic in the World, 6000 Years Old.* Washington, D.C.: Egyptian Embassy Press Department, 1954.

———. *The Suez Canal, Facts and Figures.* Washington, D.C.: Egyptian Embassy Press Department, 1956.

"Egypt since the Coup d'Etat of 1952." *The World Today* 10, no. 4 (Apr. 1954), 140–49.

"Egypt's Rural Welfare Centres." *International Labour Review* 61, no. 1 (Jan. 1950): 59–64.

"Egypt Wars on Misery." *Rotarian,* Sept. 1951, 18–20.

Feiner, Leon. "The Aswan Dam Development Project." *Middle East Journal* 6, no. 4 (1952): 464–67.

Feis, Herbert. "Suez Scenario: A Lamentable Tale." *Foreign Affairs* 38, no. 1/4 (July 1960): 598–612.

Francis, René. *Social Welfare in Egypt.* Cairo: Imprimerie Misr, S.A.E., n.d.

Gadalla, Saad M. *Land Reform in Relation to Social Development: Egypt.* Columbia: Univ. of Missouri Press, 1962.

Gallagher, Nancy Elizabeth. *Egypt's Other Wars: Epidemics and the Politics of Public Health.* Syracuse, N.Y.: Syracuse Univ. Press, 1990.

Garzouzi, Eva. *Old Ills and New Remedies in Egypt.* Cairo: Dar al-Maaref, 1958.

Georges-Picot, Jacques. *The Real Suez Crisis.* Translated by W. G. Rogers. New York: Harcourt Brace Jovanovich, 1978.

Gerges, Fawaz A. *The Superpowers and the Middle East: Regional and International Politics, 1955–1967.* Boulder, Colo.: Westview, 1994.

Ghali, Mirrit Butrus. *Al-Islah al-Zira'i.* Cairo: Dar al-Fusul, 1945.

———. *The Policy of Tomorrow.* Translated by Isma'il R. el-Faruqi. Washington, D.C.: American Council of Learned Societies, 1953.

el-Ghonemy, M. Riad. *Land, Food, and Rural Development in North Africa.* Boulder, Colo.: Westview, 1993.

———. *The Political Economy of Rural Poverty.* London: Routledge, 1990.

Girod, Roger, Patrick de Laubier, and Alan Gladstone, eds. *Social Policy in Western Europe and the USA, 1950–1980.* New York: St. Martin's Press, 1985.

Gordon, Joel. "The False Hopes of 1950: The Wafd's Last Hurrah and the Demise of Egypt's Old Order." *International Journal of Middle East Studies* 21 (1989): 193–214.

———. *Nasser's Blessed Movement: Egypt's Free Officers and the July Revolution.* New York: Oxford Univ. Press, 1992.

Hahn, Peter L. *The United States, Great Britain, and Egypt, 1945–1956.* Chapel Hill: Univ. of North Carolina Press, 1991.

Halpern, Manfred. *The Politics of Social Change in the Middle East and North Africa.* Princeton, N.J.: Princeton Univ. Press, 1963.

Heikal, Mohamed H. *The Cairo Documents.* New York: Doubleday, 1973.

———. *Cutting the Lion's Tail: Suez Through Egyptian Eyes.* London: André Deutsch, 1986.

Heyworth-Dunne, J. *Egypt: The Co-operative Movement.* Cairo: Renaissance Bookshop, 1952.

———. *An Introduction to the History of Education in Modern Egypt.* London: Cass, 1968.

———. *Religious and Political Trends in Modern Egypt.* Washington, D.C.: n.p., 1950.

Hocking, William Earnest. "The Israel-Arab Conflict and Its Origins in 1947." *New York Herald Tribune,* July 20, 1957.

Hoskins, Halford L. "Arab Socialism in the U.A.R." *Current History* 44, no. 257 (Jan. 1963): 8–12 et seq.

———. "The Guardianship of the Suez Canal." *Middle East Journal* 4, no. 2 (1950): 143–54.

Husayn, Taha. *The Future of Culture in Egypt.* New York: Octagon Books, 1975.

Hussein, Ahmed. "Egypt's New Regime: Full Sovereignty Demanded." *Vital Speeches of the Day* 19, no. 20 (Aug. 1, 1953): 610–12.

———. "Egypt's War on Poverty." *United Nations World* 5 (Mar. 1951): 69–71.

———. "The New Egypt: Domestic and Foreign Policies." *Vital Speeches of the Day* 21, no. 11 (Mar. 15, 1955): 1102–5.

———. *Rural Social Welfare Centers in Egypt.* Washington, D.C.: n.p., 1954.

———. *Rural Social Welfare Centres in Egypt.* Cairo: Ministry of Social Affairs, 1951.

———. "Some Aspects of Agricultural and Rural Life Developments in Egypt." Washington, D.C.: Department of Agriculture, 1955.

"Hussein, Ahmed." In *Current Biography Yearbook, 1956,* edited by Marjorie Dent Candee, 293–95. New York: H. W. Wilson, 1957.

"Hussein, Ahmed." In *The Annual Obituary, 1984,* edited by Margot Levy, 635–36. Chicago: St. James Press, 1985.

"Hussein, Ahmed." In *Current Biography Yearbook, 1985,* edited by Charles Moritz, 468. New York: H. W. Wilson, 1986.

Hussein, Ahmed, and Carl C. Taylor. *Report of the Mission on Rural Community Organization and Development in the Caribbean Area and Mexico.* New York: United Nations, 1953.

Hussein, Aziza. "The Role of Women in Social Reform in Egypt." *Middle East Journal* 7, no. 4 (1953): 440–50.

———. *Women in the Moslem World.* Washington, D.C.: Egyptian Embassy Press Department, n.d.

Information Administration. *The Egyptian Revolution in Three Years, 1952–1955.* Cairo: Information Administration, 1955.

———. *The Permanent Council for Public Welfare Services.* Cairo: Société Orientale de Publicité, 1955.

Information Department. *The Revolution in Thirteen Years, 1952–1965.* Cairo: Information Department, 1965.

———. *The United Arab Republic: Achievements and Future Development Plans.* Cairo: Information Department, 1960.

———. *The United Arab Republic: Achievements and Future Development Plans.* Cairo: Information Department, 1968.

Issawi, Charles. *Egypt.* London: Oxford Univ. Press, 1947.

———. *Egypt at Mid-Century.* London: Oxford Univ. Press, 1954.

———. *Egypt in Revolution.* London: Oxford Univ. Press, 1963.

Jabbra, Joseph G. *Bureaucracy and Development in the Arab World.* New York: E. J. Brill, 1989.

el-Kammash, Magdi M. *Economic Development and Planning in Egypt.* New York: Praeger, 1968.

Kandel, I. L. *The Making of Nazis.* New York: Bureau of Publications, Teachers College, Columbia Univ., 1935.

Keen, Bernard A. *The Agricultural Development of the Middle East.* London: H.M. Stationery Office, 1946.

Kellerman, Fritz. *The Effect of the World War on European Education.* Cambridge, Mass.: Harvard Univ. Press, 1928.

Kingston, Paul W. *Britain and the Politics of Modernization in the Middle East, 1945–1958.* Cambridge: Cambridge Univ. Press, 1996.

Lacoutre, Jean, and Simonne Lacoutre. *Egypt in Transition. Translated by Francis Scarfe.* New York: Criterion Books, 1958.

"Land Reform Legislation of Syria, Egypt, and Iran." *Middle East Journal* 7, no. 1 (1953): 69–87.

Lenczowski, George. "Syria: A Crisis in Arab Unity." *Current History* 42, no. 248 (Apr. 1962): 200–7.

Lens, Sidney. "The Middle East's New 'Ism'." *Christian Century,* Jan. 13, 1960, 42–46.

Lilge, Frederic. *The Abuse of Learning: The Failure of the German University.* New York: Macmillan, 1948.

Lloyd, Selwyn. *Suez 1956: A Personal Account.* London: Jonathan Cape, 1978.

Louis, William Roger. *The British Empire in the Middle East, 1945–1951.* Oxford: Clarendon, 1984.

Marei, Sayed. *Agrarian Reform Co-operatives.* Cairo: Agrarian Reform Organization Public Relations Department, 1958.

———. "The Agrarian Reform in Egypt." *International Labor Review* 69, no. 2 (Feb. 1954): 140–50.

———. *Agrarian Land Reform in Egypt.* Cairo: Imprimerie de l'Institut Français d'Archéologie Orientale, 1957.

Margold, Stella. "Agrarian Reform in Egypt." *American Journal of Economics and Sociology* 17, no. 1 (Oct. 1957), 9–19.

Marsot, Afaf Lutfi al-Sayyid. *Egypt's Liberal Experiment, 1922–1936.* Berkeley: Univ. of California Press, 1977.

Maslahit al-Isti'lamat. *The Revolution in Thirteen Years, 1952–1965.* Cairo: Maslahit al-Isti'lamat, 1965.

———. *The United Arab Republic: Ten Years.* Cairo: United Arab Republic, 1961.

Mattison, Beatrice McCown. "Rural Social Centers in Egypt." *Middle East Journal* 5 (1951): 461–80.

Mayfield, James B. *Rural Politics in Nasser's Egypt.* Austin: Univ. of Texas Press, 1971.

Ministry of Finance. *Population Census, 1937.* Cairo: Ministry of Finance, 1937.

Ministry of Information. State Information Service. *Egypt's Agricultural Policy.* Cairo: n.p., 1974.

Ministry of Local Administration. *Shrouk.* Cairo: Ministry of Local Administration and ORDEV, n.d.

Ministry of Social Affairs. *The Egyptian Social Security Scheme.* Cairo: Government Press, 1950.

———. *The Fellah Department.* Cairo: Société Orientale de Publicité, 1950.

———. *Second Social Welfare Seminar for Arab States of the Middle East: Lectures—Discussions—Reports.* Cairo: Ministry of Social Affairs, 1950.

———. *Social Welfare in Egypt.* Cairo: Ministry of Social Affairs, 1950.

———. *Souvenir Booklet: Community Councils and Social Centres.* Cairo: Government Press, 1950.

Ministry of Social Affairs. Fellah Department. *Annual Report on the Rural Welfare Centers, 1942.* Cairo: C. H. Pallemans, 1942.

———. *Souvenir Booklet: Exhibition of Rural Cottage Industries.* In English and in Arabic. Cairo: Ministry of Social Affairs, 1946.

Mitchell, Richard P. *The Society of the Muslim Brothers.* London: Oxford Univ. Press, 1969.

Monroe, Elizabeth. *Britain's Moment in the Middle East, 1914–1956.* Baltimore, Md.: Johns Hopkins Press, 1963.

Moore, Austin L. *Farewell Farouk.* Chicago: Scholars' Press, 1954.

Muller, Edwin. "Allah Helps Those." *Reader's Digest,* Aug. 1946, 91–94.

———. "New Ideas in Old Egypt." *Rotarian,* July 1946, 44–46.

Nasser, Gamal Abdel. "The Egyptian Revolution." *Foreign Affairs* 33, no. 1/4 (Jan. 1955): 199–211.

———. *The Philosophy of the Revolution.* Buffalo, N.Y.: Economica Books, 1959.

Owen, Roger. *State, Power, and Politics in the Making of the Modern Middle East.* London: Routledge, 1992.

Owen, Roger, and William Roger Louis, eds. *Suez 1956: The Crisis and Its Consequences.* Oxford: Clarendon, 1989.

Pachter, Henry M. *Modern Germany: A Social, Cultural, and Political History.* Boulder, Colo.: Westview, 1978.

Peretz, Don. *The Middle East Today.* 5th ed. New York: Praeger, 1988.

Phillips, David, ed. *Education in Germany: Tradition and Reform in Historical Context.* London: Routledge, 1995.

Radwan, Abu al-Futouh Ahmad. *Old and New Forces in Egyptian Education.* New York: Bureau of Publications, Teacher's College, Columbia Univ., 1951.

Reid, Donald M. *Cairo University and the Making of Modern Egypt.* Cambridge: Cambridge Univ. Press, 1990.

Richards, Alan. *Egypt's Agricultural Development, 1800–1980.* Boulder, Colo.: Westview, 1980.

Rizk, Hanna. "Social Services Available for Families in Egypt." *Marriage and Family Living* 17, no. 3 (Aug. 1955): 212–16.

Sayed-Ahmed, Muhammad Abd el-Wahab. *Nasser and American Foreign Policy, 1952–1956.* London: LAAM, 1989.

el-Shafii, Hussein. *Statement by Hussein el-Shafii, Central Minister of Social Affairs and Labour.* Cairo: General Organisation for Government Printing Offices, 1960.

Shalaby, Mohamed M. *Rural Reconstruction in Egypt.* Cairo: Egyptian Association for Social Studies, 1950.

Sharabi, H. B. "The Egyptian Revolution." *Current History* 42, no. 248 (Apr. 1962): 233–37.

Shuckburgh, Evelyn. *Descent to Suez: Diaries, 1951–1956.* New York: W. W. Norton, 1986.

Smith, Adam. *The Theory of Moral Sentiments.* Indianapolis, Ind.: Liberty Classics, 1976.

Springborg, Robert. *Family, Power, and Politics in Egypt: Sayed Bey Marei—His Clan, Clients, and Cohorts.* Philadelphia: Univ. of Pennsylvania Press, 1982.

Stark, Gary D., and Bede Karl Lackner, eds. *Essays on Culture and Society in Modern Germany.* College Station: Texas A & M Univ. Press, 1982.

Stephens, Robert. *Nasser: A Political Biography.* New York: Simon and Schuster, 1971.

Stevens, Georgiana G. *Egypt Yesterday and Today.* New York: Holt, Rinehart, and Winston, 1963.

"Suez Canal Agreement." *Current History* 27, no. 160 (Dec. 1954): 381–82.

Tignor, Robert L. *Modernization and British Colonial Rule in Egypt, 1882–1914.* Princeton, N.J.: Princeton Univ. Press, 1966.

The UAR: Ten Years. Cairo: Information Department, 1962.

United Arab Republic. *Ministry of Social Affairs in Eleven Years from July 23, 1952, to July 23, 1963.* Cairo: Public Relations Information Service, 1963.

———. *Ten Years of Progress and Development, 1952–1962.* Cairo: UAR Maslahit al-Isti'lamat, 1962.

———. Ministry of Social Affairs. *Social Security.* Cairo: Conference of the Ministers of Social Affairs in Africa, 1967.

United States Government. *Foreign Relations of the United States, 1952–1954.* Vol. 9, *The Near and Middle East.* Washington, D.C.: Government Printing Office, 1986.

———. *The Suez Canal Problem, July 26-September 22, 1956.* Washington, D.C.: Government Printing Office, 1956.

———. Department of State. "Agreement with Egypt on Development Funds." *Department of State Bulletin* 30 (Mar. 14, 1955): 441.

———. "Anglo-Egyptian Agreement on the Suez Base." *Department of State Bulletin* 31 (Aug. 9, 1954): 198–99.

———. "Aswan High Dam." *Department of State Bulletin* 35 (July 30, 1956): 188.

———. *Confidential U.S. Department of State Central Files: Egypt 1945–1949.*

———. *Confidential U.S. Department of State Central Files: Egypt, 1950–1954.*

———. *Confidential U.S. Department of State Central Files: Egypt, 1955–1959.*

———. "Correspondence of President Eisenhower and Premier Bulganin Concerning Reduction of International Tension and Disarmament." *Department of State Bulletin* 36 (Jan. 21, 1957): 89–93.

———. "Discussions Concerning Financing of Egyptian Dam Project." *Department of State Bulletin* 33 (Dec. 26, 1955): 1050–51.

———. "Egypt Invited to Participate in a New Middle East Command." *Department of State Bulletin* 25 (Oct. 22, 1951): 647–48.

———. "Israel Urged to Withdraw Armed Forces From Egypt." *Department of State Bulletin* 35 (Nov. 19, 1956): 797–98.

———. "Secretary Dulles' News Conference of April 2." *Department of State Bulletin* 36 (Apr. 22, 1957): 641–47.

———. "U.K.-Egyptian Agreement Regarding Suez Canal Base." *Department of State Bulletin* 31 (Nov. 15, 1954): 734–35.

———. "United Nations Considerations of Developments in the Middle East." *Department of State Bulletin* 35 (Nov. 12, 1956): 747–56.

———. "Withdrawal of British and French Forces From Egypt." *Department of State Bulletin* 35 (Dec. 17, 1956): 951–53.

Vatikiotis, P. J., ed. *Egypt since the Revolution.* London: George Allen and Unwin, 1968.

Viton, Albert. "Politics along the Nile." *Asia* 38 no. 6 (June 1938): 349–52.

Warriner, Doreen. *Land and Poverty in the Middle East.* London: Royal Institute of International Affairs, 1948.

——— "Land Reform in Egypt and its Repercussions." *International Affairs* 29, no. 1 (Jan. 1953): 1–10.

Weinryb, Bernard D. "Industrial Development of the Near East." *Quarterly Journal of Economics* 61 (May 1947): 471–99.

Wheelock, Keith. *Nasser's New Egypt: A Critical Analysis.* New York: Praeger, 1960.

Publications in Arabic

Ahmed, 'Ali Fu'ad. *'Ilm al-ijtima' al-rifi* (Rural social science). Cairo: Dar al-Thaqafa wa-al-'Ulum lil-Tiba'a wa-al-Nashr, 1960.

'Amr, 'Abd al-Rauf Ahmed. *Tarikh al-'alaqat al-misriyyah al-amrikiyyah* (The history of Egyptian-American relations). Cairo: al-Hai'a al-Misriyyah al-'Aama lil-Kitab, 1991.

Butrus, Ragheb, and Ibrahim 'Ali al-Mahlawi. *Sharah qanun al-daman al-ijtima'i* (Explanation of the Social Security Law). Cairo: Dar al-Ma'arif b-Misr, 1953.

de Schweinitz, Karl. *Al-Mashru' al-misriyyah lil-daman al-ijtima'i* (The Egyptian project of social security). Cairo: al-Mataba'a al-Sharqiyyah, n.d.

el-Ghonemy, Muhammad Riad. *Al-Islah al-rifi fi-Misr* (Social reform in Egypt). Cairo: al-Mataba'a al-Salafiyyah b-Misr, 1957.

Heikal, Muhammad Hassanein. *Milaffat al-Suwes* (The Suez files). Cairo: Markaz al-Ahram lil-Tarjama wa-al-Nashr, 1996.

Hussein, Ahmed. *Al-Mirakaz al-ijtima'iyyah al-rifiyyah fi Misr* (Rural social centers in Egypt). Cairo: n.p., 1951.

Hussein, Ahmed, and Mahmoud Riyad. *Mashru' l-taufir al-sakan lil-tabaqat al-mah-*

duda al-dakhil fi Misr (Project to increase housing for classes of limited income in Egypt). Cairo: Matabi' madkur, 1949.

'Isa, Muhammad Tala't. *Darasat al-ijtimai' al-rifi* (Rural social studies). Cairo: Maktabat al-Qahirah al-Haditha, Dar al-Hana'a lil-Tiba'a, 1960.

al-Jam'iya al-Misriya lil-Dirasat al-Ijtima'iya. *Tajriba islah al-qariyah* (The village reform experiment). Cairo: Matabi' Dar Sa'ad Misr, n.d.

———. *Al-Jam'iya al-Misriya lil-Dirasat al-Ijtima'iya: Mahdiha—hadaruha—mustaqbaluha, 1938–1994* (The Egyptian Association for Social Studies: Its past, its present, and its future). Cairo: al-Jam'iya al-Misriya lil-Dirasat al-Ijtima'iya, 1994.

Jam'iyat al-Fellah: La'hat al-nizam al-asasi (The Fellah Association: List of statutes). Cairo: Matba'at Shirka al-'Alanat al-Sharqiyyah, n.d.

al-Jumhuriya al-'Arabiya al-Muttahidda. Idarah al-malumat al—alaqat al-aama. *Wizarat al-Shu'un al-Ijtima'iya fi 25 aaman* (The Ministry of Social Affairs in 25 years). Cairo: Dar wa-Matabi' al-Sha'ab, 1964.

Muharram, Ibrahim. *Shuruq: Al-Tanmiya al-rifiya* (Shuruq: Rural development). Cairo: Matabi' Dar al-Ta'aun lil-Taba' wa-al-Nashr, 1997.

Sa'd, Ahmad Sadiq. *Mushkilat al-Fellah* (The problem of the peasant). Cairo: Dar al-Qarn al-Ishrin li-l Nashr, 1945.

Teodorovich, B. *Mushkilat al-askan fi al-rif al-masri* (The problem of housing in the Egyptian countryside). Sirs al-Layyan: al-Mirkaz al-Dawli lil-Tarbiyyah al-Asasiyyah fi Misr, 1955.

Wizarat al-Shu'un al-Ijtima'iya. *Bayan 'an mashru' al-daman al-ijtima'ii wa-al-marsum al-khas bihi* (Announcement of the Social Security Project and the regulations specific to it). Cairo: al-Mataba' al-Amiriyyah, 1950.

———. *Al-Daman al-ijtima'i fi 'ashura as'ila* (Social security in ten questions). Cairo: Matba't Shirka al-'Alanat al-Sharqiya, n.d.

———. *Halqa al-dirasat al-ijtima'iya lil-duwal al-'arabiya: Al-Muhadarat wa-al-bahuth wa-al-taqarir* (Social studies seminar for the Arab States: Lectures, research, and reports). Cairo: Mataba't Misr, 1950.

Wizarat al-Shu'un al-Ijtima'iya: Siyasatuha al-insha'iya fi nahdatiha al-hadira wa-birnamajiha lil-mustaqbal (The Ministry of Social Affairs: Its constructive policies in its current revival and its program for the future). Cairo: Matba't Misr, Shirka Masahama al-Misriya, 1949.

Wizarat al-Zira'a. *Taqrir al-ba'tha al-misriya l-mu'tamar al-ummum al-muttahida lil-agdiya wa-al-zira'a b-amrika* (Report of the Egyptian Delegation to the United Nations Conference on Food and Agriculture in America). Cairo: Matba't al-I'timad, 1944.

Unpublished Documents

Alterman, Jon. "Egypt and American Foreign Assistance, 1952–1956." Ph.D. thesis, Harvard Univ., 1997.

el-Bidewy, M. Fouad. "The Development of Social Security in Egypt." Master's thesis, Columbia Univ., 1951.

Dawood, Hassan Aly. "Economic Aspects of Land Tenure in Egypt." Ph.D. thesis, Michigan State Univ., 1950.

al-Diffrawy, Ahmad Fathi. "Local Government and Service Ministries." Unpublished paper, n.d.

Ikeda, Misako. "Sociopolitical Debates in Late Parliamentary Egypt." Ph.D. thesis, Harvard Univ., 1998.

Kinsey, David Chapman. "Egyptian Education under Cromer: A Study of East-West Encounter in Educational Administration and Policy, 1883–1907." Ph.D. thesis, Harvard Univ., 1965.

Meijer, Roel. "The Quest for Modernity: Secular Liberal and Left-Wing Political Thought in Egypt, 1945–1958." Ph.D. thesis, Univ. of Amsterdam, 1995.

Meyer, Gail E. "Egypt and the United States: The Formative Years." Ph.D. thesis, Univ. of Geneva, 1980.

Shoukri, Karim. "Strong Press Support for Ahmed Pasha Hussein as a Determining Factor in His Acceptability to the Leaders of the Revolution." Unpublished paper, American Univ. in Cairo, 1984.

Newspapers and Periodicals

In European Languages

Christian Science Monitor

The Economist

Egyptian Gazette

Evening Star (Washington, D.C.)

Newsweek

New York Times

U.S. News and World Report

Washington Daily News

Washington Post

Washington Times-Herald

In Arabic

al-Ahram
Akher Lahza
al-Anba
al-Asas
al-Ishtiraki
Ruz al-Yusuf

Interviews

al-Abd, Anwar Abdul Razzak. Cairo, Jan. 22, 1998; Jan. 4, 1999.

Abd el-Razak, Khaled Mahmoud. Cairo, Jan. 4, 1999.

al-Beili, Sabri. Benha, Qalyubiyah, June 1999.

Dawood, Hassan. Cairo, Oct. 31, Nov. 20, Dec. 11, 1996; Jan. 2, 1999; via phone, Jan. 26, 1998.

al-Diffrawy, Ahmad Fathi. Cairo, Jan. 22, 1998; Jan. 4, 1999.

Eleish, Samir. Cairo, Jan. 22, 1998; Jan. 4, 1999.

el-Ghonemy, Mohamed Riad. Cairo, Jan. 17, 22, and 27, Dec. 31, 1998.

el-Haggagi, Ali Hassan. Cairo, Jan. 22, 1998; Jan. 4, 1999.

el-Heneidy, Abdul Latif. Cairo, Jan. 22, 1998; Jan. 4, 1999; Sindiyun, Qalyubiyah, June 5, 2000.

Hussein, Adly. Benha, Qalyubiyah, May, 2000.

Hussein, Aziza. Cairo, Oct. 24, Nov. 13, Dec. 3, and Dec. 8; Jan. 17, 22, and 27, and Dec. 31, 1998; Jan. 3 and 4, 1999; May 26, 2000. At Hussein's *'izba,* Daqahliya, June 8, 1999.

al-Islam, Hami. Benha, Qalyubiyah, June 1999 and May 2000.

al-Mikawy, Omar Rashed. Cairo, Jan. 22, 1998.

Mohsen, Bahiga. Sindiyun, Qalyubiyah, May 27 and 28, 2000.

Muharram, Ibrahim. Cairo, July 2001.

el-Nimaky, Salah. Cairo, Jan. 22, 1998; Jan. 4, 1999.

Rafferty, Katherine Macguire. Interview via e-mail, Feb. 22, 1999.

Shalakany, Amr. Interview via e-mail, May 12, 1999.

Springborg, Robert. Cairo, June 1999.

al-Wardany, Kamal al-Din. Jan. 22, 1998; Jan. 4, 1999.

Yousef, Ahmad Saber. Jan. 22, 1998; Jan. 4, 1999.

Index